THIRD THOUSAND.

EPISCOPAL METHODISM,

AS IT WAS, AND IS;

OR,

AN ACCOUNT OF THE ORIGIN, PROGRESS, DOCTRINES, CHURCH POLITY, USAGES, INSTITUTIONS, AND STATISTICS,

OF THE

METHODIST EPISCOPAL CHURCH IN THE UNITED STATES.

EMBRACING ALSO

A SKETCH OF THE RISE OF METHODISM IN EUROPE, AND OF ITS ORIGIN AND PROGRESS IN CANADA.

BY

REV. P. DOUGLASS GORRIE,

AUTHOR OF "CHURCHES AND SECTS," "EPISCOPACY," ETC.

AUBURN:

DERBY AND MILLER.

1852.

STEREOTYPED BY THOMAS B. SMITH,
216 WILLIAM STREET, N. Y.

RECOMMENDATION.

"HAVING examined the manuscript of the work entitled: EPISCOPAL METHODISM, AS IT WAS, AND IS, &c., by Rev. P. Douglass Gorrie, and believing that the work contains *much useful information* in relation to the *History, Doctrines*, and *Institutions* of the Methodist Episcopal Church; and that the facts therein stated are correct, so far as we have been able to judge: we hereby cheerfully recommend the work to the attention of the public, and especially to the members and friends of the Methodist Episcopal Church.

G. C. WOODRUFF,
Presiding Elder of Potsdam District, B. R. Conference.
HIRAM SHEPARD,
Presiding Elder of Ogdensburgh District, B. R. Conference."

PREFACE.

THE only apology which the Author has to offer to his ministerial brethren, or to the public, for the appearance of this work, is, that he thinks such a work is needed; not that the Church is unsupplied with many valuable books of a historical and doctrinal character; nor yet, that there are no works on the ecclesiastical polity of Episcopal Methodism; but as the author believes, there is no *one work* now extant which embraces all these points. Such a work, containing the most important parts of Methodist history, with a brief statement and defence of its doctrines, a statement of its church polity in its various branches, and much information in regard to its statistics, all brought down to the present time, is now presented to the Church and the public. That the work has its imperfections is not impossible,—to claim otherwise would be the evidence of vanity,—but we trust that its defects are as few as might reasonably be expected in a work of this description, and if there are errors, it is to be hoped they are not material ones.

To name *all* the authors, from whom facts and statements have been obtained, would be unnecessary. Suffice it to say, that a free use has been made of facts referred to in Wesley's Journal, and in Bangs' "History of the Methodist Episcopal Church," down to the year 1840. The history of the Church for the past ten or eleven years, has not been written by any person; consequently, the author has had the entire field of history during that important period to himself. "Meacham's History,"—a Canadian work,—has also afforded some facts in relation to Methodism in Canada. On the doctrinal part, "Comfort's Articles" have been reviewed, and many important thoughts have been gleaned from that valuable work. That part of the work relating to church polity, it is scarcely necessary to say, has been chiefly borrowed from the little book called the "Methodist Discipline." Were we disposed to deny this fact, it might be said to us as to one of old,—"Thy speech betrayeth thee." The reader, however, will find much original matter even here, the arrangement of course being principally original. The statistical information has been obtained from the General Minutes, and from other reliable sources.

Hoping the work will please the public, and meet with a ready sale for the benefit of the enterprising publishers, as well as that of the reader, the book, such as it is, is committed to the mechanical skill of the one, and to the attention of the other,

By the Author.

Canton, St. Lawrence Co.,
New York, September, 1851.

CONTENTS.

BOOK I.

HISTORY OF METHODISM.

CHAPTER I.

FROM THE BIRTH OF JOHN WESLEY, TO THE INTRODUCTION OF METHODISM INTO AMERICA.

SECTION IV.

SECTION V.

CHAPTER II.

FROM THE INTRODUCTION OF METHODISM INTO AMERICA, TO THE PRESENT TIME.

SECTION I.

SECTION II.

SECTION III.

SECTION IV.

SECTION V.

SECTION VI.

SECTION VII.

SECTION VIII.

SECTION IX.

SECTION X.

SECTION XI.

SECTION XII.

BOOK II.

DOCTRINES OF METHODISM.

INTRODUCTION.

ARTICLE I.

Of Faith in the Holy Trinity.

ARTICLE II.

Of the Word or Son of God who was made Man.

ARTICLE III.

Resurrection of Christ.

ARTICLE IV.

Of the Holy Ghost.

ARTICLE V.

The Sufficiency of the Holy Scriptures for Salvation.

ARTICLE VI.

Of the Old Testament.

ARTICLE VII.

Original or Birth Sin.

ARTICLE VIII.

Of Free Will.

ARTICLE IX.

Of the Justification of Man.

ARTICLE X.

Of Good Works.

ARTICLE XI.

Of Works of Supererogation.

ARTICLE XII.

Of Sin after Justification.

ARTICLE XIII.

Of the Church.

ARTICLE XIV.

Of Purgatory.

ARTICLE XV.

Of Speaking in an Unknown Tongue.

ARTICLE XVI.

Of the Sacraments.

ARTICLE XVII.

Of Baptism.

ARTICLE XVIII.

Of the Lord's Supper.

ARTICLE XIX.

Of the Supper in both Kinds.

I. Witness of the Spirit.

II. Sanctification of Believers.

III. Possibility of Falling from Grace.

IV. Eternal Rewards and Punishments.

BOOK III.

POLITY OF EPISCOPAL METHODISM.

CHAPTER I.

SECTION I.

Introduction.

SECTION II.

Apostolic Succession.

SECTION III.

SAME SUBJECT CONTINUED.

SECTION IV.

ORIGIN OF METHODIST EPISCOPACY, &c.

SECTION V.

ADVANTAGES OF THE METHODIST EPISCOPAL FORM OF CHURCH GOVERNMENT, WHEN COMPARED WITH OTHER FORMS.

CHAPTER II.

GENERAL RULES, AND RECEPTION, AND EXPULSION OF MEMBERS.

SECTION I.

SECTION II.

SECTION III.

CHAPTER III.

OF THE MINISTERS, PREACHERS, AND OTHER OFFICERS.

SECTION I.

SECTION II.

SECTION III.

SECTION IV.

SECTION V.

SECTION VI.

2

SECTION VII.

SECTION VIII.

SECTION IX.

CHAPTER IV.

OF THE GENERAL, ANNUAL, AND QUARTERLY CONFERENCES, AND OTHER COLLECTIVE BODIES.

SECTION I.

SECTION II.

SECTION III.

SECTION IV.

SECTION V.

CHAPTER V.

OF THE PUBLIC AND SOCIAL MEANS OF GRACE.

SECTION I.

SECTION II.

SECTION III.

SECTION IV.

SECTION V.

SECTION VI.

SECTION VII.

SECTION VIII.

CHAPTER VI.

OF THE SUPPORT OF THE MINISTRY AND FINANCIAL INTERESTS OF THE CHURCH.

SECTION I.

SECTION II.

APPENDIX TO BOOK III.

BOOK IV.

BENEVOLENT AND LITERARY INSTITUTIONS, AND STATISTICS OF METHODISM.

CHAPTER I.

BENEVOLENT INSTITUTIONS.

SECTION I.

Book Concern.

SECTION II.

Chartered Fund.

SECTION III.

Missionary Society of the Methodist Episcopal Church.

SECTION IV.

Sunday School Union of Methodist Episcopal Church.

SECTION V.

Bible Society.

CHAPTER II.

LITERARY INSTITUTIONS OF METHODISM.

SECTION I.

Universities and Colleges.

SECTION II.

Biblical Institute.

SECTION III.

CHAPTER III.

STATISTICS OF EPISCOPAL METHODISM.

SECTION I.

SECTION II.

SECTION III.

SECTION IV.

SECTION V.

SECTION VI.

SECTION VII.

SECTION VIII.

BOOK I.

HISTORY OF METHODISM.

CHAPTER I.

SECTION I.

John Wesley, the father and founder of Methodism, was born on the 17th of June, A.D. 1703. He was the son of Samuel Wesley, Rector of Epworth, Lincolnshire, England, and was the descendant of a long list of learned and pious ancestors, both on the paternal and maternal side. John Wesley had two brothers; the elder, Samuel, was born in 1692, educated in Westminster school, and at the age of nineteen was elected to Christ's Church, Oxford. After a life of ministerial and literary usefulness, he died in 1739. Charles, the younger brother, was born in 1708. Besides these three sons, Mr. Wesley, senior, had several daughters, but as their biography is not necessarily connected with the annals of Methodism, we merely allude to the fact without further detail.

At the age of six years, John had a wonderful escape from death. The rectory, or parsonage house, in which the family resided, having been consumed by fire, while John, being asleep in an upper apartment, was with great difficulty saved from destruction. In allusion to this deliverance, he, in after life, frequently represented himself as being "a brand plucked from the burning."

After receiving the necessary instruction preparatory to his admission to the University, he was, in the year 1720, entered as a student in Christ's Church College, Oxford, where he pursued his studies with unwearied diligence and zeal, and where he soon after took his degree of Bachelor of Arts. In 1725, he was ordained a deacon of the established Church of England by the Bishop of Oxford, and the next year, 1726, he was elected Fellow of Lincoln College. In 1727, he obtained his degree of Master of Arts, and in 1728 was ordained Priest by the same bishop who had previously conferred upon him deacon's orders. In the meantime, John had become curate of Epworth, or assistant minister to his father. In the year 1729 he returned to Oxford and became a tutor in the college. During his temporary absence from college, his brother Charles, who had become a student of Christ's Church, and was of a serious turn of mind, had associated with himself two or three other young students, for the purpose of prosecuting with greater diligence their respective studies, and also to assist each other in the formation of a proper moral and religious character. From the strict method in which they spent their every hour, and their methodical exactness in relation to all things appertaining to morality and religion, they acquired from their fellow-students the name of *Methodists*, an appellation which was not unknown in England, as we find that the Nonconformists had long been known by that title, and even *before* the times of nonconformity—as early as 1639—we find a minor sect of Christians, who appear to have been a plain and pious people called by the same name—Methodists. But at whatever period the name was first applied to any sect of Christians, but little doubt can exist in relation to its application to Charles Wesley and his associates; that it was used as a term of reproach, and afterward adopted as a denominational title by the force of circumstances, and although at first considered disgraceful by those who applied it, yet, like the name *Christian*, which was first given to the disciples at Antioch, by way of derision, it has long ceased to be considered reproachful by those who bear it, but next to that of Christian, the Methodists glory in their name, and if any regret exists in relation to its application, it is that those who bear it are not more worthy of it.

On the return of Mr. John Wesley to Oxford, he at once joined the little band, and by common consent became its leader, and through his influence and energy, his piety and depth of learning, he gave additional vigor to their exertions to promote their own welfare and the welfare of others. Among those composing the *Godly Club*, as it was sometimes called, were shortly afterwards found, Mr. Hervey, the author of "Hervey's Meditations," and the justly celebrated George Whitfield.

During the residence of John and Charles Wesley at Oxford, the former took frequent excursions to his native town, and visited other places of note, such as London, and Manchester. He appears to have made it a point of duty, even at this early day, to preach wherever he could find an opening, and such was his success as a preacher, that on the decline of his father's health, he was strongly urged by the latter, as well as by his brother Samuel, and also by the people of Epworth, to apply for the parish of Epworth, as the next presentee. Such, however, was his attachment to the little band at Oxford, that neither the wishes of a father, nor the sterner commands of a brother, could induce him to forsake the station where God in his providence had placed him, while it is quite probable he had resolved, as a matter of duty, not to confine his labors to the limits of a single parish, but if he removed at all from Oxford, to go anywhere where the finger of God should direct, that he might do the greatest amount of good, to the greatest possible number. While actuated by this spirit of self-denial, it is not wonderful that we find him, during his stay at Oxford, visiting the prisoners in the gaol of that place; or spending several hours in each week in visiting the poor and sick, affording relief to the one, and comfort and instruction to the other. Such ministerial devotedness will not appear wonderful to *us*, but to those who lived in that day, it was a novel sight to see any man, aside from the minister of the parish, or the paid chaplain of the prison, paying any attention to either the poor, the sick, or the criminal; and indeed, so strange did such conduct appear, on the part of Mr. Wesley and his companions, that they were subjected thereby to much obloquy and reproach from the members of their own church, but being encouraged in his labors of love by his venerable father and elder brother, John and Charles continued in their course of doing good, according as their time and means would allow. After having been thus engaged for several years, the two brothers received a call to go to Georgia as missionaries. A colony had been planted here a few years previously, under the direction of Mr. James Oglethorpe, who, on visiting England for the purpose of procuring supplies, &c., invited the Wesleys to return with him. After due deliberation John consented to go, and Charles, agreeing to accompany him, received ordination prior to their departure. In the year 1735, they accordingly bid adieu to remonstrating friends, and beloved country, and committed their little all to the mercies of the deep and the inhospitalities of a savage shore. In the same ship which carried them to their field of labor, was a company of pious Germans belonging to the church of the Moravians or United Brethren, accompanied by their bishop. For the purpose of conversing with them, Mr. John Wesley applied himself at once to the study of the German language, while he also gave lessons in English to the bishop and two other persons. During the passage they encountered several severe storms, which rendered their situation dangerous in the extreme. While momentarily expecting to find a watery grave, the Moravians—both men and women—preserved the utmost composure, and even while the storm was at its height, cheerfully sang hymns of praise to God. John Wesley, who, on examining the state of his own heart, felt unprepared to die, could but wonder at such composure on the part of his German friends. On the abatement of the storm, he made inquiries for the purpose of ascertaining the ground of such composure and fearlessness of death, and learned for the first time in his life, that there is a degree of religion attainable by believers, which " casteth out fear."

On the arrival of the Wesleys in Georgia, John took charge of the church in Savannah, while Charles went to Frederica. The Colonists at the latter place were greatly depraved, and their conduct calling out strong rebuke from their faithful pastor, he became at once the object of bitter persecution and neglect, so much so, that he gladly exchanged places with his older and more experienced brother John,—Charles taking charge of Savannah, and John of Frederica. In 1736, Charles was sent to England as the bearer of despatches from the Governor to the Trustees of the Colony, and thus his missionary labors in America terminated. John, however, remained at his post, having returned to Savannah—visiting Frederica occasionally—and by the establishment of schools, private religious meetings, &c., he gave evidence of a desire to make full proof of his ministry. He even attempted carrying out his original design of laboring exclusively for the benefit of the Indian tribes, but as there was no other minister to supply his place in Savannah, he was obliged reluctantly to remain in that place. While officiating as the minister of Savannah and Frederica, his object was to bring himself and congregation to comply with the rubrics of the Church of England, and while enforcing the necessity of attending the Communion on the part of the parishioners, at the same time to repel unworthy persons from the table of the Lord. In doing so, he at once subjected himself to the most fierce opposition from the persons repelled, and from their friends and neighbors. So high did the storm rage, that complaints were made to the grand jury of Savannah, which latter body presented to the court, a bill of indictment against the Rev. John Wesley for breaking the laws of the realm, &c. &c.,

in sundry matters purely ecclesiastical. At length, having appeared seven times before the court to answer these charges, and believing that the intention of his enemies being simply to harass him and drive him from the Colony, he, after consulting with his friends, resolved to return to England by the first opportunity; and having set up an advertisement in the great square to that effect, and served personal notice on his chief persecutor to the same effect, on the 2d of December, 1737, he bid farewell to his friends in Georgia, and proceeded by land to Carolina for the purpose of procuring a passage, and on the 22d of the same month he bid adieu to America, and on the first of February following, he once more set foot on the shores of England, having been absent nearly two years and a half from his native land.

SECTION II.

The visit of Mr. Wesley to America, if not followed by all the good results which he desired, was nevertheless followed by consequences which to himself and the world may never be fully known until eternity discloses more clearly to the knowledge of man the true relation of cause and effect. We have hitherto been looking at Mr. John Wesley as a young man—a scholar—a minister—having the fear of God before his eyes, and using all his powers to bring himself into subjection to the law of God, but we have not thus far been able to discover in him the power of saving faith. His intercourse with the Moravians while on the passage to America and during his residence in Georgia, convinced him, that notwithstanding his morality and uprightness of conduct, these poor Germans had something which he did not possess, that the humility, patience, long-suffering, and kindness, manifested by them were the fruits of a certain kind or degree of faith, to which he had not as yet attained, and however desirous of possessing the same, how to attain to it he knew not. In this state of spiritual darkness and blindness, he remained until his return to England. A few days after his arrival, he proceeded to London, where he providentially met the Rev. Peter Bohler, a bishop of the Moravian church. To this man he opened his heart, and after several communications with him, he became more clearly convinced that thus far himself had been a stranger to the exercise of evangelical faith—a faith which consists of a "sure trust and confidence, which a man has in God, that through the merits of Christ, his sins are forgiven, and he reconciled to the favor of God." He also became convinced of the possibility and necessity of instantaneous conversion, and although yet a stranger to the converting grace of God in his own heart, by the advice of Mr. Bohler he resolved to preach the doctrines of faith and conversion, until he himself became the subject of that grace. For the purpose of advancing the cause of truth in his own heart, and the hearts of others, by the further advice of Mr. Bohler, Mr. Wesley and a few others formed themselves into a religious Society which met in Fetter-lane, which Society was long after known as the "Fetter-lane Society," and was composed at first of united brethren and members of the church of England. Mr. Wesley continued to walk in darkness until the 24th of May, on the evening of which day he attended a meeting in Aldersgate-street, and while a person was reading Luther's preface to the Epistle to the Romans, and while describing the change which is wrought in the heart through faith in Christ, "I," says Wesley, "felt my heart strangely warmed, I felt I did trust in Christ alone for salvation: and an assurance was given me that he had taken away my sins, even mine, and saved me from the law of sin and death." In those few words, we have recorded Mr. Wesley's account of his own conversion,—an event of greater importance to the religious world and to mankind in general, than the birth of a Napoleon or the victories of the greatest warriors the world ever knew. The immediate fruit of his conversion, and at the same time a strong evidence of its reality and genuineness, was a love for his enemies, and a desire for their welfare. "I began," he continues, "to pray with all my might for those who had in a more especial manner despitefully used me and persecuted me."

It is worthy of remark that the first time Mr. Wesley prayed *extempore*, was with a prisoner under sentence of death, by the name of Clifford; and that the Father of mercies was pleased to sanction such mode of prayer, by giving the poor criminal a knowledge of sin forgiven which he retained to his last earthly moments. It is also worthy of attention, that this incident transpired but a few days previous to Mr. Wesley's conversion.

After Mr. Wesley's conversion, he had a strong desire to visit Germany and converse with those pious Moravians who had obtained like precious faith with himself. He accordingly sailed from London, and on the 15th of June reached Rotterdam. While on his way to Hernhut—the Moravian settlement—he was hospitably entertained by Count Zinzendorf, the leader and head of the Moravians, and with him he spent some pleasant hours in conversation in regard to the doctrines of the new birth and justification by faith. On the first of August he reached Hernhut, where he spent a fortnight, visiting the brethren, listening to their preaching, and conversing frequently and freely with them on experimental subjects, faith, &c. Here he learned many things of which he had before been ignorant, and admired in many respects their temporal economy, and after having bidden the brethren a reluctant farewell, he returned to London, more than ever determined to preach Christ and salvation through faith.

Shortly before the conversion of John Wesley, he, in company with Peter Bohler, visited Charles Wesley, who was then in Oxford, confined upon a bed of sickness. Bohler proclaimed to him the way of life and salvation; but although sincerely desirous of being all that God would have him be, he was rather too much of a Pharisee to be willing to throw away his own righteousness, and throw himself all naked and helpless on the blood of Christ for salvation. After his recovery, he repaired to London, where Bohler again visited him, and succeeded in convincing him that his "own righteousness was but as filthy rags," and that while unjustified before God, his state was eminently a dangerous one. From this moment he became a sincere seeker of salvation by faith alone, and on the 21st of May, 1738—three days previous to the conversion of his brother John—he became the happy subject of converting grace. Thus the two brothers who had suffered so much together in, and for the cause of God, were brought nearly at the same time to a state of justification before God, and to the enjoyment of the blessings resulting from faith in Christ as their personal Saviour; and thus in a marvellous manner and by the most humble instrumentalities was the Lord raising up from the bosom of the church of England, men who would in future produce a greater, a mightier, a happier revolution, not only in England, but throughout Christendom, than the world had witnessed since the days of Luther—a revolution embracing the best of all objects, and attended by the best of all results, —a revival of pure religion.

At the period of the conversion of the Messrs. Wesley, vital piety was but little known in England. Indeed, the religion of the kingdom was a religion of mere forms and ceremonies, of prayers, fasts, and thanksgivings; while Sabbath-breaking, drunkenness, licentiousness, gambling, hunting, &c. &c., were not only permitted, but openly practised by the clergy of the Established Church. So greatly, indeed, had true religion declined after the Reformation, that Archbishop Leighton in speaking of the church in his time represents it as a "carcass without a spirit;" and Bishop Burnet represents the clergy of his times as having "less authority, and more contempt than those of any other church in Europe," as "more remiss in their labors, and less severe in their lives;" and such was the fact at the beginning of the labors of the Wesleys and their co-laborers. Darkness, moral, spiritual, doctrinal, covered the people. With an orthodox liturgy, there existed a semi-infidel clergy; with a formula of devotion, beautiful in its language, and sublime in its teachings, the bought or borrowed sermons of its ministers, while they vied to correspond with the beauty, were entire strangers to the sublimity, and indeed to the theology found in their book of devotion. This state of things, deplorable as it might be, was not after all among the unaccountable events of history. About the time of the Reformation under Luther, we find England with its church and clergy a nation of Papists. Soon the church becomes Protestant, and the clergy, for the sake of retaining their livings, become Protestant also. Again the church relapses into Romanism, and the clergy, with the same object in view, become Romanists. Again Protestant episcopacy becomes the religion of the nation, and the clergy, ever mindful of their own interests, become again traitors to the Pope, and the staunch friends of the Reformation. With such motives to influence the clergy in their frequent conversions, we may naturally conclude that while the *fleece* was an object of their tender regard, the flock themselves were entirely neglected. If, in fact, the religious teachers of the establishment were mere men of the world, seeking after wealth, or pursuing the rounds of pleasure and amusement, alike forgetful of their own souls and the souls of their people, what, we ask, must have been the moral and religious condition of that people? To be baptized, confirmed, and attend the communion of the Lord's Supper on Christmas day, Easter-Sunday, and perhaps once or twice more during the year, constituted in their view the obedience which Christ requires of his followers; while drunkenness, profanity, Sabbath-breaking, and their kindred vices prevailed to an alarming extent. In a word, the Church of England was principally composed of a multitude of baptized heathens, who were but little superior to the aborigines of America, either in point of religion, morals, or intelligence. Nor was the state of religion much better in the different dissenting bodies of the land. It is true that a higher tone of morality and intelligence existed in the different dissenting churches. The ministers, as a general thing, were men of morality and integrity, but through the influence of Pelagian sentiments and Antinomian errors, vital godliness was but little known either among ministers or people. If the above facts were not matters of history, the charitable reader would no doubt feel disposed to think that we had given altogether too dark a picture of the then existing state of things; but the annals of the times convince us that while infidelity prevailed among the higher classes, and even among the clergy, the grossest and most beastly passions were exhibited from time to time among the lower classes. England was indeed a "carcass without a spirit," a carcass dead, rotten, and fit only for burial in the depths of the sea. Such was the existing state of things in England when John and Charles Wesley were brought to the knowledge of the truth as it regards experimental piety; and from the knowledge of their character previously to their conversion we may reasonably suppose that after becoming Christians they would be in labors still more abundant, and would evince a still greater desire to bless and save their fellow-men. But at this time the brothers, especially John, had formed no plan of operation for their future course of action. Indeed John Wesley from the beginning to the end of his ministerial life appears to have been emphatically the child of Providence, going as far, and no farther than Providence seemed to open his way. Hence while we follow him from step to step, from one thing to another—from the formation of his first Society to the organization of his legal Conference, we can clearly trace the finger of God pointing, directing, controlling this wonderful man in all his varied movements. Not that we believe that John Wesley was the subject of plenary inspiration, but that he did act under the inspired influence of the Holy Ghost, we no more doubt than we doubt the fact of his existence, or doubt the propriety of the petition offered by the bishop who ordained him in these words—

"Come, Holy Ghost, our souls inspire,
And lighten with celestial fire;
Thou the anointing Spirit art
Who dost thy seven-fold gifts impart," &c.

Yes, John Wesley's "soul" was "inspired" to accomplish the work which God had given him to do, and acting under the influence of such inspiration he chose the "world for his parish," and "souls as his hire." Besides, John Wesley was peculiarly fitted by nature, education, and grace to become a religious reformer. With a sound physical constitution, a commanding flow of eloquence, a prepossessing appearance, a large stock of useful knowledge, and above all, a heart full of the love of God and man, panting after the redemption of his countrymen, and the salvation of the world, he was eminently qualified for the work of an apostle. Nor was his brother Charles wanting in those gifts and graces necessary to fit him to become a faithful co-worker in the vineyard of the Lord. A man of solid information, of sanctified talents, of cautious zeal, he was prepared to render great assistance to his brother in promoting a revival of pure religion. But the great qualification possessed by Charles as a religious reformer was the wonderful, we might almost say, the inspired gift of poetry evinced by him in the composition of those sacred, sublime songs which he wrote for the use of the people converted through the instrumentality of himself and fellow-laborers. These songs, or hymns, are among the most perfect specimens of genuine poetry that can be found in Christendom. Not only do we find in them good taste, but good theology; not merely a beautiful arrangement of words and lines, a body without a soul, but a hidden power, a soul-stirring pathos, a something that takes hold of the heart while it pleases the ear—that subdues the fiercer passions while it raises the flame of love—that brings down the pride of the human heart, makes a man loathe himself, and then raises his thoughts to heaven, to Christ, to God, and leads him by faith to realize a "heaven on earth begun." The poetic works of Charles Wesley, and the literary and theological productions of John Wesley, will ever remain a standing monument of their learning, their zeal, their piety, their qualifications as ministers of God, raised up for an extraordinary purpose, and endowed with extraordinary gifts, to enable them to discharge the duties of an extraordinary calling among men.

From the above remarks the reader will perceive that while we do not claim for the Wesleys the possession of the same degree of inspiration granted to the prophets and apostles of old, we do claim for them such a degree of inspiration as is not ordinarily given to the ministers of Christ, even to the most faithful of them—a degree of inspiration necessary to prepare them to produce one of the greatest moral and religious reformations known in modern times.

SECTION III.

After the conversion of John Wesley he began immediately to declare what the Lord had done for his soul, and wherever he was permitted to use the pulpits of his brother clergymen, he gladly availed himself of the privilege both in and around London. He also extended his labors to Bristol, Oxford, and other parts of England, and such was the degree of fervor and zeal with which he proclaimed the way of life and salvation, that many of the lukewarm or unconverted clergy took offence at his zeal and fidelity, and closed their churches against him. The closing of the churches in London and other places, impelled Mr. Wesley to adopt the practice of field-preaching, or preaching in the open air. His first attempt at field-preaching was in Bristol on the 1st of April, 1739. While in London he had been strongly solicited by Rev. George Whitfield, who was then in Bristol, and who had commenced the practice of field-preaching, to repair to the latter place for the purpose of holding forth the way of life and salvation. He arrived at Bristol on Saturday evening, and on the following day he, for the first time, witnessed what in his journal he calls, "this strange way of preaching in the fields." At first he could not reconcile such proceedings with his nice sense of propriety and order, but on the following day, in the afternoon, he so far overcame his scruples as to adopt the same method of doing good by preaching to a congregation of three thousand people with great effect. After spending some time in Bristol, he returned to London, and finding most of the churches closed against him, he preached to large congregations in an open space called Moorfields. On the 12th of May, 1739, Mr. Wesley laid the foundation of the first Methodist chapel. Bristol has the honor of being the place where this chapel was erected. On November of the same year, Mr. Wesley began to occupy as a preaching place an old building which had been used as a cannon foundry in Moorfields, London. From the circumstance of its having been previously used for the above purpose, it was ever after known by the name of "Foundry Chapel," or simply the "Foundry." In this same year (1739), class meetings were instituted. They originated in Bristol, and were merely a result of the erection of the chapel above alluded to. In erecting the said chapel Mr. Wesley had not designed, nor did he expect to take any responsibility as to the trouble and expense of building. Eleven persons had been selected as *feoffees* or trustees of the building. But the work had not progressed far before Mr. Wesley became satisfied that if completed at all he must become responsible for the cost. He accordingly involved himself in debt to raise means to complete the edifice, and as he had not the means to defray the expense out of his own pocket he appointed certain persons to go round among the members of the Society, and receive a penny a-week or whatever they felt disposed to give. These collectors being men of piety, when receiving the penny from each one, in return gave a word of Christian advice and exhortation. Soon, however, it was found more convenient for the members of the Society to bring in their pennies at an appointed time and place, and pay the same over to the collectors, the latter in every case giving advice and exhortation. From this circumstance arose the distinct formation of classes, and the appointment of class-leaders to take charge of a limited number of the members in Society in the absence of Mr. Wesley; and in pursuing the above plan, not only was the chapel debt in due time cancelled, but the members were individually strengthened and encouraged to persevere in the way of holiness.

About this time, or shortly after, watch-night meetings were held among the poor colliers of Kingswood near Bristol. Those men while in a state of sin and ignorance, had been in the habit of spending their Saturday evenings to a late hour at the tavern or ale-house in the most profane and boisterous manner; but after having listened to the preaching of Wesley and Whitfield, they heartily renounced their sins and became "new men in Christ Jesus." Their Saturday evenings, instead of being spent as heretofore, were spent in the more becoming manner of praying to, and praising God; and such was the success attending these late meetings of the colliers that Mr. Wesley afterward, in 1742, introduced them into the Society in London, having held them at first once a month, and then once a quarter.

In the meanwhile Societies were being raised up in differents parts of England and Wales, and new doors were continually being opened for the Wesleys. New fields of labor were constantly presenting themselves before them, and cries of a Macedonian nature were multiplying on every hand. The

Wesleys did not obey these calls without subjecting themselves to reproach and persecution. From the Archbishop of Canterbury down to the servile curate of an obscure parish, and from the peer down to the scum of the people, their motives were misjudged, their actions misrepresented, their seeming irregularities condemned, and in some cases their persons were insulted; but in spite of ecclesiastical opposition, or the rude insults of the profane, the work of God continued to spread far and wide. Congregations numbering from one to fifteen thousand were frequently collected to hear the glorious doctrine of the cross; and many of them not only heard but believed, and were saved. As many of such as desired were permitted to become members of the Society, that they might meet from time to time for mutual edification and instruction. As the Societies continued to multiply it became necessary to adopt some rule of conduct as a condition of membership, and in 1743, the general rules of the Societies were adopted and published by Mr. Wesley. These rules in substance remain the same at the present time, and we have no doubt will continue in substance what they ever have been as long as Methodism exists. As Societies multiplied it became necessary to leave the same under the spiritual guidance of some one or more pious and judicious men, who, in the absence of Mr. Wesley, would exercise a kind of pastoral supervision over them. Where the clergyman of a parish would consent to take such supervision, Mr. Wesley gladly availed himself of such aid, and it is gratifying to know that there were a few evangelical clergymen of the Church of England who became faithful laborious co-workers with Mr. Wesley in this and other respects; but when, as in most cases, the ministers of the Establishment not only withheld their co-operation, but openly and rudely opposed the work of God, it became necessary to select other persons who would act as far as they could in giving assistance to Mr. Wesley in the spiritual supervision of his Societies. Hence arose the necessity for lay-preachers, or men who had not been episcopally ordained by the authority of the Church of England. At first Mr. Wesley appears to have been opposed to the preaching of laymen, but in this as in many other respects his opposition was overcome by the seeming indications of the Providence of God. While preparing to leave London for a time he requested Mr. Thomas Maxfield, a young man of respectable talents, to pray with and advise the Society in his absence. After having exercised his gifts several weeks, according to the request of Mr. Wesley, he at length thought it to be his duty to expound a portion of Scripture, and did so much to the satisfaction and edification of the Society; but when Mr. Wesley heard at a distance of Mr. Maxfield's attempts to preach he hurried back to London with all speed to put a stop to what he considered an outrage upon order and propriety. Before, however, he approached Maxfield for the purpose of silencing him, Mr. Wesley's mother interfered by saying, "John, take care what you do with respect to that young man, for he is as surely called of God to preach as you are." Mr. Wesley hesitated, waited until he had himself heard Maxfield preach, witnessed the effects produced by such preaching, and concluded, indeed, that if not in the order of the Church of England that unordained men should preach the gospel, it was certainly in accordance with the will of heaven. From this period lay-preachers began to multiply, and it is owing to the labors of those men that the stone which first was set in motion by the Wesleys, has rolled with increasing dimensions and velocity throughout England, and other parts of the earth.

SECTION IV.

We have stated in the previous sections, that the Messrs. Wesley were the subjects of reproach and persecution, and the same is true of many of those who adopted their views and became members of their Societies. It may not be uninteresting or unprofitable to the reader, to give a few instances of bitter hostility on the part of clergymen and others, to the early Methodists, which facts we glean principally from Wesley's Journal.

While Mr. Wesley was on one occasion preaching in Bath, the notorious Beau Nash, the prince of fashion and dissipation, approached the preacher and inquired by what authority he said those things? Mr. Wesley at once replied: "By the authority of Jesus Christ, conveyed to me by the (now) Archbishop of Canterbury when he laid his hands upon me and said, 'Take thou authority to preach the gospel.'" Nash said to him, "This is contrary to act of Parliament, this is a conventicle." Wesley replied, "Sir, the conventicles mentioned in that act are seditious meetings; but this is not such, here is no shadow of sedition; therefore it is not contrary to that act." Nash replied, "I say it is; and beside, your preaching frightens people out of their wits." "Sir, did you ever hear me preach?" "No." "How then can you judge of what you never heard?" "Sir, by common report." "Common report, Sir, is not enough. Give me leave, Sir, to ask, is not your name Nash?" "My name is Nash." "Sir, I dare not judge of *you* by common report, I think it is not enough to judge by." After pausing awhile, Nash recovered himself, and said, "I desire to know what these people come here for:" on which an old lady replied, "Sir, leave him to me; let an old woman answer him: you, Mr. Nash, take care of your body; we take care of our souls, and for the food of our souls we come here." Nash, being thus confounded by the old lady, walked off without adding another word.

At a certain time, Mr. Charles Wesley visited Gloucester in company with Thomas Maxfield, and repaired to a place called Bengeworth for the purpose of seeing Mr. Benjamin Seward, an old friend and fellow-Christian. They however found that Mr. S. had been for some time sick of a fever, and that during his sickness, his relations, who were violent opposers of the truth, had intercepted all his letters and called his fever madness, and had placed servants over him to prevent any Methodist from coming near him. Instead of being permitted to see, and converse with his friends, Mr. Henry Seward, a brother of the sick man, gave Mr. Wesley plenty of abuse, by calling him a scoundrel, rascal, pickpocket, &c. Mr. Wesley made but little reply, but gave notice that on the next day he would preach near Mr. Seward's house—the usual place of preaching. Mr. H. Seward forbade his preaching near his brother's premises, and threatened his arrest if he did so, and gave him notice, that four constables were engaged to effect the arrest. At the appointed time, Mr. Wesley proceeded toward the place of appointment, but was met by the Mayor's officer, who requested Mr. Wesley to accompany him to the Mayor's office. Mr. Wesley told the functionary that he reverenced the Mayor, on account of his office, but that he "must first wait on the Lord, and then on the Mayor." As he proceeded toward the place of meeting, he was met by Mr. Seward, who threatened and reviled him in an outrageous manner. The only reply made by Mr. Wesley, consisted in singing the well-known lines,

"Shall I for fear of feeble man,
The Spirit's course in me restrain?" &c.,

but this, instead of quieting Mr. S. only served to make him more furious, and calling some vile fellows to his aid, they laid hold on Mr. Wesley and led him out of the corporation. As soon as his captors let go their hold, Mr. Wesley again commenced singing, and to the hundreds who followed as spectators of the scene, he preached with great liberty and power, from the words: "If God be for us, who can be against us?" After sermon, he went to the Mayor's office, where he also met a clergyman who was much incensed against him, and who found fault with the writings and proceedings of the Wesleys and Whitfield. Mr. Wesley told him that if he was a carnal, worldly-minded clergyman, he would leave with him the sentence of Chrysostom, "Hell is paved with the skulls of Christian priests." After some apology by the Mayor for the violence used, Mr. Wesley left the office, preferring not to enter any complaint against those who had maltreated him.

Shortly after this transaction, Mr. Charles Wesley being in Bristol, went to Temple church and listened to a sermon wherein the preacher strongly recommended religion as the best way to raise a fortune. Perceiving Mr. Wesley in the congregation, he, after sermon, caused the clerk to make proclamation that none should remain to the sacrament, who did not belong to that parish. Mr. W. while wondering at the strange procedure which drove scores of worthy persons from the church, did not suspect that the proclamation was made for his special benefit; but he was quickly informed of the fact by the clerk, who went to him and respectfully told him that Mr. B. the officiating clergyman, bade him go away, for he would not give him the sacrament. Mr. W. thinking there must be some mistake, went to the vestry door and quietly asked admission. "Are you of this parish?" inquired the minister. "Sir, you see that I am a clergyman," replied Mr. Wesley; on which, the former, dropping his pretence of not knowing him, boldly charged him with rebellion in expounding the Scriptures without authority, and in express language informed him that he repelled him from the sacrament. Mr. W. in reply, cited him to answer for such conduct before Jesus Christ in the day of judgment. This enraged the already angry minister, who called to certain constables who were present, "Here, take away this man." Mr. W. however, saved them the trouble of taking him away, by quietly leaving the *Good Shepherd* and his flock to themselves.

In this same city of Bristol, Mr. John Wesley was frequently assailed by mobs, who attempted not only to disturb his preaching, but injure his person. On one occasion, while expounding the former part of the twenty-third chapter of the Acts of the Apostles, "not only the courts and the alleys, but all the street upward and downward, was filled with people shouting, cursing, and swearing, and ready to swallow the ground with fierceness and rage." After much effort on the part of the Mayor, and chief constable, the ringleaders were arrested and brought before the court of Quarter Sessions, and receiving some slight punishment, were liberated. The decision of the Mayor prevented the recurrence of any such disgraceful proceedings in that city.

In London also, the Methodists were much exposed to persecution and the fury of an enraged and beastly population. They were frequently pelted with showers of stones, and an attempt was once made to unroof the Foundry Chapel while the congregation were assembled for worship. These things were done openly, the ignorant mob supposing that there was no law against abusing or even killing the Methodists. These London riots were, however, shortly after discontinued, by the influence of the reigning king, George III., who, in conversation with a Quaker gentleman, who had previously resided in Oxford, and who was well acquainted with the Messrs. Wesley, in answer to a question of the king, whether he knew the Wesleys who were making such a noise in the nation, replied, "I know them well, king George, and thou mayest be assured that thou hast not two better men in thy kingdom, nor men that love thee better, than John and Charles Wesley." After this conversation, the Justices of the Peace in and around London received "orders from above," to do the Methodists justice, whenever the latter should apply for a redress of grievances. Subsequently, a few arrests were made, and slight punishments inflicted, which served to put an end to violent persecution in London.

But while the liberty of worshipping God was thus being secured to the Methodists in Bristol and London, in other parts of England the storm of persecution raged with unmitigated fury. In his journal, under date of March 19, 1742, John Wesley says: "I rode once more to Pensford, at the earnest request of several serious people. The place where they desired me to preach, was a little green spot near the town. But I had no sooner begun, than a great company of rabble, hired —as we afterwards found—for that purpose, came furiously upon us, bringing a bull which they had been baiting, and now strove to drive in among the people. But the beast was wiser than his drivers; and continually ran either on one, or the other, while we quietly sang praise to God, and prayed, for about an hour. The poor wretches, finding themselves disappointed, at length seized upon the bull, now weak and tired, after being so long torn and beaten both by dogs and men, and by main strength partly dragged and partly thrust him in among the people. When they had found their way to the little table on which I stood, they strove several times to throw it down, by thrusting the helpless beast against it; who of himself stirred no more than a log of wood. I once or twice put aside his head with my hand, that the blood might not drop upon my clothes, intending to go on as soon as the hurry should be a little over. But the table falling down, some of my friends caught me in their arms, and carried me right away on their shoulders, while the rabble wreaked their vengeance on the table, which they tore bit from bit. We went a little way off, where I finished my discourse without any noise or interruption."

While visiting Epworth—his native town—at a certain time, Mr. Wesley was informed that in a neighboring town, a whole wagon load of Methodists had been carried before a justice of the peace: Mr. Wesley accordingly rode over to see the justice, and if necessary, befriend those who had been carried before him. The justice inquired of the self-constituted guardians of religion and morals, what the Methodists had done. "Why, they pretend to be better than other people; and besides, they pray from morning till night." "But have they done nothing besides?" "Yes, sir," said an old man, "an't please your worship, they have *convarted* my wife. Till she went among them, she had such a tongue! and now she is as quiet as a lamb." "Carry them back, carry them back," said the justice, "and let them convert all the scolds in the town."

At a time when Mr. Wesley, at a place called Great Gardens, went to preach, he found a great multitude gathered together, and he remarks in his journal, "Many of the worst of the people labored to disturb those who were of a better mind. They endeavored to drive in a herd of cows among them, but the brutes were wiser than their masters. They then threw whole showers of stones, one of which struck me just between the eyes, but I felt no pain at all, and when I had wiped away the blood, went on testifying with a loud voice that 'God had given to them that believe, not the spirit of fear, but of power, and of love, and of a sound mind.'"

Early in the year 1743, Mr. John Wesley again visited Epworth, the place of his birth, and the scene of his own and his father's pastoral labors in former years. The curate, Mr. Romley, owed not only his curacy, but all he had in this world to the kindness of Mr. Wesley, Sen., and yet this curate would not allow the son to preach in the church where his deceased father had administered the word of life for many years. John, however, when he could secure a congregation, was at no loss for a pulpit or a church, as long as a table or rock could furnish the one, or the wide-spread field the other. On the present occasion, he preached at eight in the morning from his father's tomb-stone, to a large assemblage, not only from Epworth, but from the neighboring towns. As it was Sacrament Sunday, these last inquired of Mr. Wesley if it would not be well for them to receive it. Mr. Wesley replied, "By all means; but it will be more respectful first to ask the curate's leave." One accordingly went to the curate in the name of the rest, to whom the curate said, "Pray tell Mr. Wesley I shall not give *him* the Sacrament, for he is *not fit*." This unpleasant incident, however, instead of begetting in Mr. Wesley a warmth of temper, or a desire to reproach and find fault, only led him to humble himself before the God of his father, and he exclaims, "How great a God is our God! There could not have been so fit a place under heaven, where this should befall me first, as my father's house, the place of my nativity, and the very place where, according to the strictest sect of our religion, I lived a Pharisee. It was also fit in the highest degree, that he who repelled me from that very table where I had myself so often distributed the bread of life, should be one who owed his all in this world to the tender love which my father had shown his, as well as personally to himself." Let the reader remember that while the Wesleys were thus denied the privileges accorded to the humblest member of the established church, they were ministers ordained by her authority, set apart by her bishops, and the only thing which rendered them unfit to be communicants at the altars of their own church, was the fact that they were zealous for the salvation of souls: that while they labored to save men from sin—from drunkenness, Sabbath-breaking, profanity, &c.—some of the very ministers who were the loudest in their denunciations of the Wesleys and their adherents were themselves drunkards and Sabbath-breakers. As an exemplification of this fact, we may state that on one occasion, while John Wesley was preaching at a place called Wednesbury, a gentleman rode up very drunk, and after using many bitter and reviling words to Mr. Wesley and the congregation, endeavored to ride over the people! And yet this gentleman was a zealous son of the church, a clergyman who ministered at her altars, and who, in his own estimation, and, no doubt, in the estimation of others of his clerical brethren, was too holy to commune at the table of the Lord with such a man as Mr. Wesley!

At the place last mentioned—Wednesbury—Mr. Wesley had frequently preached without molestation, and with such success, that in a short time, over three hundred were joined together as a Society; but the parish minister, supposing his craft to be in danger, raised such a storm of persecution against the unoffending members, as would have disgraced a community of pagans. Mr. Wesley has given in his Journal, vol. iii. pages 295–9, a brief account of the riots which followed as the result of the influence exerted by the infamous and unworthy clergyman above alluded to. As his description is as brief and correct as any that can be given, we will favor the reader by quoting his language.—" 1743, Oct. 20.—After preaching to a small, attentive congregation, I rode to Wednesbury. At twelve I preached in a ground near the middle of the town, to a far larger congregation than was expected, on 'Jesus Christ, the same yesterday, to-day, and forever.' I believe every one present felt the power of God, and no creature offered to molest us, either going or coming; but the Lord fought for us, and we held our peace. I was writing at Francis Ward's, in the afternoon, when the cry arose, 'that the mob had beset the house!' We prayed that God would disperse them; and it was so: one went this way, and another that, so that in half an hour not a man was left. I told our brethren, 'Now is the time for us to go;' but they pressed me exceedingly to stay. So—that I might not offend them—I sat down, though I foresaw what would follow. Before five, the mob surrounded the house again in greater numbers than ever. The cry of one and all was, 'Bring out the minister—we will have the minister.' I desired one to take their captain by the hand, and bring him into the house. After a few sentences exchanged between us, the lion was become the lamb. I desired him to go and bring one or two of the most angry of his companions. He brought in two, who were ready to swallow the ground with rage; but in two minutes they were as calm as he. I then bade them make way, that I might go out among the people. As soon as I was in the midst of them, I called for a chair, and standing up, asked, 'What do any of you want with me?' Some said, 'We want you to go to the justice.' I replied, 'That I will, with all my heart.' I then spoke a few words, which God applied; so that they cried out with might and main, 'The gentleman is an honest gentleman, and we will spill our blood in his defence.' I asked, 'Shall we go to the justice to-night, or in the morning?' Most of them cried, 'To-night, to-night;' on which I went before, and two or three hundred followed, the rest returning whence they came.

"The night came on before we had walked a mile, together with heavy rain. However, on we went to Bently Hall, two miles from Wednesbury. One or two ran before to tell Mr. Lane that they had brought Mr. Wesley before his worship. Mr. Lane replied, 'What have I to do with Mr. Wesley? go and carry him back again.' By this time the main body came up, and began knocking at the door. A servant told them Mr. Lane was in bed. His son followed and asked what was the matter. One replied, 'Why, an't please you, they sing psalms all day, nay, and make folks rise at five in the morning, and what would your worship advise us to do?' 'To go home,' said Mr. Lane, 'and be quiet.'"

"Here they were at a full stop, till one advised to go to Justice Persehouse, at Walsal. All agreed to this; so we hastened on, and about seven, came to his house. But Mr. P. likewise sent word that he was in bed. Now they were at a stand again; but they all thought it the wisest course to make the best of their way home. About fifty of them undertook to convey me, but we had not gone a hundred yards when the mob of Walsal came pouring in like a flood, and bore down all before them. The Daralston mob made what defence they could, but they were weary as well as outnumbered; so that in a short time many being knocked down, the rest ran away and left me in their hands."

"To attempt speaking was in vain; for the noise on every side was like the roaring of the sea. So they dragged me along till we came to town, when seeing the door of a large house open—I attempted to go in; but a man catching me by the hair pulled me back into the middle of the mob. They made no more stop till they had carried me through the main street from one end of the town to the other. I continued speaking all the time to those within hearing, feeling no pain or weariness. At the west end of the town, seeing a door half-open, I made toward it and would have gone in; but a gentleman in the shop would not suffer me, saying they would pull the house down to the ground. However, I stood at the door and asked, 'Are you willing to hear me speak?' Many cried out, 'No, no! knock his brains out; down with him; kill him at once.' Others said, 'Nay, but we will hear him first.' I began asking, 'What evil have I done? Which of you all have I wronged in word or deed?' And continued speaking for above a quarter of an hour till my voice suddenly failed; then the floods began to lift up their voice again, many crying out, 'Bring him away, bring him away!'"

"In the meantime, my voice and my strength returned, and I broke out aloud into prayer. And now the man who just before headed the mob, turned and said, 'Sir, I will spend my life for you; follow me, and not one soul shall touch a hair of your head.' Two or three other fellows confirmed his words, and got close to me immediately. At the same time, the gentleman in the shop cried out, 'For shame, for shame! let him go.' An honest butcher who was a little further off, said it was a shame to do thus, and pulled back four or five, one after another, who were running on the most fiercely. The people then, as if by common consent, fell back to the right and left; while those three or four men took me between them and carried me through them all. But on the bridge, the mob rallied again; we therefore went on one side, over the mill-dam, and thence through the meadows; till a little before ten, God brought me safe to Wednesbury, having lost only one flap of my waistcoat and a little skin from one of my hands."

Such was one of the "fiery trials" through which Mr. Wesley was called to pass; and a natural inquiry of the philosopher and Christian will be, With what spirit did the apostle of Methodism endure the rage of his enemies? In reading the

4

extracts just given, the reader may have been struck with the evident intention of Mr. Wesley to give the account in the mildest possible language, and to present every redeeming trait of character and conduct that was manifested by his cruel enemies. But let us hear him further, in relation to this instance of persecution. "I never saw such a chain of providences before; so many convincing proofs that the hand of God is on every person and thing, overruling all as seemeth him good. The poor woman of Darlaston, who had headed that mob, and sworn that none should touch me, when she saw her followers give way, run into the thickest of the throng, and knocked down three or four men, one after another. But many assaulting her at once, she was soon overpowered, and had probably been killed in a few minutes—three men keeping her down and beating her with all their might—had not a man called to one of them, 'Hold, Tom, hold!' 'Who is there,' said Tom. 'What! honest Munchin? Nay then, let her go.' So they, held her hand and let her get up and crawl home as well as she could. From the beginning to the end I found the same presence of mind as if I had been sitting in my own study. But I took no thought for one moment before another; only once it came into my mind that if they should throw me into the river it would spoil the papers that were in my pocket. For myself, I did not doubt but I should swim across, having but a thin coat and a light pair of boots."

Mr. Wesley next proceeds in his Journal to recount a few of the more remarkable incidents of the riot in the following words:—

"The circumstances that follow, I thought more particularly remarkable: 1. That many endeavored to throw me down while we were going down hill, on a slippery path to the town; as well judging that if I was once on the ground, I should hardly rise any more. But I made no stumble at all, nor the least slip, till I was entirely out of their hands. 2. That although many strove to lay hold on my collar or clothes, they could not fasten at all; only one got fast hold of the flap of my waistcoat, which was soon left in his hand: the other flap, in the pocket of which was a bank note, was torn but half off. 3. That a lusty man just behind, struck at me several times with a large oaken stick; with which, if he had struck me once on the back part of my head, it would have saved him all further trouble. But every time, the blow was turned aside, I know not how; for I could not move to the right hand or left. 4. That another came rushing through the press, and raising his arm to strike, on a sudden let it drop and only stroked my head, saying, 'What soft hair he has.' 5. That I stopped exactly at the Mayor's door as if I had known it—which the mob probably thought I did—and found him standing in the shop, which gave the first check to the madness of the people. 6. That the very first men whose hearts were turned, were the heroes of the town—the captains of the rabble on all occasions, one of them having been a prize fighter at the bear garden. 7. That from first to last, I heard none give a reviling word, or call me by any opprobrious name whatever; but the cry of one and all was, 'The Preacher! The Preacher! The Parson! The Minister!' 8. That no creature, at least within my hearing, laid anything to my charge either true or false; having in the hurry, quite forgot to provide themselves with an accusation of any kind. And lastly, That they were as utterly at a loss to know what to do with me; none proposing any determinate thing; only, 'Away with him! Kill him at once.'"

When the mob just described, began to gather, there were a few of the Society in the same house with Mr. Wesley. All but four—three men and one woman—fled for their lives. Those four persons accompanied their spiritual leader and friend wherever he was led by the mob, resolved to die with him if necessary; and it is somewhat remarkable that none of them received a single blow, except one who was dragged away from Mr. Wesley's person and knocked down. The heroic female who made one of the number was asked by Mr. Wesley after the affray ended, if she was not afraid. She replied, "No, I could trust God for you, as well as for myself. I knew God would fight for his children."

The day after, Mr. Wesley left for Nottingham, and while leaving the town, was greeted on every hand with smiles and congratulations at his providential and almost miraculous escape.

A few days after Mr. Wesley had left Wednesbury, the two magistrates before whom the mob had brought him, and who had refused to see him, saw fit to issue, what Mr. Wesley calls, "as great a curiosity of its kind, as was ever seen in England." It was directed to all constables, peace officers, &c., within the county, and read as follows:

"Whereas, we, his majesty's justices of the peace for the said county of Stafford, have received information that several disorderly persons styling themselves Methodist preachers, go about raising routs and riots to the great damage of his majesty's liege people, and against the peace of our sovereign lord the king:

"These are in his majesty's name to command you and every one of you within your respective districts to make diligent search after the said Methodist preachers and to bring him, or them before some of us his said majesty's justices of the peace to be examined concerning their unlawful doings.

"Given under our hands and seals, &c."

The reader can infer from the above warrant how ready to do *justice*, those justices were, and how absolutely contemptibe, their conduct appears in refusing to aid Mr. Wesley while in the power of the mob, and after he had left their jurisdiction, issue a warrant bearing falsehood on its face, accusing him of raising 'routs and riots;' but no surprise will be excited, when we consider that these magistrates, like their brother clergymen —who first occasioned the riot by a sermon preached against Mr. Wesley—were true sons of the church. Nor did the influence of those unworthy men end in the personal abuse of

Mr. Wesley, but persons of the baser sort were hired by them and others to break open the doors of their praying neighbors, extort money, destroy goods, beat the men, insult the women, and threaten death to every Methodist.

About two years after the above disgraceful riot, Mr. Wesley while in Falmouth was the subject of another equally disgraceful persecution. While visiting at a house where he called to see a sick person, he suddenly found the house surrounded on all sides by a large multitude of people, who made a loud and confused noise as though they were taking a city by storm. The inmates of the house endeavored to still the mob, but in vain; and fearing violence, were forced to seek shelter where they could, leaving Mr. Wesley and one other person to defend themselves as best they might. The rabble roared, "Bring out the Canorum! Where is the Canorum?"—the latter word being a common one in that part of the country to signify Methodist. "No answer being given," says Mr. Wesley, "they quickly forced open the outer door and filled the passage. Only a wainscot partition was between us, which was not likely to stand long." When they began their work with abundance of imprecations, poor "Kitty" was utterly astonished, and cried out, "Oh! Sir, what must we do?" "We must pray," replied Mr. Wesley. "But is it not better to hide yourself?" asked his companion in trouble. He replied, "No, it is better for me to stand just where I am." Among the rabble were some sailors whose vessels had lately arrived in port. "Some of these being impatient at the slowness of the rest, thrust them away, and coming up altogether, set their shoulders to the inner door and cried out, Avast, lads, avast! Away went all the hinges at once, and the door fell back into the room." Mr. Wesley stepped forward into the midst of them and said, "Here I am. Which of you has anything to say to me? To which of you have I done any wrong? To you? or you? or you?" After making his way into the street bareheaded, he placed himself in the midst of the mob, and after addressing them for some time, the captains or leaders of the mob swore that not a man should touch him, and he was suffered to depart with a few imprecations from the disappointed ones who had no doubt expected to see John Wesley sacrificed on the altar of religious hatred and bigotry.

These few instances of popular fury, are given merely as illustrations of the sufferings of these men of God who were instrumental in reviving the flame of pure religion in England and other parts of the world. A volume might be filled with the detail of wrongs and outrages inflicted upon our fathers in the gospel for conscience' sake; and however interesting to the uninformed reader the recital of other instances of persecution might be, the limits of this work will only admit of the insertion of the above. Nor should the reader infer that the Wesleys were the only persons who suffered from popular violence. Throughout England Mr. Wesley's preachers and followers were subject to even worse treatment than that above described. The preachers were not only assailed by mobs, stoned, pelted, thrown into the water, &c. but were frequently imprisoned, and were sometimes impressed into the army as though they were common vagrants.* Nor should it be forgotten that these scenes of riot were in most cases induced by the influence of clergymen, magistrates, and other zealous sons of the Church of England, and that such influence was allowed to exert itself without rebuke from the bishops and other dignitaries of the church; and that only through the authority and influence of the King and the higher judicial officers were these disgraceful proceedings in any measure stopped.

* The author has it in contemplation to prepare a work to be entitled "The Persecutions of the early Methodists in Europe and America," in which the more prominent instances of persecution and violence will be recorded for the benefit of the present and future generations.

SECTION V.

NOTWITHSTANDING the efforts made on the part of ungodly men, and more ungodly ministers, as recorded in the preceding section, to stay the progress of the work of God, the latter continued to spread from one end of the kingdom to the other, producing as might be expected, a redeeming, hallowed influence on the hearts and lives of its subjects; and on none more so than in the case of the poor miners of Cornwall, among whom the disgraceful scenes last mentioned took place. While the rich, the learned, the pious, were opposing and calumniating; the miserable, the ignorant, and wretched were embracing the gospel of Jesus Christ, and submitting themselves to its easy yoke. The drunkard forsook his cup; the swearer learned to pray; the Sabbath-breaker, who for years had not seen the inside of a church, now took delight in going to the house of God; and with a revival of religion, came a reformation of manners. It was such results as these which encouraged the hearts of the Wesleys and their compeers amidst the storms of persecution which assailed them on every hand; and who instead of quailing and retreating from the field of moral conflict, girded on their heavenly armor with greater courage and bade defiance to the powers of darkness.

Societies were raised up in different parts of the kingdom, and as before intimated, it was impossible for Mr. Wesley to be present in every place where supervision was necessary. Hence arose the necessity for assistants, and helpers, who being selected from among the lay preachers, were left in charge of the Societies raised by Mr. Wesley. As the Societies increased in number, the preachers appointed to take charge of them in Mr. Wesley's absence also increased; and as it was important that these preachers should not only see Mr. Wesley, but each other occasionally, for the purpose of conferring together in relation to the great work in which they were engaged, a necessity arose for an annual or yearly conference, the first of which was held in London in June, 1744, composed of six clergymen, and a few lay-preachers. The time at this conference appears to have been mostly occupied with "conversations," in relation to doctrine and practice, and to have closed with a determination to purge the Society of all ungodly, or unworthy members; consequently during the ensuing week the members in London were reduced to about nineteen hundred. The conferences of the Methodist preachers were ever after held annually in London, Bristol, or Leeds; and although small and feeble in their first beginning, like the Societies, the preachers have increased so much, that if the whole number of preachers who acknowledge themselves as the sons of John Wesley, were gathered together in one body, they would form of themselves a population sufficient for a respectable city, in point of size.

Mr. Wesley, in the early history of his Societies, saw the importance of providing the means of education for the children of the more ignorant and destitute portion of the membership. Hence shortly after the formation of a Society among the colliers at Kingswood, he built a small school-house for the benefit of their children, where the rudiments of an English education, blended with religious and moral instruction, might be taught; and in a few years afterward, he opened a much larger school in Kingswood, where the better class of members might send their children to acquire a classical education. In process of time this school became the nursery of education for the sons of Mr. Wesley's preachers, and although the daughters were deprived the privilege of attending it for purposes of education, yet the funds by which it has been supported, have allowed of a small annuity to be granted to the latter, as an aid toward securing an education elsewhere.

In the year 1747, Methodism was introduced into Ireland through the instrumentality of Mr. Williams, one of Mr. Wesley's preachers, who crossed the channel and commenced preaching in Dublin. Great numbers flocked to hear, and a small Society was soon organized in that city. Having written an account of his success to Mr. Wesley, the latter resolved to visit Ireland immediately, where he was kindly welcomed by the members of the Society, and by a clergyman of the church. After spending some time in "confirming the disciples," he returned to England, leaving Mr. Williams in charge of the flock. Soon after this, Mr. Charles Wesley visited Dublin, where he found the members in much trouble on account of the fiery persecutions of the Papists. But amid the storm they held on their way rejoicing. About the same time, other preachers visited different parts of Ireland, and formed Societies wherever it was practicable, until at length Methodism was found planted in every considerable town and city of the kingdom. In different places in Ireland, the persecutions which arose against the Methodists, surpassed in wickedness and animosity, any that had disgraced the English name; but as the authors and abettors of these persecutions were not ministers and wardens of the Church of England, but mostly members of the Romish communion, they were endured with less pain, and more patience, than those in England, where Mr. Wesley had a right to expect toleration, at least, from the ministers of his own church.

About this time also Methodism was introduced into Scotland; and in 1757 the latter country was visited by Mr. Wesley, where he found several Societies which had been formed by his preachers. During his stay in Scotland he preached in Glasgow, and in other towns, and was well pleased with the candor and good behavior of the Scotch; and to the honor of the latter country, it should be recorded, that notwithstanding the known attachment of the Scottish people generally to the Presbyterian creed, and their acknowledged tenacity in matters of opinion, yet no mobs or riots were ever raised to prevent the introduction of the doctrines of free grace; but Mr. Wesley and his preachers were generally treated with respect, and heard with attention. And if Methodism in the latter country has not made the same progress it has in England in proportion to the number of inhabitants, the true reason may be found to exist not so much in the aversion of the Scotch to the doctrines and peculiarities of Methodism, as in the fact that their religious and moral character rendered Methodism less necessary than in the sister kingdom.

We thus find Methodism established permanently in England, Wales, Scotland, and Ireland. The attention of the reader will, in the next chapter, be directed to the introduction of Methodism into America through the instrumentality of emigrants from Ireland, and of the unexpected prosperity of this form of Christianity in the New World.

CHAPTER II.

SECTION I.

In the year 1765, a sea-going vessel might be seen in the distance approaching the harbor of New York. As the vessel neared the wharf there might be seen leaning over the bulwarks a few Irish emigrants, observing with evident emotions of interest and pleasure their future intended home. Their appearance indicated that they did not belong to the higher circles of society in their native land, nor yet that they belonged to the poorest class of Irish laborers, but with an appearance of respectability combined with the possession of a mere sufficiency of this world's gear to meet their daily returning wants, the stranger would at once conclude that they belonged to the better class of the laboring Irish; and that they had left the shores of their own green isle, not to avoid starvation at home, but to better their condition in the far off western world. The vessel having reached the dock, the few emigrants hastily stepped on shore, and for the time being, are lost sight of amidst the general din of business, without having excited any extraordinary degree of interest or attention on the part of the inhabitants of the city in which the former had taken up their abode. In the following year, 1766, another vessel, under similar circumstances, might also have been seen making for the same port; and while her passengers were being landed, an elderly lady might be observed among them slowly and thoughtfully wending her way from the ship towards the city. "In all this there is nothing wonderful," says the "observer." Certainly not; but in that old lady's possession is a precious seed, which being deposited in American soil, will take deep root, germinate, grow to be a mighty tree, and extend its branches in time from the Atlantic to the Pacific, and from the Gulf of St. Lawrence to that of Mexico! Yea, its branches extending themselves over seas and oceans, with ripe clusters hanging over continents, and inviting the South American, the African, the Chinaman, to pluck and eat the fruits of Paradise restored. To drop the figure, that elderly matron was a Christian—a *Methodist Christian*—one who felt the power of redeeming grace in her own heart, and who was anxious to spread the knowledge of salvation by faith in Christ to others who were yet under the power of sin. This lady, soon after her arrival, learned that the company who had emigrated during the preceding year in the first-mentioned ship, having been Methodists in Ireland, but who in consequence of emigrating among strangers had become in fact backsliders from God, had among them a man, who had not only been a member of one of Mr. Wesley's Societies, but who had been a local preacher in his own country. So far indeed had these persons wandered from the path of duty that they frequently indulged in what many professed Christians would call an "innocent game at cards"—a pastime thought by many clergymen of the Establishment, to be not only innocent, but highly useful in driving away serious thoughts, but a practice which Mr. Wesley not only discouraged but forbade in his members. On one occasion the lady referred to, happening to enter the room where these persons were engaged in their favorite amusement, she seized the pack of cards and threw them into the fire. She then turned with holy indignation manifested in her countenance to Mr. Philip Embury, the local preacher just alluded to, and with all the anguish of a grieved spirit, reproved him for his unfaithfulness and said, "You must preach to us, or we shall all go to hell together; and God will require our blood at your hands." This sharp appeal to his conscience, aroused the unfaithful Embury to a sense of duty;

but as if unwilling to yield at once to the power of truth and the dictates of his better judgment, he replied, "I cannot preach, for I have neither house nor congregation." The old lady replied, "Preach in your own house, and to our own company." Not being able to resist the upbraidings of conscience and the reproofs of this mother in Israel, he consented to comply with her request, and soon after preached the first Methodist sermon ever delivered in America, to a congregation of five persons, in his "own hired house." Thus we see the "precious seed" deposited already in America through the direct influence of *woman!* and in looking at the remote results of planting this seed, as they are *now* seen, and known, and felt, could it have been possible for the most uninterested spectator of the approach of those vessels, and the landing of those unpretending emigrants, to foresee the same, would they not have acknowledged that such vessels were freighted with something more precious than the gold that perisheth, and that the influence to be, in the future, exerted by the obscure, unpretending, lukewarm Embury, and the lively zeal of that praying female, would be greater, and more important, and enduring, than would have been the emigration of a thousand Louis Philippes or Joseph Bonapartes?

As Embury was now fully committed to a course of Christian fidelity, he continued statedly to preach to the few persons who were willing to hear him; and though for some time the small company of Methodists remained in obscurity, yet their hearers gradually increased in numbers, until at length it became more generally known that there was Methodist preaching in the city, and Embury's "hired house" became too small to accommodate the congregation. They were accordingly under the necessity of procuring a larger room, the rent of which was defrayed by voluntary contributions.

On one occasion, while met for worship in their humble temple, the few members were not a little disconcerted by the entrance of an officer of the British army in full uniform. The not unreasonable conclusion at first was, that he had come in to disturb them in their worship, or, peradventure, to forbid their assembling for such purpose, or for aught they knew to arrest them, and throw them into prison. But quickly their fears were dispelled when they saw the officer reverently kneel in prayer, and participate with them with seeming delight in their simple acts of worship. On inquiry they found that he whom they feared as a persecutor, was a brother in the Lord, and also one of Mr. Wesley's local preachers. Captain Webb, for such was the officer's name, had been converted under Mr. Wesley's preaching in Bristol, England, and being remarkably zealous, and possessing an ardent love for souls, he was soon permitted to preach, which he did at first to the soldiers, and then to all who wished to hear him. Being sent by the government to America, he was stationed in Albany, where he first learned that there was a small Society of Methodists in New York. Accordingly, at the first opportunity, he made his way thither, and introduced himself as above stated. He was of course invited to preach, with which invitation he complied, and as it was customary in those days for military men to wear their regimental suit on all occasions, the appearance of this officer in the pulpit with his scarlet coat, and other articles of military apparel, created no little surprise, as well as much curiosity, with a general desire to see such a wonderful sight. As might be expected, the congregation became increasingly large, so much so, that their place of meeting had again become too strait for them. Nor was the increase in size of the congregation the only effect of Captain Webb's preaching. His bold and animated manner—his burning zeal for the conversion of souls—his frequently repeated sentence, "You must repent or be forever damned," resounding in the ears of his auditors, produced that solemnity of feeling and deep searchings of heart, which resulted in many cases, in the sound conversion of a portion of his hearers. Nor did the favorable result of his preaching stop here. Officers of the British army have always been considered as entitled to mingle with the higher classes of English society, as being gentlemen and entitled to respect. The few Irish emigrants were of course, what all emigrants are who have neither wealth nor worldly honor to bring them into notice, despised and neglected by the more respectable class in society; but the appearance of a respectable man among them, as the leader of their devotions, as the expounder of their doctrines, a gentleman, an officer in the army, gave the little Society a tone of respectability which otherwise it would not have had, and brought in from time to time a portion of the more respectable class to see and hear what was going on. As just stated, their place of worship became too small; they therefore hired a rigging-loft in William-street, which they fitted up as a chapel, and here under the labors of the now faithful and pious Embury, who sustained the relation of pastor, assisted occasionally by Captain Webb, the Society continued to meet weekly, or oftener, for prayer and mutual edification. We have said that Embury sustained the relation of pastor to the Society. By this is meant only, that he had by common consent the chief direction in the spiritual affairs of its members, for as Mr. Embury was not ordained, he could not administer the sacraments; he had no salary, but was obliged to labor through the week with his own hands to earn a subsistence, while his services on Sabbath and at other times, were freely given without money and without price.

While Mr. Embury attended at all times to the interests of the Society in New York, Capt. Webb, who had more leisure and fewer pecuniary wants, made frequent excursions to Long Island and Philadelphia, not for the sake of amusement but to preach "Jesus Christ and him crucified," to all who were willing to hear him; and these labors were not in vain. Many, through his instrumentality, were brought to the knowledge of the truth, and testified that Jesus Christ has power on earth to forgive sin. In this way the good work continued to spread from place to place, and from city to city, until at length

Methodism became a subject of much inquiry and conversation in different parts of the colonies.

During the period embraced in the above remarks the congregation in New York continued further to increase in size, until the rigging-loft, in its turn, became too small to accommodate the listening throngs who from time to time assembled to hear the word of God. To remedy this inconvenience the small Society began seriously to think of building a chapel. But there appeared insuperable difficulties in the way; the Society small, the members poor, and without much influence among the higher and more wealthy class in community, they might well despair in accomplishing such a work. Here again the agency and influence of woman appears to advantage. While well-nigh discouraged about making any attempt of the kind, a Mrs. Hick, a member of the Society, and a woman full of faith and the Holy Ghost, made the matter a subject of fervent prayer to God, and while engaged in communion with the Lord, she received the answer in her soul, "I, the Lord will do it!" In connection with this answer to prayer, the plan of operation was clearly presented to her mind, which induced her at once to lay the subject before the Society, accompanied by her warm and earnest exhortations to go on with the work, trusting in the Lord. She also presented her plan of operations, which was at once adopted by the Society. In accordance with this plan, a subscription-paper was prepared and presented to the Mayor and other wealthy citizens, to whom the object and design of the contemplated chapel was fully stated, and from these persons liberal donations were at once obtained, which encouraged the Society to go on with the enterprise. Among the more prominent and active members engaged in this undertaking, in addition to Mr. Embury, Capt. Webb, and Mrs. Hicks, were Messrs. Lupton, Source, Newton, White, and Jarvis, the first of whom being a respectable merchant, exerted himself to the utmost for the erection of the chapel, his motto being, "The church first, and then my family." The above five persons acted as trustees, or building committee, and after having purchased several lots, on what was then called "Golden Hill," now John Street, they procured materials and contracted for the building of the house on their individual responsibility.

Notwithstanding the opposition of many to the erection of a Methodist Chapel, the building gradually went up, until at length "the top-stone was put on," if not with "shoutings" at least with gratitude and thankfulness on the part of the little band of believers. The municipal regulations of the province of New York at that time were such, that dissenters from the established Church of England were not allowed to occupy a place of worship exclusively for that purpose: hence it became necessary to convert a part of this building into a dwelling-house, in order to elude the regulations on the subject. The house was sixty feet in length, and forty-two in breadth, and when finished, is said to have been capable of seating seventeen hundred persons. Mr. Embury, who was a carpenter by trade, made the pulpit with his own hands, and at length, on the 30th day of October, 1668, had the pleasure and honor of preaching the first sermon in what the Society significantly called "Wesley Chapel."

While Wesley Chapel was in process of erection, the Society felt the need of more ministerial aid; for although Mr. Embury was a good man, his preaching talents were but moderate; besides, it was desirable to place themselves more directly under the supervision of Mr. Wesley, and to be recognized by him as one of his Societies. Accordingly one of their number, who had more recently emigrated from England, and who was personally acquainted with Mr. Wesley, was appointed to address him on the subject of obtaining a preacher from England. After giving Mr. Wesley a brief account of the Society, and their success in building a house for the Lord, he entreats the former to send over "a man of wisdom, of sound faith, and a good disciplinarian," and concludes with these words, "With respect to money for the payment of the preachers' passage over, if they could not procure it, we would sell our coats and shirts to procure it for them."

On the reception of this letter by Mr. Wesley the subject was laid by him before the next conference of preachers; and two of the latter, Richard Boardman and Joseph Pilmore, volunteered their services as missionaries to America, by whom Mr. Wesley sent fifty pounds as a token of love to the Society in New York, to assist in liquidating the debt which rested on the chapel. After a passage of nine weeks the missionaries arrived in America, in the latter part of October, and were received with open arms by the brethren, who now numbered about a hundred. We have thus far traced the establishment of Methodism in the Western Continent under rather peculiar circumstances. A society of one hundred members organized, a respectable house of worship erected, a large congregation secured, and all done without the aid of the brethren at home; without missionaries; without even the knowledge of Mr. Wesley! but simply through the instrumentality of two local preachers, and the counsels and prayers of two pious females. When we consider these facts in the history of American Methodism, may we not with propriety exclaim as an inspired apostle exclaimed in reference to another subject, "Behold! how great a matter a little fire kindleth!" In these facts the Christian cannot but discern the workings of an unseen hand, performing wonders in an incredibly short space of time.

The missionaries having arrived, Mr. Boardman took charge of the Society in New York, while Mr. Pilmore, after having preached a few times in the latter city, proceeded to Philadelphia, and succeeded in collecting large congregations and organizing Societies. These brethren adopted the plan of frequently interchanging with each other between the places, alternating at first every six months, then every four months, and finally once in three months. Such was the effect of their preaching, that large as was the chapel in John Street, scarcely two thirds of the congregation could find admittance, the others being satisfied to stand outside of the door and open windows, that they might catch a word from time to time as it fell from the preacher's lips.

But while success was thus crowning the efforts of Christ's laborers in New York and Philadelphia, other pioneers were silently operating in another portion of the land. And here too, the same humble instrumentalities were employed in the planting of Methodism as in the first named city. About the same time that Mr. Embury and Capt. Webb in New York, were laboring to secure the erection of the chapel in John Street, Mr. Robert Strawbridge, a local preacher, also from Ireland, emigrated to Maryland, and settled in Frederick county. He being a man full of faith and the Holy Ghost, no sooner became settled than he began to preach to a few persons in his own house, and in other private houses. Soon a Society was formed, and a place of worship, humble in its pretensions, was erected. This chapel being built of logs, was long known by the name of the "Log Meeting-House." There is an amusing anecdote related of Mr. Strawbridge by the late Rev. Freeborn Garretson, and copied by Doctor Bangs in his History of the Methodist Episcopal Church. Mr. Garretson observes, "He came to the house of a gentleman near where I lived to stay all night. I had never heard him preach, but as I had a great desire to be in company with a person who had caused so much talk in the country, I went over, and sat, and heard him converse until nearly midnight. * * * He spent most of the time in explaining Scripture and in giving interesting anecdotes, and perhaps one of them will do to relate here: A congregation came together in a certain place, and a gentleman who was hearing, thought that the preacher had directed his whole sermon to him, and he retired home after the sermon in disgust. However, he concluded to hear him once more, and hide himself behind the people so that the preacher should not see him. It was the old story—his character was delineated.

He retired dejected; but concluded that possibly the preacher saw him, and said, 'I will try him once more;' he did so, and hid himself behind the door. The preacher took for his text: 'And a man shall be as a hiding-place, &c.' In the midst of the sermon the preacher cried out, 'Sinner, come from your scouting hole!' The poor fellow came forward, looked the preacher in the face, and said, 'You are a wizard; and the devil is in you; I will hear you no more.' Although not stated, the supposition is, that the preacher alluded to was Mr. Strawbridge himself, and that his humility alone prevented him from acknowledging the fact. Such was the searching power of the gospel!"

About this time, also, two other local preachers arrived in the country—Robert Williams and John King—both from England. Although not sent by Mr. Wesley, they nevertheless proved a great acquisition to the few gospel laborers in America, and were, soon after their arrival, engaged fully in the work of preaching the gospel as travelling preachers. But with the addition of these two, there was still a great demand for more preachers. Accordingly, in 1771, Mr. Wesley resolved to send additional help to the brethren in America, and Francis Asbury and Richard Wright having volunteered their services as missionaries, were dismissed amidst the prayers of their brethren at home. These also proved a great blessing to the Societies in the New World; and as the former—Francis Asbury—may emphatically be styled the apostle of American Methodism, a brief notice of him may not be out of place in this connection.

Mr. Francis Asbury was born near Birmingham, England, in 1745. His parents were respectable, but not pious. At the age of thirteen, Francis was indented as an apprentice to a gentleman for the purpose of learning a trade, and while residing with this man, he heard much said about the Methodists, and he inquired of his mother who, whence, and what the Methodists were. His mother, having imbibed a favorable opinion of the sect everywhere spoken against, gave him the necessary information, and in a short time he proceeded to Wednesbury for the purpose of seeing and hearing for himself. He entered the place of worship, and soon found that it was not *the* church; but to him a better place; men and women kneeling down, and in an audible voice saying, Amen! The preacher had no prayer-book, and yet he prayed wonderfully; he read his text, and preached a sermon; and more wonderful still, he had no sermon-book! He talked about assurance, confidence in God, &c.; all this was strange to young Asbury, but it led him to self-examination, and although never immoral, he felt he was a sinner, shut up in unbelief. This view of himself led him subsequently to look to Christ for salvation, and he received the forgiveness of sin, and the witness of adoption. He joined the Society, met in class, and in a band, and in a rather private way, exercised his gifts, and talents, and graces, in frequently warning men to flee from the wrath to come. In this way, almost imperceptibly to himself, he became a local preacher, until finally he ventured to come out more publicly as such, and proved a valuable assistant or helper to the preachers regularly appointed by Mr. Wesley, as he frequently preached from three to five times every week, visiting distant places for that purpose, and at length, after having acted in the above capacity from the seventeenth to the twenty-second year of his age, he gave himself wholly to the work, as a regular travelling preacher. After travelling about four years under the direction of Mr. Wesley, the latter, at the conference held in Bristol, 1771, proposed that volunteers should offer themselves for America. Mr. Asbury proposed himself, and was accepted, and after having spent a few weeks in visiting his friends, he came to Bristol, for the purpose of taking ship. On his arrival at Bristol, he had not a single penny in his pocket, but his Christian friends in that place soon supplied him with clothes and money, and accompanied by Mr. Wright, he bid a long and last adieu to his native land, and in October of the same year landed safely in Philadelphia, where they were received with open arms by the brethren in that city.

SECTION II.

THE number which had been gathered into the Methodist Societies in America previous to the arrival of Mr. Asbury, was about six hundred—three hundred in New York, two hundred and fifty in Philadelphia, and fifty in New Jersey. After spending a short time in Philadelphia, Mr. Asbury proceeded to New York, and preached with great acceptability. But now commenced a new era in the history of American Methodism. The preachers who had preceded Mr. Asbury, had confined their labors entirely to the cities, and seem to have thought that it was their duty to do so; but Mr. Asbury, fortunately for the cause of Methodism in America, entertained different views, and in accordance with these views, he spent his time alternately in city and country, visiting neighboring towns and villages, and being everywhere received as the messenger of God, although sometimes meeting with opposition from the "baser sort." As might be expected, good was accomplished by these visits, Societies being formed by him in different places. Another good result was, the example he set the other preachers; which, being followed, they also extended their labors to the country places.

In the latter part of the year 1772, Mr. Asbury visited Kent county, Maryland, where Mr. Strawbridge had opened the way for him. Before preaching, however, a clergyman of the Church of England came to him, desiring to know who he was; and whether he was licensed to preach. After Mr. Asbury had informed him who, and what he was, the minister replied, that having authority over the people, &c., he—Mr. Asbury—could not, and should not preach, and if he did, he should be proceeded against according to law. Mr. Asbury, however, gave the gentleman to understand, that he had come to preach, and preach he should; and asked him if he had authority to bind the consciences of people, or if he was a justice of the peace. The parson replied by charging Asbury with making a schism, and with hindering people from their work, &c. Mr. Asbury, however, informed him, that he was not an enemy of the church; that listening to preaching would occupy no more time than attending fairs and horse-races, and instead of designing to injure the parson or his business, he had come to assist him in his work of saving souls. "I did not hire you for an assistant, and do not want your help," said the parson. After more conversation of a similar character, Mr. Asbury, nothing daunted by the frowns or threats of his clerical opponent, proceeded to preach, and urge upon the people the duty of repentance and reformation. The parson, who came into the house in a rage, after hearing Mr. Asbury preach, went out and cautioned the people against hearing him any more. In this incident, unimportant in itself, we see the spirit with which the established clergy welcomed the labors of the self-denying itinerant, and from it we learn, that if the clergy in England were mere formalists, "denying the power of godliness," the clergy in America were scarcely less formal, or less opposed to the revival of the work of God.

In spite of all opposition, however, the work of God spread throughout the land—from Maryland to Virginia, North and South Carolina, and Georgia, all which places were visited first by Mr. Pilmore, and then by other Methodist preachers, who entered in at every open door, and successfully preached the gospel to the people. Among those who followed Mr. Pilmore in his visits to Virginia, was Mr. Williams, who went to Norfolk, and without giving any public notice of his intention to preach, he stood on the steps of the court-house, and began to sing, which soon brought a congregation around him, to whom he preached. Some of the people attempted to raise a disturbance, thinking, no doubt, that the preacher was mad more especially as he made a frequent use of the words *hell* and *devil*, while appealing to the consciences of his impenitent hearers—words which their own ministers seldom if ever used—perhaps because they did not believe in any such things—which, sounding strange to the ear, as coming from the pulpit, made them think that Mr. Williams must be a very wicked, swearing man, and although some parts of his discourse sounded like the gospel, yet they had so little charity for the preacher, that when he had concluded, no one invited him to their house. Not discouraged, however, Mr. Williams preached a second time, and shortly afterward had the privilege, not only of being hospitably entertained, but of forming a Society in Norfolk, which has remained in a flourishing condition to this day.

The year after Mr. Asbury's arrival in America, he received a letter from Mr. Wesley, in which the latter designated Mr. Asbury as his General Assistant in America—an office which involved the stationing of the preachers, and the general oversight of the entire work. In accordance with the requirements of the letter of appointment and instructions, Mr. Asbury, without calling a conference of all the preachers, proceeded to the work of assigning the preachers their respective fields of labor, which was usually done at *Quarterly* meetings.

In the summer of 1773, Messrs. Thomas Rankin and George Shadford arrived in Philadelphia, as missionaries sent over by Mr. Wesley. Mr. Rankin, having travelled several years longer than Mr. Asbury, was appointed to supersede the latter as General Assistant, and was invested with authority to call a conference, which was accordingly held in Philadelphia, July 4, 1773. The number of preachers in the connection at this time was ten, and the number of members had increased to 1,160.

As some of the preachers, especially Mr. Strawbridge, had departed from the instructions of Mr. Wesley in regard to administering the ordinances of baptism and the Lord's Supper, it was at this conference resolved that each preacher should avoid administering these ordinances. The members, also, were to be exhorted to attend the Episcopal church, and receive the ordinances there at the hands of the ministers thereof. At this conference, also, the preachers were all regularly stationed by Mr. Rankin, and measures were adopted for a more systematic prosecution of the work, and especially for a more rigorous enforcement of the discipline. The carrying out of the latter, met with some opposition, especially in New York, but Mr. Rankin, who was himself stationed there, by a prudent, yet steady course, overcame every obstacle, and succeeded in introducing system and method in the management of the Society and congregation. The same system of vigorously carrying out the requirements of the discipline being generally adopted by the preachers, was not without its wholesome influence, as at the next conference, we find the preachers increased to the number of seventeen, and the memberships reported to be 2,073.

From the session of the above conference in 1774, until the beginning of the revolutionary war, which separated the American colonies from the mother country, the work of God went on with increased power and success, notwithstanding the political storm raged with such violence over every part of the land. As some of the preachers laboring in the colonies were natives of Britain, it may be supposed that they would naturally espouse the royal cause. Mr. Wesley, who was always on the alert in reference to anything which might injure the influence of his preachers, or mar their usefulness, wrote to them at this juncture, advising them to addict themselves to no party, and to say not a word against one side or the other. This advice was seasonable, and no doubt in most cases exerted a salutary influence, but as the war proceeded, several of the English preachers felt it to be their duty to leave the theatre of strife, and return to their native land; and among them Mr. Rankin, the general assistant, sailed for England in 1777.

In the year 1775, there was a remarkable revival of religion in the southern portion of Virginia. It was principally effected through the instrumentality of Mr. George Shadford—one of Mr. Wesley's missionaries. Justice, however, to the memory of a great and good man, Rev. Mr. Jarratt, of the Episcopal church in that part of the country, requires us to say that no one contributed more to the progress of this work than he, by preaching, administering the ordinances among the Methodists, meeting the classes, holding love-feasts, &c. &c. As Doctor Bangs well observes, "Had all the clergy of that day manifested a kindred spirit, how much more extensively would the work of God have prevailed!" and *we* may add, that if all the clergymen of that day had manifested a proper Christian spirit, the probability is, that in less than ten years afterward the Methodist Episcopal Church had not been organized, at least on its present basis, but opposition on the part of clergymen created a necessity for its organization.

SECTION III.

On the 4th of July, 1776, the American colonies were declared by Congress to be free and independent States. The Declaration of Independence, however, while it asserted, did not secure the political independence of the colonies. A long and bloody war between the contending parties must exist, before such independence is acknowledged by the mother country, and such a war did exist for six long years after Congress issued the above document.

The continuance of the war, rendered it peculiarly trying to most of the Methodist preachers in America. Four of the leading ones were known to be from England, and some of them, contrary to the advice of Mr. Wesley, did not hesitate to avow their attachment to the British cause. Notwithstanding the prudent reserve of others in relation to these matters, the whole body was suspected of being in the interest of the

British monarch, and were consequently the subjects of political hatred and persecution; so much so, that it was with extreme difficulty the preachers could travel their circuits from appointment to appointment. Mr. Asbury, than whom there never was a more prudent man in relation to political matters, was nevertheless on one occasion fined five pounds, not for uttering anything against the cause of liberty, but for preaching the gospel in the vicinity of Baltimore without having taken the oath of allegiance to the State of Maryland, which he could not conscientiously do; and for the same reason during the next year he was forced to retire beyond the borders of Maryland, and seek an asylum in the house of his friend Judge White of Delaware, where he remained secluded for nearly a year. In the place of his retreat, however, he was not inactive, for although it was considered imprudent for him to attempt speaking in public, during the height of the political storm, he would frequently go out in the evening and visit from house to house, and enforce privately the truths of the Gospel.

Nor was Mr. Asbury the only sufferer; those of the preachers whose patriotism could not be doubted, were frequently maltreated by the magistrates and others. Mr. Freeborn Garretson, a native born American, and a man of some influence and note in society previous to his conversion, and not less so after he became a Methodist preacher, was on one occasion while riding peaceably along in the State of Maryland, arrested by an ex-judge of the county, who seized his horse's bridle, and who although assured by Mr. Garretson that the latter was a preacher of the Gospel peaceably engaged in his calling, began to strike him over the head and shoulders with a stick, all the while calling for help. As some were approaching with a rope, perhaps for the purpose of binding Mr. Garretson, the judge let go his hold on the bridle, on which Mr. Garretson gave his horse the whip and got beyond the reach of his foes. He was however pursued and overtaken by his persecutor, who again struck him and threw him from his horse with great violence, wounding him severely, and rendering him insensible. While in this condition a lady passed by having a lancet in her possession, and Mr. Garretson being carried into a house near by, was freely bled, which restored him to consciousness. His persecutor fearing that he had killed him, stood over him with some degree of anxiety and sorrow, but as Mr. Garretson revived and began to exhort him to repent, his rage returned with redoubled violence, and he immediately went out and brought a magistrate more wicked than himself. "With a stern look," says Mr. Garretson, "the magistrate demanded my name. I told him; and he took out his pen and ink and began to write a mittimus to commit me to jail. 'Pray, sir,' says I, 'are you a justice of the peace?' He replied that he was. 'Why then do you suffer men to behave in this manner?' 'You have,' said he, 'broken the laws.' 'How do you know that?' said I, 'but supposing I have, is this the way you put the law in force against me? I am an inhabitant of this State, and have property in it; and if I mistake not, the law says for the first offence, the fine is five pounds, and double for every offence after. The grand crime was preaching the Gospel of the Lord Jesus Christ, in which I greatly rejoice. My enemy conducted himself more like a highwayman than a person enforcing the law in a Christian country. Be well assured that this matter will be brought to light in awful eternity.' He dropped his pen, and made no farther attempt to send me to prison." Meanwhile the lady who bled Mr. Garretson coming with her carriage, took him off where he was properly taken care of till partially restored from the effects of the maltreatment, when he went on his way rejoicing, being instrumental in bringing scores and hundreds of souls to the knowledge of the truth.

In the year 1780, Mr. Garretson having had an invitation to preach in a portion of the country in Maryland where political feeling ran very high, and persecution against the Methodists prevailed to an alarming extent, made the matter a subject of earnest prayer, and also asked the advice of Mr. Asbury. The latter advised him to accept the invitation, which he did; but while on his way had fearful forebodings of trials and persecutions, so much so, that he felt half inclined to turn back. However, putting his trust in the Lord, he pursued his way towards the place of his destination. Having arrived, Mr. Garretson preached in the neighborhood to large and attentive congregations during three successive days, and then went to the county-seat where the court was in session, and preached also. Some of the leading men connected with the court, were offended with Mr. Garretson for daring to preach, and determined in some way to get him out of the place. For a pretence they charged him with toryism, and as Mr. Garretson was informed, procured the liberty of a very wicked man who was in prison, for the purpose of taking his life. This he was to do by lying in wait for Mr. Garretson the next day, but providentially Mr. Garretson heard of it, and privately withdrew to a friend's house where he remained two days. Although convinced in his own mind that something uncommon would transpire, he nevertheless left his place of retreat and preached with freedom and power to a weeping congregation, but while returning to his friend's house in the evening, he was waylaid by a company of mèn who had embodied themselves for the purpose of taking him to jail. They accordingly surrounded him, and called him their prisoner. They beat his horse, cursed and swore, and took him before a magistrate who was his avowed enemy, by whom he was judged and condemned for preaching the gospel, and ordered to jail. His horse was brought, and twelve men appointed to guard him to prison. Being placed on his horse, a man on each side held his horse's bridle. The night was very dark, and when about a mile from the magistrate's, an uncommon flash of lightning dispersed his foes, so that he was left alone. The night being still dark he called several times, but no answer was given. Soon the friend at whose house he had been entertained and secreted, and who accompanied him throughout the whole affair, approached him, and they both rode on cheerfully together. At length they overtook two of the guards, who had fled and sought shelter in a little cottage by the road-side, and were frightened almost out of their wits. Mr. Garretson told them that if he was to go to jail that night, it was time they were on their way, as it was getting late. "O! no," said one of them, "let us stay until the morning." Mr. Garretson and his friend however rode on, and the sky having become clear they were soon surrounded again by his guards. They appeared however to be somewhat fearful on account of the flash of lightning, and one of them inquired, "Sir, do you think the affair happened on our account?" Mr. Garretson replied he must be his own judge of the matter, but reminded him of the day of judgment and the necessity of being prepared for it. While proceeding toward the jail, one of the company swore an oath, but he was immediately reproved by another, who exclaimed, "How can you swear at such a time as this?" At length the company stopped and concluded they had better give him up for the present, and turned their horses and went back, but soon they rallied again saying, "We cannot give him up," but after accompanying them for a few moments longer, they finally left them.

The next day being Sunday, he went forth to preach, and to give his own words, "Many came out to hear the word, and it was expected my enemies would be upon me. I was informed that not a few brought short clubs under their coats, to defend me in case of an attack, for many had just about religion enough to fight for it. As I was giving out my hymn, standing between the hall and room doors, about twenty of my persecutors came up in a body. I was amazed to see one of them who was an old man, and his head as white as a sheet. The ring-leader rushed forward, presented a pistol, and laid hold of me. Blessed be God! my confidence was so strong in him that I feared none of these things. Some of the audience who stood next to me, gave me a sudden jerk; I was presently in the room and the door shut. As soon as I could, I opened it, and beckoning to my friends, desired that they should not injure my enemies; that I did not want to keep from them, but was willing to go to jail. If I had not spoken in this manner I believe much blood would have been shed. I began to exhort, and almost the whole congregation were in tears. The women in particular were amazingly agitated. I desired my horse to be got, and I was accompanied to Cambridge, where I was kept in a tavern from twelve o'clock till near sunset, surrounded by the wicked, and it was a great mercy of God that my life was preserved.

"When we came to the hotel, my friend and I were permitted to occupy a room adjoining the large public room. The inhabitants of the place seemed to be coming and going the whole day, and kept the room filled the whole of the time, drinking and rejoicing over their prey. My friend was a young soldier, and the trial was too great for him. One of the company, a stout man, was about to break into the room to abuse him, for their hatred against him was almost as great as it was against me—and actually did strike at him with all his force with a large, loaded whip, and in all probability would have killed him, had not the whip struck the top of the door. My friend was young and active, and he instantly sprung and as quickly sent his fist into the fellow's temple, who, like a Goliah under David's sling, fell flat to the floor, and there was a roar of laughter through the house and a declaration, 'The Methodists will fight.' At a convenient time I got my friend round the neck and wept, and told him he had grieved my spirit. He said he was sorry on account of grieving me; but that it was almost as sudden as thought, that it appeared to him that his arm was nerved for the purpose, and that he did not feel as if he had done wrong. And I must say I think they behaved rather better afterwards.

"A little before night, I was thrust into prison, and my enemies took away the key that none might minister to my necessities. I had a dirty floor for my bed, my saddle-bags for my pillow, and two large windows open, with a cold east wind blowing upon me; but I had great consolation in the Lord, and could say, 'Thy will be done.' * * * Many, both acquaintances and strangers, came to visit me from far and near, and I really believe I never was the means of doing more good for the time: for the country seemed to be much alarmed, and the Methodists among whom I had labored, to whom I had written many epistles, were much stirred up to pray for me. I shall never forget the kindness I received from dear brother and sister Arey. They suffered much for the cause of God in Dorset county, for which, if faithful, they will be amply compensated in a better world.

"Mr. and Mrs. A. were remarkably kind, and sent me everything which was necessary. My brother Thomas, who lived about an hundred miles off, heard of my imprisonment and came to see me, and brought a letter from Judge White to Mr. Harrison, a gentleman of note, who was the greatest enemy I had in town. After reading the letter he not only invited my brother to put up at his house, but went and got the prison key, and my brother came in, and next morning he came to the jail and invited him out to breakfast, and told me he would do anything he could for me. Before this he was as bitter as gall. One day, when an old Quaker friend came to see me, he came and abused him, and strove to drive him away. The Quaker made him ashamed of his conduct. My enemies sent a spy who feigned himself a penitent, and as I was coming down stairs to converse with him through the window, it came powerfully to my mind, 'he is an enemy, sent if possible to draw something out of you concerning the war.' He cried, and said he was a miserable sinner; that he was afraid he would go to hell, and wanted to know what he should do to be saved. I told him to leave off swearing and drunkenness, and return, and I would give him farther directions. I afterwards found he was the very character I had supposed.

"My crime of preaching the gospel was so great, that no common court could try my cause. There appeared to be a probability of my staying in jail till a general court, which would not convene in nearly twelve months. My good friend, Mr. Asbury, went to the governor of Maryland, and he befriended me; had I been his brother he could not have done more for me. The manner in which he proceeded to relieve me was this—I was an inhabitant of Maryland by birth and property. I could likewise claim a right in the Delaware state, which state was more favorable to such *pestilent fellows*. I was carried before the governor of Delaware. This gentleman was a friend to our Society. He met me at the door, and welcomed me in, assuring me that he would do anything he could to help me. A recommendatory letter was immediately despatched to the governor of Maryland: and I was entirely at liberty. O! how wonderfully did the people of Dorset rage; but the word of the Lord spread all through that county, and hundreds, both white and black, have experienced the love of Jesus. Since that time, I have preached to more than three thousand people in one congregation, not far from the place where I was imprisoned, and many of my worst enemies have bowed to the sceptre of our Sovereign Lord."

The reader can infer from the above statements of Mr. Garretsòn, the state of public feeling in different parts of the country in relation to the Methodists, and how the great Head of the church overruled the persecutions, for the good of his own cause, and made even "the wrath of man praise him," while "the remainder of wrath he restrained." As a farther exhibition of the opposition of the wicked to the preaching of the early Methodists and the good effects resulting therefrom, an additional instance of persecution may be given.

In 1778, Mr. Joseph Hartley, a Methodist preacher, was arrested in Queen Ann's county, Maryland, for no crime except preaching the gospel. He gave bonds to appear at the next court for trial, and in the meantime was forbidden to preach.

He, however, felt it his duty to attend his appointments, and after singing and prayer, he would remain upon his knees and exhort the people to repent, with so much effect, that his enemies said that he might as well preach standing on his feet, as on his knees. He went from Queen Ann's to Talbot county, where he was again apprehended and committed to jail. His being confined in prison, however, did not silence him. The people, anxious to see the man who was imprisoned for conscience' sake, frequently gathered around the jail, and he, desirous of promoting their spiritual good, preached to them through the iron grates, and with such zeal and power, that some were awakened to a sense of their sinful condition, and began in earnest to seek the Lord. This state of things alarmed the ungodly, and induced some of them to say, that unless Mr. Hartley was released from jail he would convert the whole town. He was at length set at liberty, but the seed sown by him through the grates of his prison was not lost, but took deep root in the hearts of many, and resulted in the formation of a flourishing Society. Thus, notwithstanding the opposition of the wicked to the preaching of the Methodists, the word of God continued to operate on the hearts and consciences of men, bringing them into "captivity to the law of Christ," so that during the Revolution, the Methodist Societies continued to multiply, and the doctrines of the Methodists to become more generally known and appreciated. The increase of the Societies, both north and south, demanded an increase of preachers, so that notwithstanding the ravages of war, and the distracting state of public affairs, yet on the cessation of hostilities, it was found at the conference of 1783, that the preachers had increased to eighty-two, and the members to 13,740, making a net gain during the war of the Revolution—reckoning from 1775—of sixty-five preachers, and 10,592 members!

We have stated on a previous page, that during the prevalence of hostilities, Mr. Rankin, the General Assistant—with some other English preachers—felt it his duty to return to

England, and as no one had been appointed by Mr. Wesley to fill his place as superintendent of the Societies in America, Mr. Asbury, at the conference of 1779, was, by a vote of the conference, chosen to act as the General Superintendent, which he afterwards did to the great satisfaction of the preachers and members.

Notwithstanding the general prosperity of the work during the Revolution, various perplexing questions agitated the Societies and Conferences, especially in the southern portion of the field. Among the most important and perplexing of these questions, was one which related to the administration of the ordinances by the preachers. For it will be borne in mind by the reader, that the preachers were not ordained, and consequently had no right to administer the ordinances of baptism and the Lord's Supper. In fact, Mr. Wesley being himself a minister of the Church of England, looked upon his preachers, whether in England or America, not as ministers—fully set apart to the work—but as *lay-preachers* simply. In England, where there was one or more clergymen in every parish, no necessity seemed to exist for the ordination of Mr. Wesley's preachers, but in America, it was far otherwise. Many of the Episcopal clergy, on the breaking out of hostilities, left their churches and their flocks and went to England, so that for hundreds of miles around no one could be found properly qualified to administer the ordinance of baptism to the children, or the sacrament of the Eucharist to the dying. In consequence of this scarcity of ministers, the Methodist preachers were frequently importuned by the people to celebrate those ordinances, and so loud became the demand in this respect at the south, that at a conference of southern preachers, held in Virginia in 1779, a committee was appointed to ordain ministers, who, having first ordained each other, proceeded to ordain others by the imposition of hands and prayer. Mr. Asbury, who was not ignorant of the feeling existing at the south on the above subject, endeavored, with the concurrence of the northern preachers, to dissuade the preachers and people of the south from carrying their design into execution, and a delegate fróm the northern preachers was appointed to meet the above conference in Virginia to prevent, if possible, by argument and entreaty, the carrying out of their proposed measures. All efforts, however, were unavailing, and the preachers were ordained as before stated. This circumstance caused a temporary breach between the northern and southern preachers, and at the next session of the conference held in Baltimore in 1780, at which the northern preachers were present, the southern preachers, as a condition of union, were required to suspend the administration of the ordinances for one year. On the adjournment of the Baltimore Conference, as the southern preachers were not present but had called a separate conference in Virginia—Mr. Asbury and other prominent members went to meet the latter in their separate capacity, and after having laid the matter before them, a reconciliation was happily effected, the Virginian brethren agreeing to desist from the administration of the ordinances for the present.

At length the war of the Revolution was at an end; peace was declared between Britain and her rebellious subjects in America; the political and national independence of the latter was secured; Church and State were divorced; and the Americans were in ecclesiastical, as well as in civil matters, left to provide for themselves. Under these circumstances the Methodists, who now numbered about 14,000 members, and probably had twice that number of adherents, thus constituting at least one-sixth part of the population of the United States, could not remain indifferent to their future condition as an ecclesiastical body. The advice of Mr. Wesley was sought, and freely and frankly given; and such advice, and the provision made by him for the separate, independent existence of the American Societies resulted, as hereafter shown, in the organization of the Methodist Episcopal Church.

SECTION IV.

Until the acknowledgment of American independence, the Methodists in America, as well as in England, were considered by Mr. Wesley, and the preachers who acted under his authority, as a *Society* within a *Church*, or to speak more properly, as a religious Society, the members of which belonged to various Churches. The preachers, as a general thing, professed to be nothing more than lay, *i. e.*, unordained preachers, with no authority to administer the ordinances. In America the want of a ministry properly qualified and authorized to administer baptism and the Lord's Supper, had been long and severely felt. Mr. Wesley had before the acknowledgment of American independence been importuned to provide for the exigencies of the case by appointing *ministers* for America, but as a presbyter of the Church of England, and such a step being foreign from his original design in forming Societies, he resisted such applications for a separate ecclesiastical existence.

The colonies, however, having become civilly and ecclesiastically independent of Great Britain, Mr. Wesley began to think seriously of the frequent requests made by his American children for a ministry of their own, and his scruples being at length overcome by the seeming necessities of the case, and the advice of judicious friends, he finally resolved to adopt measures by which pastors might be provided for his distant flocks, measures by which a fold might be made for the security of those sheep who otherwise would be in danger of losing, not only their way in the wilderness, but their spiritual if not eternal life. Accordingly at the conference held in Leeds in the spring of 1784, he made arrangements to send the Rev. Thomas Coke, LL.D., and some other preachers to America, for the purpose of carrying out his parental designs. He also, previously to their departure, abridged the Common Prayer-Book of the Church of England for the use of his Societies in

America; and also by the imposition of hands—being assisted by other ordained clergymen of the Church of England—set apart Dr. Coke, himself a presbyter of the English Church, to the office of superintendent or bishop, that he might feed and preside over the flock of Christ in North America, and appoint such men to the ministry as he thought fit to ordain for that purpose. Mr. Wesley also set apart Mr. Richard Whatcoat and Mr. Thomas Vasey to the office of elders in the church.

These ministers being furnished with proper credentials by Mr. Wesley, left England for their distant field of labor, and arrived in New York on the 3d of November, 1784. Notice was immediately given of their arrival through all parts of the connection, and a conference was called to meet at Baltimore on the 25th of December following. The conference accordingly assembled at the time appointed. At this period there were eighty-three preachers in the travelling connection, and sixty of these appeared in answer to the call. The first act of the conference was to appoint Dr. Coke and Mr. Asbury joint superintendents, for although the former had been appointed to that office by Mr. Wesley, yet he declined officiating as such, except he could obtain the consent of the conference. This consent was cheerfully and unanimously given; and Dr. Coke, by virtue of the authority vested in him, ordained Mr. Asbury, first as a deacon, then as an elder, and lastly as a superintendent of the Methodist Episcopal Church; and by a unanimous vote of the conference, they resolved themselves into a Methodist Episcopal Church. The organization of the Church gave great satisfaction to the Methodist people generally, for now instead of being dependent as they had heretofore been on the ministers of different churches for the ordinances of Christianity, they could look to their own church and to their own ministers for these appendages of a Christian Church. Nor had it been, as before stated, at all times possible for the Methodists to avail themselves of these things, even through the ministers of other churches. On the breaking out of the revolutionary war, as already shown, most of the English Episcopal clergy had left their flocks, and the greater part of them who remained, were anything but fit, in point of moral character, to preach the gospel, much less to administer the sacred ordinances of the church. The Presbyterian and Congregational ministers would not baptize a child unless at least one of the parents professed faith in the doctrines of Calvin; nor would they admit the Methodists to the Supper of the Lord. While the Baptists, as a matter of course, would neither baptize the children nor admit to the communion any but those who had been immersed. And besides all these considerations, by each and all of the denominations just mentioned, the Methodists were looked upon not as a Christian community, but as a Society of heretics; a band of wild enthusiasts; a company of dangerous fanatics. In addition to these considerations, the Methodists had been converted through the instrumentality of men who were above all others the most proper persons to feed the flock of Christ, of whom the "Holy Ghost had made them overseers." It need not therefore create surprise that at the organization of the Methodist Episcopal Church, with a ministry fully qualified to administer all the ordinances of the gospel, a sensation of joy and gratitude should be experienced throughout the entire connection, and that the provision made by Mr. Wesley, the father, the founder, the APOSTLE of Methodism, for the perpetuation of the privileges of Christianity should be hailed by all, both preachers and people. Nor was the step taken in the organization of the church hailed with greater pleasure than it was followed by the most beneficial results. The great Head of the Church sanctioned the doings of his ministers and servants, and by the frequent outpourings of his Spirit upon the people gave evidence of his divine approbation, and applied his own seal to the ministry of the church.

After a harmonious session of several days the ministers, of whom twelve were ordained at this conference, and the preachers separated for their respective fields of labor. Mr. Garretson and Mr. Cromwell having been appointed to Nova Scotia, soon after left for that distant part of the north to labor for the benefit of the loyal refugees who had fled from the United States, during the war, to that province, and who, notwithstanding their attachment to the British cause, were many of them sincere Christians. These and other Methodists from England required pastoral care, and Mr. Garretson willingly consented to leave his own land for their sakes and the gospel's, and in that province had the satisfaction of seeing the work of God revived, and men's souls converted.

Dr. Coke and Mr. Asbury as joint superintendents of the Methodist Episcopal Church, soon commenced a course of arduous labors for the advancement of the cause of Christ in different parts of the land. Instead of being confined to a small State, or territory, as their diocese, they considered the continent as their parish. Hence they were almost constantly engaged in travelling from State to State, preaching the gospel of the Kingdom and making full proof of their ministry. One important work which the superintendents had in view even before the church was organized, was the establishment of a Methodist college for the benefit of the children and youth of the membership. After soliciting donations, &c., a sufficient sum was secured to warrant the erection of a proper building, and the week after the adjournment of the conference just alluded to, a site was selected about twenty-five miles from Baltimore, and orders given to commence the building; and in a short time a beautiful, yet modest structure arose to grace the banks of the Chesapeake Bay, and to throw its commanding outlines along the course of the Susquehannah River. In due time the college was opened under the most flattering auspices, and in honor of the two superintendents who were its actual founders, it was named Cokesbury College. After flourishing for about ten years from the time of its commencement, it was consumed by fire in the year 1775, and the Connection thus lost the entire sum expended upon its erection, amounting to ten thousand pounds, or forty thousand dollars.

After this calamity, Mr. Asbury became discouraged about the educational interests of the church, and thought it useless to make any farther attempts at rebuilding; but Dr. Coke, whose love of sound learning, and zeal in its behalf, surpassed that of his pious colleague, at once determined to make another effort; and being encouraged by the liberality of a few wealthy friends in Baltimore and other places, a large building in that city was purchased for the sum of twenty-five thousand dollars, and the college was again opened under even more favorable circumstances than the former one; but, alas! a fate similar to that which befell the former one awaited it, and in a short time the college and the church connected with it were burned to the ground. This latter calamity more than ever discouraged the friends of education among the Methodists, and for a number of years little or nothing was done to revive an interest in this direction.

Shortly after making provision for the erection of the first college and after the adjournment of the Baltimore Conference in June, Dr. Coke, having fulfilled his mission for the present, returned to Europe, where he was exposed to much obloquy and reproach from the High Church Episcopalians of England, who thought, or pretended to think that his agency in the organization of the Methodist Episcopal Church was inconsistent with his relation as a Church of England minister. Historical fidelity also requires us to notice that Mr. Charles Wesley, who had been opposed to the course pursued by his brother John in the ordination of Dr. Coke to the superintendency of the American Societies—not only was dissatisfied with Dr. Coke on that account, but in an anonymous publication commented severely on the doctor's proceedings in America as it relates to the organization of the church, and especially the reasons given by the doctor for such organization, in his sermon preached at the consecration of Mr. Asbury. In this sermon he animadverted in severe terms upon the conduct and morals of the American Episcopal clergy, as well as reflected in plain language upon their political and parasitical character, and gave the above, with the altered political condition of the country, as reasons for the separate existence of the Methodists as a body. It was said by the anonymous writer referred to, that the doctor had condemned the constitution of his own country; that he had vilified his clerical brethren in America; that he had contradicted the uniform declarations of John and Charles Wesley in relation to separating from the church, &c. To these severe charges the doctor replied in substance: that he believed the constitution and government of England to be superior to any other for the British empire, but that both were liable to abuse, and had been abused in the case of the American Colonies; that the churches in America were, in general, filled with the parasites and bottle companions of the rich and great; and that the drunkard, fornicator, and extortioner triumphed over bleeding Zion, because they were faithful abettors of the ruling powers; and he indignantly denied that the Episcopal clergy in America were his brethren, that while he would esteem it an honor to sit at the feet of several of them, generally, they were the most wretched set of men that ever disgraced the Church of God; that he had done nothing in relation to the organization of the Methodist Church but by delegated power received from Mr. Wesley. These charges against Dr. Coke by such a man as Charles Wesley not only show the High Church, and ultra-loyalist principles of the latter, but the difficult position which the former sustained as a clergyman of the English establishment, and at the same time as the joint head of an independent church in the American Republic. The reply also vindicates the doctor in the fullest manner from the charges preferred against him by his anonymous accuser.

While Dr. Coke was thus defending himself against the misrepresentations of mistaken brethren in England, Mr. Asbury remained at his post in America, travelling from place to place and overseeing the work as a faithful superintendent. The great increase of preachers made it inconvenient for all to meet together in one conference; accordingly, in 1786, three conferences were held, one in North Carolina, one in Virginia, and another in Baltimore. In the following year, 1787, three conferences were also held, being presided over by Dr. Coke and Mr. Asbury, the former of whom had again visited America, but as the doctor did not design to make his stay permanent, and as some dissatisfaction arose from his having changed the place and time for holding the conference, it was agreed that the doctor should only exercise the Episcopal office when in America.

This year also the title *Bishop* was inserted in the Discipline instead of the title *Superintendent* as before used, probably for the following reasons among others: It is a shorter word, and consequently more convenient for address; it is more expressive of the actual relation sustained by the persons to whom it was applied than superintendents; it has precisely the same signification as overseer, which latter relation was sustained, and is sustained by the Episcopacy of the Methodist Episcopal Church; it was also more scriptural; and lastly, the title was better understood by the people generally than superintendent or overseer could be, when applied to an officer in the church. Another reason may also have induced the preachers to bestow, and the superintendents to accept the title of Bishop —a disposition to claim for the newly organized church an episcopacy as scriptural at least in its character as any other episcopacy upon earth; and this claim not only the bishops, but the conference, and even Mr. Wesley himself were willing to avow everywhere, openly and boldly; although it must be admitted that the latter, while he viewed himself to be a scriptural *Episcopus* or Bishop, as much so as any man upon earth, was, nevertheless, prejudiced against the use of the term; and while he ordained Dr. Coke, and gave him authority to ordain Mr. Asbury, and provided a form of service for such ordination to the office of a bishop in the Church of God, he preferred the more modest title of superintendent. Hence he expresses his fears in a letter to Mr. Asbury, that the latter was getting proud, and even reproves him for suffering himself to be called a bishop; not that he doubted the fact of his being such, but doubted the propriety of using such terms or having them applied to each other as Methodist ministers. This, however, was a mere matter of taste with Mr. Wesley, whose extraordinary humility would not allow him even to call a college established in America by his preachers, by a more dignified name than *School.* Notwithstanding the objections of Mr. Wesley to the assumption of the title, and his fears that the Methodist Episcopacy would become lordly and overbearing like the hierarchies of Europe in consequence of such title, the preachers continued to employ the term; and although over sixty years have passed since the use of the same, and the original bishops have long since been numbered with the dead, and although important changes have been effected in relation to the persons filling the episcopal chair, and in regard to the duties of their office; yet we have failed to see the lordly air, the pompous pride, the gorgeous vestments, which, by the opposers of the title, were no doubt held in reserve for the Methodist Episcopacy, but have reason to thank God that the purity and simplicity of the episcopal character have thus far been preserved among us, and not merely preserved, but modified and rendered still more simple and acceptable to the church and the ministry.

During the war, the Methodist Chapel in the city of New York—while the British troops remained—had been forcibly converted into a soldiers' barracks, by which the Society was deprived of a place of worship, and the interests of religion suffered materially from this and other causes. Indeed while the war lasted, the Methodist Society in New York became almost extinct. For several years, such was the difficulty of holding communication with the city, that no preachers were appointed by the conference: hence the Society in New York, though not forgotten or lost sight of, occupied no prominent place in the history of the church during the above period, neither had any conference been held north of Baltimore since the commencement of the war; but in the year 1787, Bishops Coke and Asbury in company, visited the city, and by their preaching and other labors, awakened a new interest in behalf of the cause of Methodism. The Methodist preachers also began to extend their labors to the north and east of New York city, and in 1788, several new circuits were formed on the banks of the Hudson river and Lake Champlain. Mr. Garrettson, who had returned from Nova Scotia, was requested by Bishop Asbury to penetrate the country north of New York and form as many new circuits as possible. To aid him in this work, several young and zealous preachers were placed under his direction, and these going forth in the name of the Lord, were abundantly successful in their labors, as is proved from the fact, that a number of circuits were added to the list at the conference held the ensuing year in New York city. Among these new circuits, were Newburgh, Columbia, Coeyman's Patent, Schenectady, and Stamford, Conn.

SECTION V.

As the year 1789 was the one in which Methodism was introduced into New England, a brief account of the obstacles to be overcome in its introduction may be interesting to the reader. From the earliest settlement of New England by the "pilgrim fathers," Congregationalism had been the established form of religion in all the New England Colonies, with the exception of Rhode Island. Churches were built, and ministers were supported by law. The people were taxed for such support; nor did the change of civil government during the revolutionary war effect any material change in the ecclesiastical affairs of New England. For many years after the Independence of the United States, Congregationalism remained the established religion of several of the Northern members of the Confederacy. Besides the above facts the churches were not only Calvinistic, but were severely rigid and tenacious in their religious tenets, and peculiarly hostile to the doctrines of general redemption and free grace, as taught by the Methodists. In addition to these opposing influences which the Methodists had to encounter, was another, still more formidable than either—the low state of religion in the New England churches, and the prevalence of Unitarianism among their members.

In this state of things the Rev. Jesse Lee, who may well be called the apostle of New England Methodism, was sent by Bishop Asbury to proclaim the doctrines of free salvation to the inhabitants of New England. He immediately repaired to his new field of labor, and his reception by the people may be learned more perfectly if we quote his own words. He says in his journal: "I arrived in Norwalk, and went to one Mr. Rogers, where one of our friends had asked the liberty for me to preach. When I came Mrs. R. told me her husband was from home, and was not willing for me to preach in his house. I told her we would hold meeting in the road rather than give any uneasiness. We proposed speaking in an old house which stood just by, but she was not willing. I then spoke to an old lady about speaking in her orchard, but she would not consent, but said we would tread the grass down. So the other friend went and gave notice to some people, and they soon began to collect and we went to the road where we had an apple-tree to shade us. When the woman saw I was determined to preach she said I might preach in the old house; but I told her I thought it would be better to remain where we were. So I began on the side of the road, with about twenty hearers. After singing and prayer, I preached on John iii. 7, '*Ye must be born again.*' I felt happy that we were favored with so comfortable a place. Most part of the congregation paid particular attention to what I said, and two or three women seemed to hang down their heads as if they understood something of the new birth. After preaching I told the people that I intended to be with them again in two weeks, and if any of them would open their houses to receive me I should be glad, and if they were not willing, we would meet at the same place; some of them came and desired that I should meet at the town-house the next time; so I gave consent. Who knows but I shall yet have a place in this town where I may lay my head?"

From Norwalk he went the next day to Fairfield, and put up at a tavern. On declaring his errand the women of the house asked him if he had a liberal education. He replied he had just education enough to carry him through the country. After some difficulty he obtained permission to preach in the court-house to between thirty and forty people, among whom was his hostess. On his return to his lodgings he prayed with the family, tarried all night, and left in the morning without charge; and received a hearty invitation to call again. After preaching in several places he went to Stratford, and put up as usual at a tavern. He applied to the person who had charge of the town-house for liberty to preach therein. The man said he did not know much about the Methodists; they might be like the New Lights. Mr. Lee told him he did not know much about the New Lights, but some thought the Methodists preached like them. "Well," said the man, "if you are like them, I would not wish to have anything to do with you." Mr. Lee inquired what objection he had to the New Lights. "Why," said he, "they went on like madmen: there was one Davenport that would preach, and holloa, and beat the pulpit with both hands, and cry out, 'Come away, come away to the Lord Jesus Christ. Why don't you come to the Lord?' till he would foam at the mouth, and sometimes continued it till the congregation would be praying in companies about the house." "For my part," says Mr. Lee, "I wished the like work was among the people again." He at last gained consent to use the town-house, where he preached to a large congregation, and at the close of the service was hospitably entertained for the night.

Thus this pioneer of Methodism went from place to place, and from State to State, generally meeting with a cold reception at first, and some opposition from the ministers of the "standing order," but leaving a favorable impression behind him on the minds of the people, and forming small Societies in different places. The first Methodist Society formed in Connecticut was in Stratford, and consisted of only three females; but this small number was the germ of a large and flourishing Society which remains to the present day. On Stratford Circuit also was erected the first Methodist church ever built in New England. It was called Lee's Chapel, in honor of the first Methodist preacher who visited those parts.

Before the session of the ensuing conference, Mr. Lee visited the city of Boston, and immediately after his arrival there, endeavored to find some house in which he might preach. He conversed with many on this subject, but every expedient to find a place failed. None would encourage him, none would put themselves to the trouble of assisting him in finding a place to preach. He accordingly gave as extended a notice as possible, that on the day following,—Sabbath,—at 6 o'clock in the afternoon, he would preach on Boston Common. At the time appointed, a large congregation attracted by the novelty of the occasion assembled on the Common, and heard the word with considerable attention and solemnity. On a second visit made in a short time after the first, he had the privilege of preaching in a private house, and in a vacant Baptist meeting-house. He also preached on the Common to an assemblage of five thousand people.

After visiting different cities and towns in Connecticut, Massachusetts, Vermont, and New Hampshire, embracing a circuit of hundreds of miles in extent, and requiring several thousand miles' travel, Mr. Lee attended the conference held in the city of New York in the year 1790, and at this conference was appointed by Bishop Asbury to the city of Boston. On his arrival at the latter city, he tried in vain to get a place in which to preach. He applied to the high sheriff and clerk of the court for liberty to use the court-house, but was peremptorily refused. One of his friends next tried to obtain a school-house but a plain and positive refusal was the result of the application. Disheartened with the attempt to introduce Methodism into Boston, he went to Lynn and organized a Society, and after spending a few days in that place, returned to Boston again for the purpose of renewing his efforts; but everything remained as dark and forbidding as before, having no place to preach in, no friendly voice to welcome the youthful preacher to their home, and he having but two shillings in his pocket to pay for his board and lodging. Mr. Lee under these circumstances, instead of confining himself to Boston, visited several towns and villages in the State, and occasionally returning to his appointed field of labor, and making an attempt to secure a place wherein to preach. At last a room in a small private house in the north end of the city was obtained, where he occasionally preached to a small number of hearers, but it was not until July, 1792, that a Society was organized in Boston, consisting of but a few poor members. The Society thus formed obtained at length liberty to worship in a school-house, and after having used it a few times, it was taken from them. They next rented a chamber in the skirts of the city, and finally undertook to build a small meeting-house, but being poor they could do but little toward paying for it. Aid, however, was procured for them in Baltimore, Philadelphia, New York, and other places, and in 1795, the corner-stone of the first Methodist Chapel in Boston was laid, since which period Methodism in that city and the surrounding country has increased its numbers and influence so much, as to render the Methodist Episcopal Church one of the most respectable denomina-

7

tions in New England, having hundreds of able ministers and thousands of intelligent members.

SECTION VI.

On the 2d day of March, 1791, the venerable and apostolic John Wesley, the father and founder of Methodism, died in the 88th year of his age, in his own house, in the city of London, after having preached the gospel for sixty-four years. The death of this distinguished man produced much sorrow, not only in England where he was best known, but in America. The tidings were received with undissembled sorrow, especially by the ministers and preachers of the Methodist Episcopal Church. A great man had fallen in Israel, and it was but proper that his sons in the gospel should weep when their spiritual father and head was taken away from them. None however received the afflictive intelligence with greater sorrow than Bishops Coke and Asbury. The former, on first hearing of the sad event, began to make preparations for his departure for England, that he might mingle his tears and sorrows with those of his brethren in his native land. On his way he stopped at Baltimore and preached a sermon on the occasion, and shortly after set sail for Europe where he arrived in safety after a short and pleasant voyage. Having mentioned the death of Mr. Wesley, whose dying words were, "The best of all is, God is with us," and the departure of Dr. Coke for England, we will resume the thread of our narrative in relation to the extension of the work in America.

While Mr. Lee was operating at the north and east, Bishop Asbury, Mr. Garretson, and others were laboring in other parts of the land, entering into new fields of labor, organizing many new Societies, and forming new circuits. The work had spread so much, that it became quite inconvenient for the preachers to meet together in one general conference; hence district conferences, so called, were held in different parts of the country to the number of thirteen or fourteen in each year; but as no *one* of the conferences possessed legislative powers, it became necessary to adopt some plan by which the conferences might be represented, when it became necessary to legislate on the affairs of the Connection. Bishop Asbury recommended a council to be composed of the bishops and presiding elders, and after some debate among the preachers, the advice of the bishop was approved of, and the council was accordingly formed. After two sessions, however, of the council, it was found that a majority of the preachers who had voted for it had changed their minds in reference to its utility and propriety, and it consequently was disorganized, and in its place a general conference was called, which met in Baltimore, in November, 1792, and was composed of all the travelling preachers then in full connection. At this conference several important alterations in the economy of Methodism were proposed by some of the preachers, and among these, one which would limit the power of the bishops in stationing the preachers. The leading advocate of these alterations was the Rev. James O'Kelly, a popular and highly gifted presiding elder from Virginia; but as a large majority of the ministers present objected to such changes, the mover of the same felt grieved, and withdrew from the church, and having many friends in Virginia, he succeeded in inducing many to follow his example, and with those seceders he organized during the next year a church with the title of Republican Methodists, which however soon became merged in the Unitarian Baptist, or Christian denomination, and thus lost its identity, while the leader of the secession himself, at last lost his influence, and died in obscurity.

At the above conference the presiding elder's office was established, for although the bishops had previously appointed presiding elders, it had been done without the action of the conferences, and as some had objected to the usage of the bishops in this respect, a majority now fully sanctioned their doings, and formally authorized their appointment in the future. Various other important rules were passed, and after a session of some days, the conference adjourned, having resolved to have another General Conference in four years from that time.

Between the sessions of the General Conferences of 1792–6, the Methodist preachers continued in their work of saving souls and forming Societies, gradually extending the borders of the church, and embracing within its fold entire states and the inhabited portions of the adjoining territories. A considerable foothold was obtained in Rhode Island, where the first Methodist sermon had been preached in Charlestown in 1789. In 1794, a church was erected in Warren, and was opened for worship on the 24th day of September of that year. A Society was also formed in Provincetown in 1795, and soon after, an attempt was made to build a church. The timber was procured at a distance and brought to the place by water. In the meantime, persecution began to rage, and a collection of those hostile to the Methodists met in the night, and taking the most of the timber to the bottom of a large hill, they cut it to pieces and made a pen of it. They then procured a sailor's old hat, jacket and trowsers, and stuffing them so as to represent a man, they fastened the effigy on the top of the pen, and then tarred and feathered it. These persecutions, however, did not discourage the members, but laying their plans anew, they procured more timber and soon built themselves a comfortable house of worship.

The first Methodist church in Maine was erected in the town of Readfield in 1704–5. The first Society formed in New Hampshire was in the town of Chesterfield in 1795, and the first circuit formed in Vermont was in 1796, and was called Vershire circuit; and for the first time in the history of the Methodist Episcopal Church, Societies were found to exist in all the United States.

At the session of the General Conference of 1796, there were one hundred and twenty ministers present. At this conference it was agreed that the annual conferences, which had previously been called district conferences, should be reduced to six in number, and be called yearly conferences, as follows: New England, Philadelphia, Baltimore, Virginia, South Carolina, and the Western Yearly Conferences. The Chartered Fund was also instituted, and after introducing a few changes in the discipline, the conference adjourned to meet in the year 1800.

At the General Conference of 1800, Bishops Coke and Asbury presided, as they had done at the two previous ones: but Dr. Coke having received a very urgent call from the British Conference to labor more especially for the benefit of the Wesleyan Missions in the West Indies, and in Ireland, the General Conference with some regret consented to give up the doctor for a short time, and in reply to the British Conference, state, that in compliance with their request, "We have lent the doctor to you for a season, to return to us as soon as he conveniently can, but at the farthest by the meeting of the next General Conference." To supply the doctor's lack of service, Richard Whatcoat—who accompanied Doctor Coke in his first visit to America, and who had been ordained a deacon and an elder by Mr. Wesley in 1784—was elected and ordained a bishop of the Methodist Episcopal Church.

It was about this period that camp-meetings first began to be held. Although at present mostly confined to the Methodists, they originated among the Presbyterians and Methodists under the labors of two brothers by the name of M'Gee, the one being a Presbyterian and the other a Methodist minister. In the year 1799, these two brothers set off on a tour from Tennessee toward the state of Ohio. On their way they stopped at a settlement on the Red River to attend a sacramental occasion in a Presbyterian congregation. The Methodist brother was invited to preach by the pastor of the church. He consented, and was followed by his Presbyterian brother, and then by another Presbyterian minister. During the preaching of the latter, a woman in the congregation shouted aloud the praises of God. This shouting offended the pastor and the minister who was preaching when it took place, so that they and another minister present left the house, but the two brothers remained, and such were the continued manifestations of the power of God, that the entire congregation was moved by the mighty invisible impulse. William M'Gee, the Presbyterian, felt such a shock of divine power, that not knowing what he did, he left his seat and sat down on the floor, while John his brother sat trembling under a consciousness of the divine presence. Although expected to preach again, he arose, and told the people that his feelings would not allow him to do so, but exhorted them to surrender their hearts to the Lord. Such was the effect of this meeting, that the people came in crowds from the surrounding country to see and hear for themselves, the wonderful works of God. But as no house could contain the multitude, and the people wished to remain for several days, and accommodations for board, lodging, &c., could not be readily obtained, they saw the propriety of bringing provisions and bedding; and some built temporary huts or tents, as places of shelter; and thus we see the beginning of camp-meetings—a precious means of grace which has been blessed to the conversion of tens of thousands of sinners and the sanctification of hundreds of believers.

The results of this first camp-meeting casually convened, induced the ministers above named to appoint another, and still another in different parts of the country; at each of which, the power of God was displayed in the most wonderful manner, and it has been stated by an eye and ear witness of the scenes alluded to, that the people under the power of the Word, fell like corn before a storm of wind; and what added greatly to the interest of such meetings, was the spirit of union and brotherly love exhibited by ministers and members of different denominations, for each other. Here the Presbyterian, the Methodist, the Baptist, all coöperated heartily in the work of

God; and as they thus coöperated, the revival flame rose higher and higher, and spread wider and wider, and such was the excitement produced by these meetings, that in Kentucky, from three to twenty thousand were frequently in attendance, and although no doubt many went merely from motives of curiosity, and others to mock and sneer, yet many attended with a sincere desire to be benefited, and frequently, those who went to scoff, returned to pray. An amusing, yet instructive incident of this kind occurred at one of these meetings, held we believe in Kentucky. A gentleman and lady of note in the fashionable world, attended the Caneridge camp-meeting, and while they were on their way amusing themselves at the expense of the deluded worshippers—as they thought them to be—and while they saw, in *their* imagination, numbers falling to the ground all around them, they, in a moment of hilarity and glee, made a sportive agreement that if either of *them* should fall under the power, the other should by no means forsake the fallen one. They at length arrived on the ground, but had not been present long, before the lady fell under the word. The gentleman, frightened at the sight of his fallen companion, and regardless of his agreement, and afraid probably that a similar fate awaited him, fled with the utmost precipitancy, but he had not proceeded far, before he shared the fate he so much dreaded, was prostrated upon the earth, and was soon surrounded by a praying circle of friends.

Such large meetings, composed as they were of all classes in society, could not be expected to pass off without great irregularity of conduct on the part of some, and of violent opposition on the part of others. Many exaggerated statements were made in reference to the spiritual exercises at such meetings, and many of the cold-hearted ministers, who were opposers of the revival, were among the most prominent enemies of camp-meetings, but in spite of the opposition of the professedly good, and the hostility of the openly wicked, God sanctioned these feasts of tabernacles; and such has been their acknowledged utility among the Methodists, that while the Presbyterians have long since discarded them, as unsuited to their mode of operation for the advancement of religion, the former have continued them in most parts of the country from year to year, and at [illegible] former time have camp-meetings been more frequent, better attended, or followed by more beneficial results than at the present time.

About this time also, Methodism began to take deep root in the provinces of Upper and Lower Canada, where it had before been introduced by several zealous preachers of the Methodist Episcopal Church, and other Methodists from England; but as the author intends to speak of Canadian Methodism in a separate section of this work, he will in this place only state, that at the period of which we are now treating, regular circuits were in existence in different parts of these provinces. (See Section XII.)

In 1804, the fourth regular General Conference assembled in the city of Baltimore. It was composed of the three bishops, Coke, Asbury, and Whatcoat, as presidents, and one hundred and twelve members. Among the most important acts of this conference was one establishing the Book Concern in the city of New York, there having previously been published a few Methodist books in Philadelphia, at which place the Book Concern was first located, but on a small scale. At this conference also, the bounds of the several yearly conferences were fixed and printed in the Book of Discipline. The British Conference having again requested the labors of Dr. Coke in behalf of their missions, he was permitted to go under the same restrictions as before imposed upon him—that he should return by the next General Conference.

As nothing very extraordinary transpired in the interim between this and the succeeding General Conference of 1808, we pass to notice the proceedings of the latter, so far as matters of importance are concerned.

The fifth General Conference assembled in the city of Baltimore, Bishop Asbury being the only bishop present. Bishop Whatcoat had died two years previously, in the 71st year of his age, and Bishop Coke, for certain reasons, had not found it convenient to leave his work in Europe for the purpose of attending this conference. He, however, wrote to the conference expressing his willingness to come over and labor, and live and die with them, but that unless his services were *necessary* to the church in America, he preferred remaining where he thought they were more needed, and where he could render himself more useful. In accordance with these wishes, the conference adopted resolutions commendatory of their absent bishop, and consenting to his remaining in Europe until called to America by the General Conference; or all the annual conferences. At this conference also, the Rev. Wm. M'Kendree was elected and consecrated a bishop; and provision was made for a delegated General Conference, to be composed of one delegate for every five members of an annual conference. It was also resolved, that the General Conference should meet on the first day of May, 1812, and thenceforward on the first of May, once in four years perpetually. Restrictive rules were also adopted, which have remained the same as originally adopted till the present time, excepting the one which relates to the ratio of representation. As the constitution and powers of the General Conference will be referred to in a proper place, it will be unnecessary to enlarge upon the same in this section.

The bishops at this conference were authorized—if they deemed it expedient to do so—to organize another annual conference, in addition to the seven already organized by the General Conference. Accordingly, in 1810, the Genesee Conference was formed, embracing within its bounds the whole of Central and Western New York, and the province of Upper Canada, which province Bishop Asbury visited in the year 1811. Crossing from the Indian village of St. Regis to Cornwall in Canada, the bishop, after having been a citizen of the United States since the independence of the same, and having lived and preached in the colonies for a few years prior thereto, amounting in all to forty years, at length sets foot upon a soil protected by the flag of his native country, and it is no wonder that under such circumstances the old man should have "strange feelings come over him."

The bishop proceeded up the province along the banks of the St. Lawrence, and preached in most of the towns between Cornwall and Kingston. After preaching in the latter place, he re-crossed the river, or lake, to Sackett's Harbor, and soon after, in conjunction with Bishop M'Kendree, he attended the session of the Genesee Conference, which was held in Paris, Oneida County, New York, and on its adjournment, the bishops returned again to their travels through the Connection, holding the conferences in Kentucky, and in Tennessee, and also in South Carolina.

SECTION VII.

The first delegated General Conference of the Methodist Episcopal Church assembled in the city of New York on the first of May, 1812. Bishops Asbury and M'Kendree were present, and presided alternately. There were ninety delegates in attendance. No bishop was elected at this conference, but several important rules in relation to local preachers were adopted, as also resolutions in regard to raising money for missions, the publication of a monthly periodical, &c. &c., and after a session of three weeks, the conference closed its labors; and soon after the adjournment, the United States declared war against Great Britain. This unhappy event produced pernicious effects upon the interests of true religion in the United States, and brought the Methodists in the States and in the Canadas into an unfriendly relation, and frequently into actual collisions with each other. In consequence of this state of things, the American preachers appointed this year to Canada, either obtained permission to remain in the States, or having gone there, returned home. The Canadian preachers, who of course remained at their posts in Canada, were also prevented from attending the sessions of the Genesee Conference, to which they belonged, and were thus left to take care of themselves and their flock in the best way they could, during the war.

In the year 1813, a small secession from the Methodist Episcopal Church took place in Vermont, which resulted in the organization of the "Reformed Methodist Church." The originator of this secession was the Rev. Pliny Brett, a member of the New England Conference, who this year located, and succeeded in luring from the church several local preachers, in the vicinity of Cape Cod. From thence he proceeded to Vermont, and succeeded, through the assistance of Elijah Bailey, a local preacher in Readsboro', in drawing off a number of Societies in that town and vicinity, and after having called a general convention of all the disaffected ones, the Rev. Mr. Bailey was chosen President, the Reformed Methodists became a distinct body, and Mr. Bailey became the apostle of the new movement. Many local preachers and exhorters having joined them, they at one period in their history gave some promise of becoming quite a respectable denomination, having formed circuits in different parts of Vermont, New York, and Canada, but like some other secessionists, they finally became merged in other bodies distinct from the above, so that at present the Reformed Methodists have scarcely an existence in any part of the United States or Canada, although at the time of their greatest prosperity, they had five annual conferences, nearly a hundred preachers, and several thousand members.

In the year 1814, the sad tidings reached the shores of Europe and America, that Bishop Coke had departed this life. After having been more fully released from his engagements to the American Connection, Dr. Coke gave his especial attention to the cause of missions in the British Connection, of which missions he had the superintendence. He at length resolved to establish a mission in British India, and in company with seven others, whom he had selected as assistants, he left England on the first of January. After being absent about four months, and as the vessel which conveyed him neared the port of destination, the doctor, while in his berth, was seized with a fit of apoplexy, and on opening the door of his cabin in the morning, was found dead upon the floor. His body was consigned to the bosom of the great deep, with appropriate religious services by his surviving colleagues. Thus ended the life and labors of Bishop Coke, who, although having some enemies while he lived, had many warm friends, and who was himself the true friend of Methodism, in America, and in his native land,—a man whose life was entirely spent in the service of the church of God, and who, no doubt, exchanged the trials of this life for the inheritance of the sanctified in heaven.

Before the session of the next General Conference, a still greater calamity than the preceding one befell the Methodist Episcopal Church. This was nothing less than the death of the apostle of Methodism in America—Bishop Asbury—which occurred on the 31st of March, 1816, near Fredericksburg, in Virginia—aged seventy years. His health, for several years, had been declining, in consequence of his constant exposure to heat and cold, and all the hardships and vicissitudes of an itinerant life. His remains were finally deposited under the pulpit in a vault, in the Eutaw-street church, Baltimore. Thus perished the mortal existence of a man, a Christian, a Christian minister, and a truly apostolic bishop, who, during the forty-five years of his ministry in America, preached, probably, not far from twenty thousand sermons, and travelled not less than two hundred and seventy thousand miles—a distance equal to more than ten times the circumference of the earth!

In the year 1815, another secession from the Methodist Episcopal Church took place in Philadelphia, the subjects of it being colored people. At an early period in the history of the Methodist Episcopal Church, its ministers had taken a lively interest in the spiritual welfare of the colored people, whether bond or free. Under the preaching of these ministers, many hundreds and thousands of the African race were converted to God, and very generally gave good evidence of such conversion, by an upright course of conduct. Of those thus converted, a considerable number, possessing both gifts and grace, were licensed to exhort and preach, and a few had been ordained to the offices of deacon and elder. Among these last was Richard Allen, a local preacher of Philadelphia, who had once been a slave, but had procured his freedom, and had acquired wealth and influence among his colored friends. By the aid of the whites, the colored Methodists succeeded in building a neat and commodious church, and were regularly recognized as a Methodist Episcopal Church, and were placed under the pastoral charge of a white minister, stationed by the presiding Bishop of the Philadelphia Conference. For some years everything went on prosperously and harmoniously between the white and colored Methodists, but at length mutual distrust and dissatisfaction succeeded, which resulted in the distinct organization of the "African Methodist Episcopal Church," which has continued to exist with more or less success till the present time. There were about one thousand persons who seceded as above, and since that period they have increased to some fifteen or twenty thousand members, having congregations and churches in nearly all the cities and large towns of the free States where the colored people are numerous.

In the year 1816, the second Delegated General Conference assembled in the city of Baltimore, Bishop M'Kendree, the only surviving bishop of the church, presiding. After being in session a few days, the Episcopacy was strengthened by the election and consecration to the office of bishop of the Revs. Enoch George, and Robert R. Roberts; and after a harmonious session of twenty-four days, the conference adjourned. Several alterations of the Discipline were adopted at this conference, but as such alterations, and the reasons assigned for their adoption, would occupy too much space in the body of this work, we are obliged to pass them over without further notice.

In the year 1818, the Methodist Magazine was resuscitated, after having lain dormant for a number of years. Joshua Soule and Thomas Mason, being the Book Agents, were the publishers and editors of the same. The year 1819 gave birth to the Missionary Society of the Methodist Episcopal Church. Rev. Dr. Bangs had the honor of having presided at the meeting in the city of New York when such Society was first organized. The bishops were subsequently elected as chief officers of the Society, Dr. Bangs being one of the Vice Presidents.

During this latter year, also, there was a large secession of colored members from the Methodist Episcopal Church in the city of New York. This secession embraced fourteen colored local preachers, and nine hundred and twenty-nine members, including many Class Leaders, Stewards, and Exhorters. The principal cause of such secession was the refusal on the part of the whites to employ colored men as travelling preachers. They have always retained, however, a degree of love and affection for the parent Church, which speaks well for their sincerity and piety.

SECTION VIII.

In 1820, the General Conference again met in Baltimore, Bishops M'Kendree, George, and Roberts, being the presidents thereof. As difficulties had existed for some time in relation to the Societies in Upper and Lower Canada, there being English and American preachers appointed to both provinces by their respective conferences, and as these preachers sometimes came into collision with each other in their work, this General Conference appointed Rev. John Emory a delegate to attend the ensuing session of the British Conference and adjust all difficulties in relation to these matters. Accordingly at the proper time, Mr. Emory went to England, and happily succeeded in bringing matters to a successful issue. The result of these negotiations was, that the lower province of Canada was to be in future left to the care of the English Conference, while the upper province was to be consigned to the exclusive care of the American Church. These measures were cordially assented to by the preachers of the Methodist Episcopal Church, and the ministers appointed to churches or circuits in Lower Canada were shortly after withdrawn.

This General Conference also created a *District Conference* for the benefit of the local preachers in each district. The object of creating such Conference was to place all matters relating to them as a body as much as possible under their own jurisdiction and control. These meetings, however, did not answer the purposes for which they were intended, and after a few years a succeeding General Conference repealed the clause by which they were created.

Provision was also made at the conference of 1820, for the establishment of a separate branch of the Book Concern to be located at Cincinnati, Ohio, and the Rev. Martin Ruter was appointed to the agency of the same; while Rev. Nathan Bangs and T. Mason were appointed agents of the parent establishment in New York.

The year 1820 gave birth to another secession in the city of New York, of about three hundred members of the Church, headed by Rev. Wm. M. Stilwell, a travelling preacher in the New York Conference, at that time stationed in the city. The difficulty originated in 1817, and grew out of the rebuilding of John-street church, and involved various questions of administration and other matters, which ended in the formation of an independent congregation. This new sect, however, did not flourish, but soon began to dwindle away, many of the members who had seceded seeking an asylum again in the old church which they had too hastily left.

The necessity of providing the means of education for the youth of our church began to be seriously felt throughout the

Connection, and during the year 1820, and a few succeeding years various academic institutions were opened in New York and New England, for the education of the children of Methodist members. Institutions of a like character, and of a higher grade, have since been very generally founded in every part of the widely-extended field of Methodism.

At the General Conference of 1824, the Revs. Joshua Soule and Elijah Hedding were duly elected and consecrated bishops of the Methodist Episcopal Church. Such had been the extension of the work and continued prosperity of the church, that two bishops in addition to the former three were thought to be necessary, and the above ministers were selected for this important office. At this conference also the preachers laboring in Upper Canada were, at their own request, formed into an annual conference by themselves. They had, indeed, asked to be formed into an independent organization, with authority to elect their own bishops: but the General Conference conceiving that it had not the power to sever the connection, merely allowed them a separate Conference, which was afterwards presided over by the bishops of the Methodist Episcopal Church, as long as the connection continued to exist.

During the interval between this and the succeeding General Conference, several important enterprises were commenced; one, the founding of Madison College in Uniontown, Pennsylvania, under the presidency of Rev. Henry B. Bascom; another the establishment of the Christian Advocate, a weekly paper, in the city of New York. The first number of this well-known and extensively circulated periodiocal was issued on the 9th of September, 1826. In 1827 the Sunday School Union of the Methodist Episcopal Church was organized in New York, which from that period has been slowly and gradually gaining influence and strength, especially under its recent organization.

The General Conference of 1828, met in the city of Pittsburgh, the five bishops being present and presiding alternately. Among the more important acts of this conference was one which, yielding to the importunities of the brethren in Canada, dissolved the compact existing between the Canada Conference and the General Conference in the United States; and authorized one of the bishops to attend the Canada Conference in its independent capacity, and ordain as bishop the person who might be elected by the Canada Conference to that office.

A great part of the session of this conference was occupied with the reception and reading of petitions, and in discussing matters referred to in the same. These petitions were sent up to the conference from a convention of private members and local preachers, who assembled in November, 1827, in Baltimore. The great object sought to be obtained by these and other petitioners was a representation of the local preachers and lay members in the councils of the church. For a number of years, the question of lay delegation had been discussed in conventions, in conferences, in periodicals, and in pamphlets, by those who took an interest in the matter; but as the great body of the preachers and people were decidedly opposed to such innovations, the General Conference had not thought it proper to take the desired action. This refusal of the General Conference to grant the prayer of the members of the "Union Societies," as the petitioners were generally called, produced great dissatisfaction among them. From arguments and requests, they proceeded to harsher measures to accomplish their ends; and it was at length found necessary by the authorities of the church in Baltimore where the disaffected mostly belonged, to call some of the leading ones among them to an account for disturbing the peace of the Societies. The trial of these persons resulted in their expulsion from the Methodist Episcopal Church, and their subsequent organization under the title of "Associated Methodist Reformers."

As these matters all passed in review of this General Conference while listening to the petitions and remonstrances of the expelled and disaffected preachers, and the discussion elicited thereby, a disposition on the part of the members of the conference was manifested to forgive past offences by authorizing preachers to receive those who had been expelled, and who desired to be restored again into the bosom of the church, provided that a promise was given by the expelled persons to desist from undue agitation of the matter. This disposition on the part of the General Conference to heal dissensions, and restore to the privileges of the church those who had been excluded, does not appear to have been received with much favor by the reformers; on the contrary, a very considerable secession took place not only in Baltimore, but in New York, Philadelphia, Pittsburgh, Cincinnati, and other places, where congregations were organized and ministers appointed to the charge thereof.

The secession above referred to, finally resulted in the organization of the "Methodist Protestant Church." In which the main features of Episcopal Methodism are retained, excepting the composition of the conferences, and the rejection of an Episcopal form of church government. The feelings of animosity which so long existed between the two churches have, it is to be hoped, given place to kindlier and more affectionate ones; and it is by no means impossible, but that the ministers and members of both of these branches of the church, may yet see eye to eye, and again be embraced in the same fold.

At this conference was formed the Oneida Annual Conference, making in all nineteen annual conferences in the Connection, which were attended in rotation by the bishops of the church, who were, shortly after the adjournment of the General Conference, reduced to four in number by the sudden death of Bishop George, who departed this life in Staunton, Va., aged sixty-one years. Bishop George was a good man, and a truly apostolic bishop; and his death was severely felt throughout the entire church.

The most important events connected with the history of the church which occurred in the interval of the General Conferences of 1828, and 1832, were the establishment of a Seaman's Mission in the city of Boston, under the spiritual direction of Rev. Edward T. Taylor, the world-renowned sailor-preacher, who had himself been a seaman for a number of years; but who was happily converted to God, and became a pious, zealous, and successful minister of Jesus Christ, and who since his first appointment to that mission has been continued from year to year down to the present time in the same important relation of Bethel Chaplain. Before this period also, a Mariner's Church had been established in the city of New York, which also remains in a prosperous condition, and is regularly supplied with Methodist preaching. Another event of importance was the founding of no less than three Methodist colleges in the year 1831. These colleges were the Wesleyan University in Middletown, Connecticut, under the presidency of Wilbur Fisk, D.D., who had the honor of being the first graduate of a collegiate institution among the American Methodist preachers; the Randolph Macon College, in Boydston, Virginia, under the presidency of Stephen Olin, a graduate of Middlebury College, Vermont, and at the present time, the highly popular President of Wesleyan University;* and La Grange College, in La Grange, Alabama, under the presidency of Rev. Robert Paine. The establishment of these literary institutions, all in the course of a single year, gave good evidence that although the Methodist Episcopal Church had been for many years in an apparently dormant state in reference to education, she had now awakened in good earnest, and was about to atone for past remissness by increased energy and zeal in this important department of her work.

The General Conference of 1832 met in the city of Philadelphia on the 1st of May. At this conference two additional bishops were elected and consecrated, namely, James O. Andrew and John Emory. Measures were taken at this confer-

* Since the above was written, Stephen Olin, D.D., LL.D., departed this life in Middletown, Conn., on the 16th August, 1851, greatly and deservedly regretted.

ence for the establishment of a mission in Liberia, on the western coast of Africa; and in October of this year Rev. Melville B. Cox sailed as a Missionary of the Methodist Episcopal Church, to that distant and benighted shore. But alas! for all human calculations, he had scarcely entered on his field of labor before he became a victim to the malaria on the coast, and after a long sickness with African fever, he fell in the arms of death on the 21st July, 1833, in the 33d year of his age. His dying words were—" Let thousands fall before Africa be given up!"—memorable words, and worthy of the man!

During the year 1833, two other colleges were established under the patronage of the Methodist Episcopal Church:—Dickenson College, in Carlisle, Penn., of which Rev. John P. Durbin was appointed President, and Alleghany College, in Meadville, Penn., of which Martin Ruter, D.D. was appointed President. A large and flourishing Seminary, in Lima, Livingston Co., N. Y., was also established in 1833, Dr. Samuel Luckey being its first Principal.

In addition to the establishment of the Liberia Mission, and the sending out of five additional missionaries to fill the place of the departed Cox, another important mission was commenced in the distant territory of Oregon. The Flathead tribe of Indians inhabiting that territory had heard in their native wilds of the white man's God, and had sent a deputation of four of their principal men eastward, across the Rocky Mountains, to make the necessary inquiries about the Being whom the white men worshipped. The singular errand on which these Indians came, awakened in the bosom of the Christian Church a strong desire to send to these heathen the Gospel of Jesus Christ. A call was made for volunteers, and in answer to that call, two young ministers of the Methodist Episcopal Church, announced their readiness to go. Accordingly, the Revs. Jason and Daniel Lee—uncle and nephew—were appointed missionaries to that far off field, and on the 10th of April, 1834, they commenced their journey of over three thousand miles on horseback, and on the 28th of the following September, they had the privilege of preaching the first gospel sermon ever delivered in that part of the country. The prospects of this mission were so flattering, that the Board of Missions, in 1836 and 1837, sent out large reinforcements for the benefit of the same. This mission still exists, and although all the good has not been effected which was desired, and hoped for among the Indians, yet the mission has proved a great blessing to that part of the land, especially since it began to be settled by a white population.

In 1835, a mission was established in Rio Janeiro, and Buenos Ayres, in South America, the Rev. Fountain E. Pitts, of the Tennessee Conference, being appointed a missionary to that field. Through his labors, and those of his successor, Rev. Dr. Dempster, a small but flourishing Society has been formed, and a handsome and commodious church has been erected in the latter city.

During the year 1835, the church lost two of her bishops by death, namely: William M'Kendree, the senior, and John Emory, the junior bishop, the former having filled the office for twenty-seven years, and the latter only since the previous General Conference. Bishop M'Kendree was seventy-eight years of age at the time of his death—he had served the church faithfully, and was much beloved by both preachers and people. His last dying words were, "All is well;"

> "Not a cloud doth arise
> To darken my skies,
> Or hide for a moment
> My Lord from my eyes."

Bishop Emory was comparatively a young man, being only forty-seven years of age at the period of his sudden and untimely death. For twenty-five years of his life he had been a Methodist preacher, and had filled some of the highest and most responsible offices in the church previously to his being elected bishop, and during the short time he filled the latter office, he gave evidence of his fitness for "the work of a bishop," and promised great usefulness to the church in that important capacity, but on the 16th of December, 1835, while on his way to Baltimore, his horse ran away with him, and he was thrown from his carriage, and received such a wound on the head, as caused his death on the evening of the same day. Being deprived of his senses, the only word he was heard to say before he died, was "Amen!"

SECTION IX.

THE General Conference of 1836, assembled in the city of Cincinnati, Ohio. At this conference, three additional bishops were elected, namely, Rev. Beverly Waugh, Rev. Thomas A. Morris, and the Rev. Wilbur Fisk. The two former being present, were consecrated, but the latter being absent in Europe, was simply advised of his election. He, however, after his return to the United States, declined accepting the appointment, preferring to remain at the head of the Wesleyan University.

The great and exciting topic of discussion at this conference was that of slavery. For a number of years the public mind had been called up to the subject of slavery as existing in the United States, and to the duty of immediate emancipation. The advocates of the immediate abolition of slavery in the General Conference, had been elected delegates by their respective annual conferences, with strict reference to their opinions on this subject. Among the most able of these advocates was the Rev. Orange Scott, of the New England Conference, who lost no opportunity of introducing at suitable times during the session, this—to him—all-important subject. Eloquent and able as he was acknowledged to be, he met a staunch opponent in the Rev. W. Winans, of the Mississippi Conference. At length after a stormy and lengthy discussion of the subject, *pro* and *con*, the conference passed resolutions condemnatory of modern abolitionism, so called. These resolutions were carried by a large majority of the delegates, while a small but respectable minority not only voted against their passage, but opposed them otherwise, as far as they could.

This General Conference made provision for the publication of several additional weekly periodicals. Several new conferences were also formed, and among the latter the Black River Conference, so called, because the Black River—an important stream in Northwestern New York, emptying into Lake Ontario near Sackett's Harbor—runs nearly through the centre of it. Several important alterations were also made in the discipline, and the conference, having completed its work, adjourned after a session of four weeks, to meet again in Baltimore, May 1st, 1840.

After the adjournment of the General Conference of 1836, the anti-slavery excitement continued not only to exist, but to increase in intensity, especially in the New England States, and in the western part of the State of New York; but while the church was thus convulsed from centre to circumference, she did not forget her appropriate duty of sending the gospel to distant lands. During the interval between this and the succeeding General Conference, several talented and useful missionaries were sent out to different parts of the world, under the direction of the missionary board of managers. Among those thus sent out during the above period, were the Rev. Daniel P. Kidder, as missionary to Rio de Janeiro, accompanied by a male and a female teacher; Rev. John Dempster, of the Black River Conference, to Buenos Ayres; Rev. John Seys, of the Oneida Conference, to Liberia; Rev. J. B. Barton, of the Georgia Conference, to the same field; Rev. Squire Chase, of the Black River Conference, to Liberia, to assist Br. Seys, who having returned to America for the benefit of his health, on his return to Africa was accompanied by his friend and colleague last named; Rev. Geo. Brown, a colored local preacher, to the same field; Doctor S. M. E. Goheen, as physician, Rev. J. Burton, as teacher, and Rev. W. Stocker, as missionary, were all sent to the same field, to labor, and if need be, to die for the benefit of the colored race. All the persons sent to the coast of Africa, as above, after their arrival, were more or less prostrated by disease, while undergoing the process of acclimation, and one of their number, shortly after his arrival, fell asleep in the arms of death, with the hope in possession of a glorious resurrection from "Afric's burning plains." In 1837, Dr. Ruter, president of Alleghany College, and two other preachers, were appointed missionaries to Texas—at that time an independent State by itself. These missionaries, being abundantly successful in that distant field of labor, were soon followed by others who assisted them in planting the standard of the cross in different portions of Texas. The year 1836 witnessed the establishment of the first German Mission in America, for the benefit of the German population. It was commenced in Cincinnati, and was placed under the charge of Rev. William—now Doctor—Nast, a young native German preacher, of sound education, and deep piety. This was the beginning of a great and glorious work among the Germans, thousands having since that time been converted, and added to the church in different parts of the United States, and from among these, scores of pious, intelligent Methodist preachers have been raised up, some of whom have since gone to their *fatherland*, to preach a spiritual gospel. In 1838, a mission for the benefit of the French population was established in the city of New York, under the care of Rev. Mr. Williamson, a native Frenchman. This mission, in consequence of the prejudices of the Roman Catholic French and others, has not succeeded as it otherwise would have done, but has, notwithstanding, done much good.

During the latter part of the year 1839, the *Centenary of Methodism* was celebrated with all due solemnity in all parts of the Methodist Connection in Europe and America. The first Methodist Society having been formed in London in November of 1739, a hundred years had thus transpired since the "*eight or ten persons* came to Mr. Wesley," and with him formed the reproached band of Methodists. During the lapse of a century, God had done great things for this people; the small one had become a thousand; more than a million of members, and three millions of adherents, had shared in the blessings of a gospel which declares a *free* and FULL salvation to the lost sons and daughters of men. The 25th day of November was accordingly set apart as a day of thanksgiving and rejoicing before the Lord. Sermons were preached in all parts of the land—collections were made, free-will thank-offerings were presented to God for the benefit of his Church, and more than half a million of dollars were raised for missions, education, and the worn-out preachers, and the widows and orphans of deceased ministers.

The General Conference of 1840, met in Baltimore—the bishops of the church all being present. There were also several distinguished visitors from England and the Canadas, among whom may be named the Rev. brethren Newton, Stinson, Harvard, Richey, John and E. Ryerson. Several important alterations were made in the Book of Discipline at this session; the subject of slavery was also introduced, and discussed in all its various aspects, but without arriving at any point whereby the growing agitation in the church could be quelled, and after a session of five weeks, the conference adjourned, to hold its ensuing session in the city of New York, on the first of May, 1844.

After the adjournment of the General Conference of 1840, the anti-slavery excitement in the church assumed a new phase. Hitherto the abolitionists so called, had been satisfied with complaints, petitions, &c., to the general and annual conferences, but many of them now began to evince a desire to leave the church and form independent organizations among themselves, or join such other existing branches of the church as favored their peculiar views in relation to slavery. That the reader may more fully understand the state of feeling then existing on this subject, and the partial results of the anti-slavery movement as it relates to the Methodist Episcopal Church, the author will give a brief history of the same in the form of extracts, from a work entitled the "CHURCHES *and* SECTS of the United States," written by the author.

"On the introduction of Methodism into the Southern portion of the American provinces, many of those who sought admission to the fellowship of the Societies were slaveholders, and as some of them at least, were so involuntarily, having come into possession of slaves by inheritance or bequest, and not having the legal power to manumit them even if they desired to do so, it was not thought proper to debar those who, in all other respects, gave evidence of sincerity and piety, from the privileges of the Societies; consequently, although there existed a rule of discipline against slaveholding, many masters were received, and in the course of time slaveholding ministers were even allowed to preach. In the year 1784, through the advice of Bishop Coke, stringent rules were adopted by the conference which organized the church, against slavery and slaveholding; and among these rules, one which required every slaveholding member to emancipate his slaves within the period of five years at most, or if the slave was under twenty years of age, when he should arrive at the age of twenty-five; likewise that all children born thereafter should be free from their birth. In order to bring these rules into practical operation, the slaveholding members were required to execute deeds of manumission within twelve months or be expelled from the church. Such, however, was the strong hold which slavery had already obtained, that it was found impossible by the preachers to enforce the rules, and at the succeeding conference the rules were suspended, and remained so until the year 1796. At the conference of this latter year, rules were adopted requiring *official* members of the church who held slaves to emancipate them;

and in the year 1800, it was enacted that when any travelling preacher became the owner of slaves he should forfeit his ministerial standing, unless he executed, if practicable, a deed of manumission for such slaves, according to the laws of the state in which he lived. It was, however, soon found that some of the preachers who had become involved in slaveholding could not legally execute such deeds of emancipation without a special act of legislation authorizing them to do so; and in the year 1812, in view of the above impediment, a rule was passed by which the annual conferences respectively, were empowered to form such regulations in regard to slaveholding as their wisdom might dictate and the laws of the states admit of being put in execution. This rule remained in force until 1820, when it was repealed, it being found in the meantime that the interference of the annual conferences in the matter of slavery was attended with considerable difficulty and embarrassment. From the year 1820 to the year 1844, no new rules on the subject of slavery were adopted by the General Conference. Meanwhile a large number of the travelling preachers in the Southern States had become possessed of slaves, some by purchase, some by bequest, and others by marrying slaveholding ladies. While slavery was thus being introduced more and more into the body of the ministry, many, perhaps a majority of the ministers and members in the non-slaveholding states and conferences, were ignorant of the true state of things in the South, and little imagined that there were actually thousands of slaveholding members, and scores, if not hundreds of slaveholding ministers in the Southern portion of the church.

"About the year 1832, the great anti-slavery excitement commenced in the North. Ministers of different religious denominations had their attention directed to the existence of this evil in the nation and in the churches. Sermons were preached and lectures delivered on the subject. Anti-slavery societies were formed, and anti-slavery periodicals were established.

The attention of the entire nation was solicited to a consideration of the subject. The ministers and members of the Methodist Episcopal Church began to examine the true relation which slavery held to the religious body of which they formed a part. A few zealous ministers began lecturing and preaching on the subject, and a paper was established in the city of New York for the ostensible purpose of showing forth in all its varied features the abominations of slavery. This paper, "Zion's Watchman," established in 1835, being edited by a Methodist minister, and being patronized by thousands of Methodist members, created an intense abhorrence of the entire system of slavery, and an active personal opposition to all its apologists and abettors. The conservative portion of the church in the North opposed the measures of the abolitionists, as the anti-slavery men were then generally called, but in spite of all attempts to quell excitement on the subject, the agitation still continued. Petitions and memorials were presented by hundreds to the annual and general conferences. These petitions, in many cases, were received unwillingly, in some cases not at all, but still the flame spread wider and rose higher, until the very existence of the church was threatened. Secessions became frequent; thousands of (hitherto) worthy members had left the church of their early choice on account of its connection with slavery, and thousands of others were only retained by the hope that action would be had upon the subject by the General Conference" (of 1844.)

Among the most zealous and prominent of the Northern abolitionists, were the Rev. Orange Scott, George Storrs, Le Roy Sunderland, Jotham Horton, Cyrus Prindle, Luther Lee, and Lyndon King, all being members of annual conferences. Mr. Sunderland was the editor of the paper above alluded to, but as it advocated the immediate and unconditional emancipation of all the slaves, especially those held by members of the Methodist Church, or the expulsion of those slaveholders from the church, and the enactment of rules absolutely forbidding the holding of slaves by members of the same, it was feared, and no doubt justly, that the measures of the abolitionists tended to anarchy and confusion, and to the disruption of the church if not the disunion of the states. Under these circumstances the bishops and leading men in the church thought it to be their solemn duty, as far as they could, to arrest the tide of evil by which the institutions of the church were threatened. Such a course of procedure awakened unkindly feelings towards them, and these feelings of hostility, which at first had reference to their official acts only, soon extended to the men themselves, and then to their office; hence in the course of the excitement, not only was a hatred of slavery openly avowed, but of Episcopacy and various other institutions of the church.

While some, as before stated in the extract made, were waiting with patience the acts of the General Conference of 1844, the leading ones among the abolitionists were devising the organization of a new church, which would harmonize more perfectly with their views in regard to the subjects alluded to. But before the organization of the new church, large numbers had withdrawn in different parts of New York and New England, and it was no doubt confidently expected by the leading secessionists that if a church based on anti-slavery and non-episcopal principles could be formed, not only the greater part of those who had left the Methodist Episcopal Church would unite in it, but that tens, if not hundreds of thousands of those who had not as yet withdrawn, would eventually do so. Accordingly, in 1843, a call was issued for a convention of abolitionists favorable to the organization of a Methodist Church that should be free from slavery and Episcopacy. This convention met in the city of Utica, N. Y. on the 31st day of May, 1843, and after some days' deliberation they succeeded in organizing the Methodist Wesleyan Church in the United States. The members who composed this convention were not all ministers or members of the Methodist Episcopal Church, nor had they all been such. Large numbers were in attendance from the Reformed Methodist, the Methodist Protestant, and Independent Methodist Churches; these all united together, and the result was the formation of six annual conferences, with about three hundred preachers (mostly local) and a reported membership of about six thousand.

Candor requires us to state that however promising the affairs of this church might have been at the time of its organization, it has not succeeded according to the hopes and expectations of its friends and adherents, in gaining a very large membership; indeed so far as we can learn by information, and our own observation, this branch of the Methodist Church, especially in the east and north, is rapidly on the decline. This is to be attributed mainly, perhaps, to the decease or defection of some of the most prominent ministers who headed the secession movement. Orange Scott, of whose piety and sincerity we cannot reasonably doubt, after having fought manfully for the Wesleyan Church, and who, in fact, was the leading spirit among them, has been called to the spirit world. Mr. Sunderland has not only ceased to be a minister, but has become a complete visionary and an abettor and agent of the "Spiritual Knockings!" Mr. Horton has recently returned to the church he left, and so with some other choice spirits, who, having taken a false step, have magnanimity enough to acknowledge and retrace the same. Mr. King and others having tried the new ship awhile and found it not suitable for their accommodation, have long since left it, and sought for better accommodations somewhere else.

This secession, however, and the state of the public mind at the North, was not without its influence on the composition and action of the next General Conference of the Methodist Episcopal Church. The Northern preachers and members had reason to fear that unless something was at least *attempted* on the part of the supreme council of the church to free the latter from the slave power and influence, the church at the

North would be rent into fragments. Such was the state of things when the time for the next session of that body had arrived.

SECTION X.

The General Conference of 1844, assembled in the city of New York. The bishops present were Soule, Hedding, Waugh, Morris, and Andrew. Bishop Roberts—the senior bishop of the church since the death of Bishop M'Kendree—had, since the last session, been called to his reward. He died at his residence in Lawrence County, Indiana, in the 66th year of his age, and the forty-second of his ministry, on the 26th of March, 1843. The continued extension of the work and the decease of Bishop Roberts, made it necessary to elect two additional bishops, and the choice fell on Rev. Leonidas L. Hamline and Rev. Edmund S. Janes.

This conference, in some respects, was the most important, so far as the results of its acts are concerned, of any conference which had ever been held since the one which organized the church in 1784. The reader will bear in mind the state of public feeling in the North in relation to the subject of slavery in the church, and that under this state of feeling the conference had assembled from all parts of the country to legislate on the affairs of the church.

At an early period in the session, it became apparent that there would be a conflict not only between the ultra-pro-slaveryism of the South, and the ultra-abolitionism of the North, but between the former and the conservative portion of the delegates from the northern, middle, and western portions of the church.

After a few days of the session had passed away, an appeal was presented by the Rev. Francis Harding, formerly a member of the Baltimore Annual Conference, who had a short time previously been located without his consent, in consequence of his connection with slavery. Mr. Harding was a young man who had been admitted to the travelling ministry but a few years before, and after being thus admitted, contracted marriage with a slaveholding lady, by which he became the nominal, if not the actual owner of slaves. The Baltimore Conference, although situated in slaveholding territory, had never favored the holding of slaves by travelling preachers, but had occupied a conservative position in relation to the slaveholding principles and practices in the more southern portion of the work, and the ultraism of the North. They accordingly required Mr. Harding, as a condition of retaining his membership among them, to emancipate his slaves according to the laws of the state of Maryland, which he refusing to do, was deprived of his membership in the annual conference. To this action of the conference, he demurred; hence his appeal. When the case came before the General Conference for a re-hearing, it was evident that there existed much excitement on the subject, both among the Northern and Southern preachers. A storm began to gather, the Northern delegates, almost to a man, were for dismissing the appeal: the Southern delegates, just as unanimously and decidedly, were in favor of sustaining the appeal, and reinstating the appellant. After a lengthy and warm debate on the subject, the moment for decision arrived; a deathlike stillness pervaded the assembly, as each delegate's name was called, and he answered yea or nay. After counting the votes, it was found that there was a large majority in favor of dismissing the appeal, and the action of the Baltimore Conference was sustained. This, however, was but the "beginning of the end;" for while this cause was pending, it came to the knowledge of some of the Northern delegates, that Bishop Andrew, then present and presiding alternately with the other bishops over the deliberations of the conference, had recently come into the possession of slaves in a manner similarly to Mr. Harding—by marriage. Upon being interrogated on the subject, the bishop candidly acknowledged all the facts in the case.

Whereupon, the subject was brought formally before the body for adjudication. After an exceedingly stormy and protracted debate, the General Conference passed a resolution, the substance of which was, that it was the sense of the conference, that Bishop Andrew should desist from exercising the functions of the episcopacy, until such time as he had released himself from the embarrassment arising from his connection with slavery. Against this action of the conference, the Southern delegation entered a warm protest, which had been drawn up by Dr. Bascom of Kentucky. It was signed by fifty-three members from the Southern States, and by seven from the Middle States, in behalf of thirteen annual conferences. In this lengthy document they protested against the acts of the majority in the case of Bishop Andrew: 1st. As being extra judicial; as being both without law, and contrary to law, and 2d. As being subversive of the union and stability of the church, because it involved a departure from the compromise law of the church in relation to slavery, and asserting in the plainest terms, that if the compromise law were repealed, or allowed to remain a dead letter, the South could not submit, and the division of the church was absolutely necessary.

To this protest, Doctors Durbin, Peck, and Elliott, presented a lengthy reply, which was read to the conference, and ordered to be spread on the Journal, by a vote of 116 yeas to 16 nays. The reply, in forcible terms, reviews the action taken on Bishop Andrew's case, and denies most emphatically that any law of the church has been violated, or that any injustice has been done to the bishop or to the Southern portion of the church. In the reply, they quote the law on the subject, which reads as follows: "When any travelling preacher becomes an owner of a slave or slaves by *any means*, he shall forfeit his ministerial character in our church, unless he execute, if it be practicable, a legal emancipation of such slaves, conformably to the laws of the state in which he lives." This law, it was alleged, covered the case of Bishop Andrew, and aside from this law, it was claimed as an admitted fact, that he was elected to the episcopacy in preference to more gifted ministers, because of his not being a slaveholder, and that being elected under such circumstances and with the expectation of his remaining free from all connection with that evil, he had no right to embarrass his administration by voluntarily connecting himself with slavery as an owner by marriage, or in any other manner.

The reply failed to convince the minority of the propriety of the proceedings in the above case. Indeed, before the reply had been read, a division of the church had been determined upon by the Southern delegation, and there appeared no disposition on their part to prevent the threatened disruption, unless Bishop Andrew was unconditionally reinstated in his office. The majority could not agree to this, and as division or separation was by both parties now deemed inevitable, it was thought best, that if they must part, it should be done in peace. Accordingly, a plan of separation was agreed upon, the substance of which was, that Conferences and Societies on, or near the line separating the slaveholding from the non-slaveholding states, might elect to which portion of the church they would adhere, and that when such election was formally made, they should be considered as an integral portion of that church to which they adhered, and that the other church should not in any manner interfere with such Conferences or Societies after such election had been determined, neither should either portion invade the territory of the other, by appointing preachers to labor therein.

It was also stipulated and agreed, that the funds of the church, consisting principally of the Book Concerns and Chartered Fund, should be divided between the two bodies, according to the number of preachers in each; Provided the several annual conferences by a constitutional majority of three fourths of all the members should concur in removing the sixth restrictive rule, which declares that the General Conference "shall not appropriate the produce of the Book Concern nor of the Chartered Fund to any purpose, other than for the benefit of the travelling, supernumerary, superannuated, and worn-out preachers; their wives, widows, and children."

Having adopted the above articles of agreement, and requested the bishops to lay the same before the annual conferences, after the completion of their business, and an arduous session of six weeks, the General Conference adjourned to meet again in the city of Pittsburgh, Pennsylvania, on May 1st, 1848.

After the adjournment of the General Conference of 1844, a general anxiety existed in the North, East, and West, in relation to the course which would be pursued by the Southern preachers generally, in regard to the separation. Hopes were entertained by many, that after the delegates had gone home, and had coolly reflected upon the matter, they and their constituents would finally conclude to prevent, if possible, a final separation of the two portions of the church. These hopes, however, were doomed to disappointment. Soon after the return of the Southern delegates, a mode of action was announced by them to produce the disruption which they had so loudly threatened, and confidently predicted. A convention of Southern ministers was called by these delegates to meet in Louisville, Kentucky, on the 1st of May of the next year. At this convention, the proceedings of the Southern delegates in the General Conference were sanctioned, and it was decided that a separation of the church was not only desirable, but unavoidable, and arrangements were made for holding a General Conference of the Southern church in May, 1846. Accordingly, during the course of the year 1845, at the sessions of the several annual conferences which adhered to the Church South, delegates were chosen to represent them in said General Conference. When the time arrived for the session of the latter, and after the opening proceedings by Bishop Andrew, Bishop Soule, the senior bishop of the Methodist Episcopal Church, gave in his adherence to the Church South, and two additional bishops were subsequently elected, namely, Capers and Paine. The separatists made no material alterations in the discipline, and such as were made, were rendered necessary by their local circumstances. Commissioners were appointed by this conference to treat with the Book Agents and others, in relation to the division of the church funds, and Dr. Pierce of Georgia was appointed a delegate to the General Conference of the Methodist Episcopal Church, to be held in 1848. The name of the new organization was declared to be "The Methodist Episcopal Church South;" and after having completed their business, they adjourned to meet in four years, namely, May 1st, 1850.

Thus we see the largest protestant body in the United States rent asunder from east to west, because of the pro-slaveryism of the one portion, and the anti-slaveryism of the other; for although the action of the majority, in the cases of Mr. Harding and Bishop Andrew, were the immediate and apparent cause of separation, yet as every reader will see, the real cause lay back of any such action. It existed in the fixed determination of the South to have slaveholding ministers and bishops at all hazards; and the equally fixed resolution of the North, to keep the episcopacy and the travelling ministry, as far as possible, free from the accursed evil.

After the adjournment of the General Conference of the Church South—as indeed since the General Conference of 1844—a violent controversy was carried on in all the religious papers of the two churches in relation to the action of the respective portions of the church. The entire connection, both north and south, was greatly agitated. This is especially true in regard to the Conferences and Societies on, or near the line of separation. As it was for the interests of the Church South, to gain as large a membership as possible, the most unjustifiable means were resorted to by a portion of her ministry, to draw off as many as possible from the Methodist Episcopal Church. One of the leading separatists, Wm. A. Smith, of

Virginia, held public meetings from place to place along the line, and in the grossest and most offensive manner impugned the motives of the majority. As might be expected, he, and other spirits of congenial nature, succeeded in drawing off some from their allegiance to the Methodist Episcopal Church, while the great mass of the members in the free, and many of those in the border slave states, retained their attachment foı the authority and ministry of the Northern church.

Meanwhile, the bishops of the Methodist Episcopal Church, in accordance with the instruction of the General Conference of 1844, submitted to the several annual conferences, the resolutions of the former body in relation to the proposed alteration or suspension of the sixth restrictive rule before alluded to, so as to allow a division of the funds of the church, according to the plan of separation adopted by the conference of 1844. But although the presiding bishops at these conferences generally advised a concurrence of the latter in the recommendation of the General Conference, it was found when all the votes were counted that the constitutional majority of three fourths had not been obtained in favor of the measure. The whole number of votes given on this subject was 3,185; the number of votes in favor of the alteration was 2,135; against it, 1,070; thus showing a deficiency of 253 votes to constitute the required three fourth majority. While therefore a majority of the ministers were in favor of dividing the funds, yet as the constitutional majority had not been obtained, it became impossible for the agents at the North, legally to divide the same. Various were the causes which operated to prevent the obtaining of the requisite number of votes. The most of the preachers at the North, believed the South to have manifested a disposition to perpetuate the institutions of slavery, and to incorporate the same into the episcopacy and ministry, for the purpose of so perpetuating the evil. They were also aware of the ungentlemanly course pursued by some of the leading Southern ministers in fomenting divisions and strife along the border; that the South had, in fact, already violated the agreement made at the General Conference of 1844 by the above course. But the chief reason which induced so many to give an adverse vote on the subject, was a belief that the General Conference had transcended its authority in consenting to a separation of the South from the North, and much more so, in making provision for the same in the plan mutually agreed upon. Others, again, indulged a hope that if the South were denied a share in the funds of the church, the Southern preachers might be induced to retrace their steps, and consent to remain under the jurisdiction of the General Conference of the Methodist Episcopal Church. It is proper also to remark, that many of the ministers who voted *for* the alteration, did so, not because they thought the South were entitled legally or morally to any portion of the funds of the church, or that they acknowledged the power of the General Conference to rend the church in twain, but they were anxious that the slaveholding conferences and ministers should form a separate connection, so as to free the Northern Church as much as possible from the stain of slavery, and if dividing the funds would induce them to do so, they were more than willing they should have a pro-rata share; they would prefer even to give them the whole rather than remain in connection with them. To use the language of one who thus voted, they "were willing the South should go; and if need be, pay them for going."

SECTION XI.

THUS matters remained at the opening of the General Conference of 1848 in the city of Pittsburgh, Pennsylvania. At this conference were present Bishops Hedding, Waugh, Morris, Hamline, and Janes; Bishops Soule and Andrew having adhered to the Southern Church as before stated. Several distinguished visitors were present; and among the latter was the Rev.

Dr. Dixon, the representative of the British Wesleyan Conference in England, and Drs. Richey and Green, and Rev. John Ryerson of the Canada Conference. Dr. Pierce, the delegate of the Church South, was also present, but the conference refused to recognize him in his official capacity as delegate, but cordially invited him to a seat among them as a minister of the gospel. Bishop Soule was also present a portion of the time, but was not recognized in his Episcopal capacity. On the eleventh day of the session Bishop Soule sent a communication to the conference, requesting that if there were any charges against him for his administration during the two years after the former General Conference, or until his connection with the Church South, these charges might be investigated, he having an opportunity of defending himself. The following day the conference voted that Bishop Soule having withdrawn from the church, the General Conference could exercise no ecclesiastical authority over him. There were also present as commissioners of the Church South, the Rev. Drs. Green, Early, Pierce, and Rev. C. B. Parsons, who preferred a formal claim to a pro-rata division of the funds of the church. This claim, as based upon the action of the previous General Conference, was taken into consideration, and while the conference by a vote of 133 to 9 declared the plan of separation to be null and void, because unconstitutional, at the same time evinced a strong desire to divide the funds with the South, if it could be legally and constitutionally done; but as the requisite majority in the annual conferences had not been obtained, it was evident to themselves that they had not the power so to divide it. They, however, passed resolutions to the following effect: That the Book Agents in New York be authorized to ask the opinion of eminent legal counsel, whether they could legally and constitutionally submit the matter to a Board of Arbitration to be chosen by both parties, and if the opinion of said counsel was, that such arbitration would be legal, the agents were further authorized to submit such claims to such Board, and abide the decision of the same; or if the Southern Commissioners should commence a civil prosecution the agents were authorized to refer the whole matter to arbiters under the direction of the court before which the case might be brought. Thus matters remained at the close of the General Conference of 1848; and since that period actions have been commenced before the United States District Courts in New York and Pennsylvania, for a division of the funds of the Book Concern and Chartered Fund, but as yet neither claim has been decided by the Court.*

We have thus endeavored to give the reader an impartial and connected account of the division of the church, and of the causes which led to the same; and the intelligent and disinterested will be able to judge of the policy of both branches of the church in relation to slavery. They will perceive that while the settled policy of the Northern branch is to discountenance that evil, especially among its members, the policy of the South is to perpetuate both in State and Church what Mr. Wesley, the founder of Methodism, pronounced to be "the sum of all villanies." It is true, there are still a few slaveholders in the Methodist Episcopal Church who reside in slaveholding territory, but the policy of the church in relation to such is, not to justify them in sustaining such a relation irrespective of circumstances, but to induce them, as soon as it can be done with justice to the slave, and safety to themselves, to emancipate them accordingly as the laws will admit.

* Since the above was written, the Southern claim on the Book Concern has been argued before the United States District Court for the Southern District of New York, Judge Nelson presiding. After hearing the argument the court advised a settlement by arbitration, or some other way. The Book Agents having the power, according to their instructions, to make a proposal for an arbitration, did so; but the Southern Commissioners would not consent to the same, unless the Agents would previously admit their right to a division of the funds, and would submit only the question—How much they were entitled to?—to the decision of the Referees. To this of course the Agents could not submit.

Having, for the sake of connection, passed over several important facts worthy of notice in the history of the church during the interim of the General Conferences of 1844–1848, we will now resume our narrative of events, as they transpired from time to time. Late in the year 1843, the Rev. George Gary of the Black River Conference, having been appointed superintendent of the Oregon mission, took his leave of his friends, and sailed for that distant shore for the purpose of "setting things in order," as connected with that part of the work. He arrived in Oregon in the early part of June, 1844, and immediately began a course of operation with the concurrence of the resident missionaries for the purpose of retrenching, as far as practicable, the expenses of that mission. Mr. Lee, the former enterprising and faithful superintendent, had in the meantime returned to the United States, and had received at the New England Conference of 1844 the appointment of Agent for the "Oregon Institute." His health, however, soon declined, and on the 12th of March following he departed this life. Thus died the Missionary Pioneer of the Valley of the Columbia, in the 42d year of his age. Mr. Gary remained in Oregon about three years, and then returned to the United States, having in the meanwhile accomplished the object of his appointment to the entire satisfaction of the Missionary Board. Such was the success attending the labors of the missionaries of the Methodist Episcopal Church in Oregon that at the conference of 1848 an Oregon and Californian Mission Conference was established on the Pacific coast, and the Rev. William Roberts, of the New Jersey Conference, was appointed superintendent of the same. Mr. Roberts, and Rev. James H. Wilbur of the Black River Conference, had two years previously been appointed to that mission, and, with other self-denying men, were laboring to build up Messiah's Kingdom in that part of the world. The missions in Oregon and California have now obtained a prominent position, there being not less than eighteen missionaries employed by the Board in these fields at the present time.

In the year 1847, a mission was established in the empire of China by the appointment of the Rev. Judson D. Collins and Rev. Moses C. White, as missionaries to that foreign field; and since that period the missionaries have been increased in number, so that there are at present five missionaries of the Methodist Episcopal Church in the Celestial Empire.

In 1849 the Board of Managers resolved to establish a mission in Germany, and the Rev. L. S. Jacoby, of the Illinois Conference, was appointed to the work. He was instructed to make the city of Bremen the centre of operations. In nineteen days after leaving New York he arrived in Bremen, and found many who were willing to receive him as the messenger of God. He immediately caused some Methodist tracts to be printed in German for gratuitous distribution. He then rented a large saloon capable of holding five hundred persons in which to celebrate public worship. He published a German hymn-book, and having suggested to the Board the importance of publishing a Methodist periodical in Bremen, he was authorized so to do, the Messrs. Baker & Brother of Baltimore having directed the Treasurer to draw on them for the whole expense of press, &c., $500. Since then, other missionaries have been appointed to Germany, and the success which has already attended the efforts of the Methodist Episcopal Church in this department of her foreign work gives assurance of being able to reap a plentiful harvest in that field; while the German missions in the United States, commenced as before stated, through the labors and instrumentality of Dr. Nast, have more than met the most sanguine expectations of the warmest friends of the enterprise, as may be judged from the fact that in 1850 there were in the United States nine German mission districts; ninety missions or circuits; one hundred and fifteen churches, or meeting-houses; forty-five parsonages; one hundred and seventeen German ministers, or preachers engaged in the regular work; eighty-eight local preachers and exhorters; over seven thousand members, and nearly four thousand Sunday-school scholars, under the care of the Methodist Episcopal Church, besides those under the care of the Methodist Episcopal Church South.

While the efforts of the church were thus being directed to foreign fields, the poor and destitute in sparse settlements of our own land, besides the German emigrants, were by no means forgotten. Many domestic missions within the last eight or ten years have been established within the bounds of the respective conferences, and in many instances have resulted in the permanent organization of large and flourishing churches. Neither has the "poor Indian" in his native wilds, or in the midst of civilization, been forgotten by the church. In different parts of the land are large tribes of Indians residing on reserved portions of land secured to them in perpetuity by the general or State governments. Among these tribes, missions have at different times been established and sustained by the liberality of the whites. Among these tribes of Indians located on such reservations is the St. Regis tribe, whose lands lie in the extreme north-east corner of the State of New York, called the St. Regis Reservation. A village counting a thousand Indian inhabitants stands partly on this reservation, and partly on land granted by the British government to those who reside on the Canada side of the line. For nearly a century a Roman Catholic mission has existed in St. Regis, and a large church has long been erected for their use; but still, although converted nominally from paganism to Christianity, they were sunk in ignorance, superstition, and vice. In the language of their priest in answer to the inquiry of a Methodist minister if the Indians were pious and sober—"They are very pious, but not very sober," was the characteristic reply. And such indeed was the truth; they were very pious in the Romanist sense of the word, attending upon all the ordinances and sacraments of the Roman Church, and living a life of debauchery, drunkenness and crime. In the year 1847–8 Rev. Ebenezer Arnold of the Black River Conference, who was laboring on a contiguous charge, providentially was led among them, and after preaching to them for a few times the requirements and blessings of a pure gospel, succeeded in arresting the attention of some, and in prevailing upon them to come to Jesus Christ by repentance and faith. The result was, that a small but flourishing Society was formed among them, and the succeeding conference witnessed the appointment of a regular missionary among them in the person of the Rev. J. P. Jennings. Through the indefatigable exertions of this young minister and others, especially through the kind concern of Bishop Janes who has had the charge of the Indian missions for the time being, a large and beautiful chapel was soon erected at an expense of over $1,500, being furnished with a fine-toned bell, and having a neat and commodious parsonage attached, with land for garden, pasture, &c., the whole costing not less than $2,000 or $2,500. Although the success of the missionary in the upbuilding of the spiritual part of the mission must necessarily be small at first, and gained only by slow degrees, yet sufficient encouragement has been given by the sound conversion of numbers of these Indians to warrant a continued effort for the special benefit of this degraded people.

Missions have also, since the division of the church, been established in different cities and towns for the benefit of the French, Swedish, Danish, and Norwegian population, and the signs of the times clearly indicate that the Methodist Episcopal Church, always missionary in her character, and aggressive in her movements, is destined to become more emphatically a MISSIONARY CHURCH.

Great advancement has also been made in the cause of Sunday-school instruction, within the few past years. The General Conference, more than ever convinced of the importance of Sunday-schools, has wisely made provision for the increased wants of the young in this respect. The Sunday School Union of the Methodist Episcopal Church was organized on the 2d day of April, 1827, but we are not to infer that the Methodists had no Sunday-schools in their church until the latter date. At the time of the organization of the church in 1784, the preachers were instructed especially to give their attention to the children and youth, and in 1790 the preachers were further required to establish Sunday-schools in, or near the place of worship, but it was in the year 1827 that the cause received a new impetus by the organization of the "Union," and in 1840 still greater efficiency was given to the exertions of the church by the reorganization of the Sunday School Union of the Methodist Episcopal Church, and since the appointment of the present able and talented corresponding secretary, Rev. D. P. Kidder, the prosperity and increase of schools, scholars, and Sunday-school books, is probably without a parallel in the history of any branch of the Church of Christ, so that at present, there is no doubt, that not less than five hundred thousand children and youth are connected with the Sunday School Union of the Methodist Episcopal Church.

We have thus, kind reader, given you a brief historical account of the rise of Methodism in Europe, and of its introduction into America, and its progress from that time until the present. Further information in regard to its present state will be obtained in the account to be given of the institutions and statistics of the Methodist Episcopal Church in the latter part of the book. We now proceed to give an account of the introduction of Methodism into Canada; and of its rise and progress in that province.

SECTION XII.

Methodism appears to have been introduced into the province of Canada in the year 1780, during the Revolutionary war between Great Britain and her North American colonies. A number of the soldiers who were sent over to Quebec at that time, were members of Mr. Wesley's Societies in England. Among these pious soldiers was a commissariat officer belonging to the forty-fourth regiment of foot, who had been a helper or local preacher under Mr. Wesley, and who immediately upon his arrival in Quebec began to preach, as occasion offered, to the officers and soldiers of the garrison. Mr. Tuffey, for such was this gentleman's name, remained in Quebec for about three years, and at the close of the war was recalled to England with a portion of the troops. The most of his Methodist associates in Quebec, having with other soldiers the privilege of returning to England, or of being disbanded in America, chose the latter, and soon scattered themselves over different parts of the province. But as yet no *Society* of Methodists had been formed in Canada, Mr. Tuffey thinking it best under all the existing circumstances not to attempt the formation of any Society.

After the declaration of peace between the two countries, the tide of emigration began to flow from the eastern shore of the St. Lawrence and the great lakes towards the British possessions, and in the winter of 1788–9, a young man by the name of Lyon, an exhorter in the Methodist Episcopal Church in the United States, engaged a school in the township of Adolphustown, Upper Canada. He soon began to hold meetings for prayer, and exhortation, and in a short time a revival of religion took place, in which some were converted, others were reclaimed, and lukewarm professors were aroused; but no Societies were formed by Mr. Lyon.

Shortly after this, an Irishman by the name of M'Carty, who had for some years lived in the United States, and who was a Whitfieldian Methodist, repaired to Canada and settled in the township of Earnestown. He soon began to preach written sermons according to the practice of the Church of England, but with such deep feeling and earnestness, that many were converted through his instrumentality. In this great work he was cheered and aided by numerous Methodists who had either belonged to Mr. Wesley's Societies in England, or to the Methodist Episcopal Church in the United States. The success of Mr. M'Carty and the Methodists who co-operated with him, aroused as usual the ire of some of the established clergy. A minister of the Church of England meeting one of these revivalists one day, said to him abruptly, "You are going to hell!" "How do you know that?" "Ah! I am sure of it; for you run out against dancing, card-playing, horse-racing, &c., and you'll go to hell for it." Such being the character of the *priests*, it is not to be supposed that the morals of the *people* were of any higher order, so that it was not without opposition that Methodism gained a foothold in Canada.

The most active opposers of the work of God in the neighborhood where Mr. M'Carty preached, were the sheriff of the county, a captain of militia, and an engineer, who employed their power and authority in abusing and maltreating the Methodists. On a certain Sunday while Mr. M'Carty was preaching in a private house, four men armed with muskets came to arrest him. On the solemn promise of the gentleman of the house that the prisoner would make his appearance the next day before the sheriff in Kingston, the men left him and returned. The next day he repaired to Kingston, and although the sheriff at first refused to take charge of him, he was the same day thrown into prison, but released for a certain time on bail. When the time for which he had been bailed expired, he again repaired to Kingston to receive his destiny, where by the orders of the chief engineer, he was put on board of a boat manned by four French Canadians, who were directed to leave him on an uninhabited island in the St. Lawrence. The boat's crew attempted to comply with their directions, but through the resistance of Mr. M'Carty, they were obliged to land him on the main shore, from whence he returned to his family. While thus persecuted by his enemies in Kingston, to the honor of the late Sir John Johnson be it recorded, that the latter furnished Mr. M'Carty with funds to carry on a prosecution against these vile wretches, and a kind-hearted attorney in

Montreal offered to lend him all necessary assistance in that respect. But before legal redress could be obtained, Mr. M'Carty was suddenly and strangely missing, and has never been heard of from that time to the present. He might have been murdered, or what we should prefer believing, he may have been accidentally drowned beneath the green waters of the St. Lawrence. His chief persecutors in Kingston soon ended their career also, the engineer and sheriff both having died in a few weeks afterward, while the militia captain subsequently wrote a confession of his crime, in which he stated that he had wrongfully persecuted an innocent man, and presented it to the judge of the court. He afterward became insane, and continued so until his death.

Two years passed away after the arrival of Mr. Lyon before any steps were taken to secure the services of a Methodist preacher from the States. At length in 1790 a message was sent to the conference of the Methodist Episcopal Church assembled in New York, for a missionary to be appointed for Canada, and the Rev. William Losee was accordingly despatched to the aid of those few sheep. He repaired to the scene of the revival before alluded to, and succeeded almost immediately in forming Societies in different townships with a membership of about two hundred persons, who attached themselves to the Methodist Episcopal Church. He also formed a circuit extending from Kingston to the head of the Bay of Quinte, embracing the townships of Earnestown, Fredericksburgh, and Adolphustown. The circuit was called Cataraqui Circuit. In 1792 the Rev. Darius Dunham was appointed to this circuit, and Mr. Losee proceeding down the St. Lawrence formed another circuit which was called the Oswegotchie, which at the next conference reported a membership of ninety persons. In 1794 the Rev. James Coleman and Rev. Elijah Woolsey were appointed by the New York Conference to Canada. The next year 1795, Rev. Sylvanus Keeler was appointed to the same field, and in 1796 Revs. Coate and H. C.

Wooster were also appointed preachers to the Canadian brethren, and thus the cause of Methodism began gradually to extend itself over the Upper Province, so that in the year 1800 there were four large circuits with a membership of eleven hundred and fifty embraced in a presiding elder's district, and attached to the New York Conference.

In the year 1802, Montreal was visited by the Rev. Joseph Sawyer. He found a few persons in that place, who had belonged to the Methodist Society in the city of New York before the revolutionary war. By these he was cordially received and assisted in procuring a school-room for preaching. A Mr. and Mrs. McGinnis were among the first who attached themselves to the Society in Montreal, and who remained faithful in the cause of Christ and of Methodism during all its vicissitudes in that place, until they joined the church triumphant. In 1803, Revs. Samuel Merwin, Elijah Chichester, and Laban Clark, were sent as missionaries to Lower Canada; and Montreal, St. Johns, and Sorel, are found included ameng the stations of the New York Conference. Mr. Merwin went to Quebec, where he stayed only about six weeks without being successful in organizing a Society, and he returned to Montreal, where he remained during the rest of the year, and was succeeded the next year, 1804, by the late Dr. Martin Ruter.

This same year also, the Rev. Nathan (now Doctor) Bangs was sent as a missionary to a new settlement on the river Thames in Upper Canada, and that the reader may know something about the hardships endured by these pioneers in the early days of Canadian Methodism, we will take the liberty of presenting the account Dr. Bangs gives of his introduction to his new field of labor, as found in his History of the Methodist Episcopal Church. Having requested the appointment of missionary to that place, and having obtained the same from Bishop Asbury, he "left the city of New York in the latter part of the month of June, went into Upper Canada by way of Kingston, thence up the country along the north-western shore of Lake Ontario to the Long Point Circuit, and thence on through Oxford to the town of Delaware on the river Thames. Here he lodged for the night in the last log hut in the settlement, and the next morning as day began to dawn, he arose and took his departure, and after travelling through a wilderness of forty-five miles, guided only by marked trees, he arrived at a solitary log hut about sunset, weary, hungry, and thirsty, where he was entertained with the best the house could afford, which was some Indian-pudding and milk for supper, and a bundle of straw for his bed. The next day about twelve o'clock he arrived at an Indian village, on the north bank of the Thames, the inhabitants of which were under the instructions of two Moravian missionaries. While there, the Indians were called together for worship, which was performed in a very simple manner by reading a short discourse, and singing a few verses of a hymn. The missionaries and the Indians treated him with great respect and affection, and seemed to rejoice in the prospect of having the gospel preached to the white settlements on the banks of the river below.

"About three o'clock P.M., he arrived at the first house in the settlement, where the following conversation took place between the missionary and a man whom he saw in the yard before the house. After the introductory salutation, the missionary inquired, 'Do you want the gospel preached here?' After some deliberation it was answered, 'Yes, that we do. Do you preach the gospel?' 'That is my occupation.' 'Alight from your horse, then, and come in, will you?' 'I have come a great distance to preach the gospel to the people here, and it is now Saturday afternoon, to-morrow is the Sabbath, and I must have a house to preach in before I get off from my horse.' After a few moments of consideration he replied, 'I have a house for you to preach in, provender for your horse, and food and lodging for yourself; and you shall be welcome to them all if you will dismount and come in.'

Thanking him for his kind offer, the missionary dismounted and entered the hospitable mansion in the name of the Lord, saying, *Peace be to this house.* A young man mounted his horse and rode ten miles down the river, inviting the people to attend meeting at that house at ten o'clock A.M. of the next morning.

"At the time appointed the house was filled. When the missionary rose up, he told the people that whenever a stranger makes his appearance in a place the people are generally anxious to know who he is, whence he came, where he is going, and what his errand is among them. 'In these things,' said he, 'I will satisfy you in a few words.' He then gave them a short account of his birth and education, of his conversion and call to the ministry, and the motives which induced him to come among them, and concluded in the following manner: 'I am a Methodist preacher, and my manner of worship is to stand up and sing, and kneel in prayer; then I stand up and take a text, and preach while the people sit on their seats. As many of you as see fit to join me in this method you can do so; but if not you can choose your own method.' When he gave out his hymn they all arose, every man, woman, and child. When he kneeled in prayer they all, without exception, kneeled down. They then took their seats and he stood up and gave out his text, 'Repent ye therefore and be converted, &c.,' and he preached, as he thinks, with the Holy Ghost sent down from heaven. Having concluded his discourse, he explained to his audience his manner of preaching by itinerating through the country, his doctrine, and how supported, &c. He then said, 'All you who wish to hear any more such preaching rise up,' when every man, woman, and child stood up. He then told them that they might expect preaching there again in two weeks."

He then sent on appointments through the settlements along down the river, and was everywhere received with great cordiality. He proceeded down the shore to Lake St. Clair, crossed over to Detroit and down the shore to Lake Erie, and preached to people who had never heard a gospel sermon, and to Methodists who had not heard a sermon preached in seven years. Thus we see Methodism introduced into that part of Canada, where it has since taken deep root and prevailed extensively.

In the year 1806, this self-denying missionary volunteered his services for Quebec. After spending a few weeks in Montreal to supply them until their preacher, the Rev. Samuel Coate, arrived, he sailed down the river St. Lawrence and reached Quebec on Saturday morning. Having a few letters of introduction he delivered them, and after great exertions, succeeded in renting a room and in getting it provided with temporary seats during the same day, and on the morrow he preached to a "tolerable congregation." The inhabitants of the city were mostly French Catholics, English Episcopalians, or Scotch Presbyterians, and all manifested a deadly hostility to Methodism. A few pious people however—and among them a Scotch missionary by the name of Dick—received him cordially and affectionately. After laboring amidst many discouragements for a length of time, with only about a dozen of stated hearers, he succeeded in forming a small Society in the capital of British North America, since which time the Methodists have not only had an organized Society in existence, but have become respectable both as it regards numbers and influence, as the author of this work, in subsequent years, has had an opportunity of knowing by a personal residence in the place.

In the year 1812, the last war between Great Britain and the United States commenced, and in consequence thereof the cause of Methodism in these provinces suffered greatly. At this time the work in the Canadas was divided into two districts, namely, the Upper and Lower Canada districts, the former of which was attached to the Genesee Conference recently formed, and the latter to the New York Conference. From each of these conferences the annual supplies of preachers were sent to the respective portions of the work. At the session of the General Conference in 1812, the preachers were appointed, as usual, to the Upper Canada district. Before the formal declaration of war, some of the preachers reached their appointments in safety, others, however, after the announcement was made, abandoned the design of going to Canada, and some of those who had already reached their circuits returned to the United States. The Rev. Henry Ryan, presiding elder of the Upper Canada district, with a few other brethren, remained at his post, and was, during the continuance of the war, the sole director and superintendent of this part of the work. He attended regularly all his quarterly meetings, and called the preachers together each year and stationed them as he judged best from time to time until 1815, when peace was declared to the joy of every pious heart. The authority and power invested in Mr. Ryan by the necessities of the case, no doubt laid the foundation of the many troubles and dissensions which existed for many years subsequently, in which Mr. Ryan was a chief actor, and which finally led to his abandonment of the Methodist Episcopal Church in 1827, and the organization of an independent body of Methodists in Canada known by the name of "Ryanites."

After the close of the war of 1812–15, intercourse between the people on both sides of the line was resumed. Preachers from the United States were again appointed to the Canadas, and were permitted to mingle freely with the inhabitants and preach wherever they could collect a congregation, and as the work had suffered materially during the continuance of the war, these preachers and the members saw the necessity of laboring zealously to recover what had been lost, and their labors were crowned with abundant success throughout different parts of the provinces.

Previous to the commencement of hostilities, Bishop Asbury in 1811, made a short visit to Canada. He, after attending the session of the New England Conference in Barnard, Vt., crossed the Green Mountains and Lake Champlain, and from Plattsburgh made his way through the wilderness known as the "Chateaugay Woods," and passing through "French Mills" (Fort Covington) reached the Indian village of St. Regis. He, from this place, crossed the St. Lawrence to Cornwall, and passed along up the banks of the latter river, stopping and preaching in different places as he went on his journey, until at length he arrived in Kingston, where he tarried several days and preached in the new chapel recently erected in that place, with great acceptability to the people. From Kingston he crossed to Sackett's Harbor, having made a flying visit to a colony then and since under the protection of the flag of his native country. It was fortunate that this visit was made at this time, as hostilities soon after commenced, and before the cessation of the same the venerable bishop was called to his rest in heaven.

While the war was raging, and the Societies in Canada were, some of them, left without ministers, the Society in Quebec sent a request to the Mission Committee in London to be supplied with English preachers; accordingly, in 1814, a missionary from England was sent to them, and Quebec, in future, was left off from the American Minutes. For the same or a similar reason that an *English* preacher was sent to Quebec, it was thought best by the Wesleyan Mission Committee to send English preachers to other points in the provinces; accordingly, Montreal, Kingston, and other prominent places were soon occupied in part by English missionaries, while at the same time American preachers were duly stationed among them. This state of things induced jealousy and bickerings, not only between the members in the Societies in these places who favored the ministrations of the one or the other, but between the preachers also, who, unfortunately for themselves, were required to occupy common ground. Complaints and remonstrances to the Wesleyan Committee on the one hand, and to the American Conferences on the other, were made for a redress of grievances. But as in the large Societies, especially the one in Montreal, there were two distinct classes of Methodists (the English Wesleyan and the American Episcopal), it was not an easy matter to effect an adjustment of existing difficulties under these circumstances, as one party preferred their own countrymen to preach the gospel to them, and the other as tenaciously insisted for the same reason, on having their old pastors remain among them. At the General Conference of the Methodist Episcopal Church in 1816, an affectionate letter written by the Wesleyan Committee was received at the hands of the Rev. Messrs. Black and Bennett, who were appointed delegates to effect an adjustment of difficulties. In this letter a request was made that the Methodist Episcopal Church should withdraw her preachers from those places occupied in whole or in part by the English missionaries. The General Conference, however, could not see the way clear to relinquish ground which had been so long occupied by them, and wrote an answer to the committee, in which they respectfully state that they could not consistently give up any part of the Societies or chapels in the Canadas to the superintendence of the British connection. The result of this refusal was that those Societies circumstanced as above described were supplied with both British and American preachers for a number of years. This was particularly the case with Montreal. At the succeeding General Conference of 1820, numerous memorials and petitions were presented from several circuits in Upper Canada, protesting against the occupancy of the ground by the British missionaries, and praying for the supply of preachers from the United States. The conference passed a resolution to the effect that the bishops still continue to exercise their Episcopal charge over the Societies in the Canadas, all except Quebec.

At this conference also, was received another address from the General Secretaries of the Missionary Society in London, in which they respectfully express their regret that any misunderstanding had taken place between the two bodies in relation to the above matter, and also state that it never was the design of the committee to have their missionaries interfere with those preachers sent by the American Conferences. The committee, in connection with the above, sent a copy of the instructions given to each of their missionaries in relation to their acts when brought in contact with the American preachers. This document was sufficiently explicit to convince the General Conference that, however any of the missionaries or preachers had erred in judgment, the designs of the committee and of the British Conference were of the most friendly and pacific character, and in order that all cause for future misunderstanding might be removed, the Rev. John Emory was appointed by the General Conference as a delegate to attend the ensuing session of the English Conference, with full powers to negotiate a settlement of all existing difficulties. In accordance with his instructions, Mr. Emory sailed immediately for England, and attended the session of the latter body, held in Liverpool in August, 1820. He was received with great respect and cordiality by his English brethren, and after due consultation, and on the recommendation of Mr. Emory, it was resolved that all the Societies and chapels in Upper Canada should be given up to the exclusive charge of the American preachers, and that all the Societies and chapels in Lower Canada should be resigned to the care of the British missionaries. For the purpose of carrying out the provisions of this plan, three ministers or preachers from each conference were appointed to meet when and where convenient, and make the necessary transfers, &c. The settlement of these difficulties in the above manner gave very general satisfaction to both preachers and people in the Canadas, and has been productive of great, and we trust, permanent good, while it affords an evidence of the Christian desire of both connections to maintain peace and unity between the two great bodies of Methodists.

The number of travelling and local preachers in the Upper

Province having become considerable, a strong desire began to be expressed on the part of many, that a separate Canada Conference should be organized, with authority to elect a bishop of their own, who should reside among them, and superintend their affairs. A petition to this effect was presented to the General Conference of 1824, and the conference so far granted the prayers of the petitioners, as to erect a separate conference for Canada, but retaining the same under the supervision of the bishops of the Methodist Episcopal Church. This disposition of the case was not, however, satisfactory to all, and especially to Mr. Ryan, before alluded to, who speedily began the work of fomenting divisions and discord among the preachers, and especially among the local preachers in the Canadian department of the work. Through his agency, a convention of local preachers was called, a conference organized, and a plan of future operations adopted. On the assembling of the conference, however, in Hallowell, U. C., peace was measurably restored for the time being, through the instrumentality of Bishops George and Hedding, who pledged themselves to sanction measures in the future for the organization of an Independent Canada Conference.

Accordingly, in 1828, the matter having again come before the General Conference at its Quadrennial Session in Pittsburgh, resolutions were adopted dissolving the compact existing between the Canada Annual Conference, and the Methodist Episcopal Church in the United States, and authorizing the bishops to ordain a superintendent or bishop for the Canada Conference, whenever elected by the latter. At the next session of the Canada Conference, held the same year in Earnestown, U. C., the proceedings of the General Conference in respect to the separation having been read and explained, it was resolved that the Canada Conference of the Methodist Episcopal Church "do now organize itself into an independent Methodist Episcopal Church in Canada." The separation was thus rendered complete; so much so, that as soon as the resolution passed, the presiding bishop rose, and declared that he no longer had any jurisdiction over them, and that they must elect a president before they could proceed to farther business; accordingly, the Rev. William Case was elected General Superintendent *pro tem.*

The Canada Conference, although claiming to be a Methodist Episcopal Church, did not succeed in electing a permanent superintendent or bishop in the interim of the sessions of the General Conference of 1828–1832, so that at the latter period resolutions were passed, allowing the bishops of the Methodist Episcopal Church in the United States to ordain any such superintendent within the ensuing four years, should one be elected, but for reasons which will hereafter be apparent, no such officer was ever elected.

The province of Canada being subject to the British crown, a jealousy had long existed on the part of its statesmen in relation to the institutions of the United States. This jealousy ripened into hatred during the war of 1812–15, and although at the close of the same actual hostilities ceased, feelings of animosity still remained. This rendered the situation of the American preachers an unpleasant one, and led, as we have just stated, to the final separation of the Canada Conference from the parent body. A desire to be identified with whatever is British in its nature and origin, led the members of the Canada Conference to seek a union with their brethren in the English Conference. Such a union was formed in 1833, the Canada Conference changing its title of Methodist Episcopal Church, to that of the Wesleyan Methodist Church in Canada. In changing their title, they also changed their church polity in several respects, and in forming the union with the British Conference, they consented to receive their president annually from the latter body.

Although this union gave satisfaction to the majority of the travelling preachers and members of the Methodist Church in Canada, it produced much uneasiness and dissatisfaction in the breasts of many who were ardently attached to the usages and ecclesiastical government of the Methodist Episcopal Church. While proposals for a union were being made, several conventions were held, in which it was resolved, on the part of those dissatisfied with the contemplated arrangements, not to consent to the union, if it should be effected. The most prominent opposer of the union was the Rev. Joseph Gatchel, a superannuated member of the Canada Conference, who, with numerous local preachers and members, resolved to adhere as far as possible to the discipline and polity of the Methodist Episcopal Church. Accordingly, in June, 1834, or about eight months after the union, Mr. Gatchel, who refused to consent to it, and retained his name of Methodist *Episcopal* minister called an annual conference, to be held in Young Street. In answer to the call, several located and local preachers met together, but no member of the Wesleyan Conference obeyed the summons to attend. Mr. Gatchel, claiming that the main body had seceded from the Methodist Episcopal Church, and that he only constituted the Conference of the Methodist Episcopal Church in Canada, proceeded in due form to re-admit several located preachers, and receive other preachers on trial. The time and place of the next annual conference were fixed upon, and a special General Conference was appointed to meet in Belville, Feb. 12, 1835, for the purpose of electing a General Superintendent, *pro tempore.* At the General Conference thus appointed, Rev. John Reynolds was elected to this office, and at a subsequent General Conference, held in June of the same year, he was elected a bishop, and ordained by the elders present. Since the above period, the Methodist Episcopal Church in Canada has gained many adherents and members, so that at the present time it may be said to be in a flourishing state, having a large number of chapels and Societies embraced in several presiding elders' districts, and two annual conferences.

In the meanwhile, the Wesleyan Methodist Conference in Canada, while repudiating the action of the "Episcopals," proceeded, according to the plan of union, in holding her annual conferences, and administering her discipline, for several years, until at length dissatisfaction arose on the part of the British Conference, in relation to some of the acts of the Canadian brethren, and the action of the Canada Conference in relation thereto, which led to a disruption between the two bodies. In consequence of this disruption the British Conference included the territory in the upper province within her field of missionary operations, and appointed preachers to the most important places in Canada. This state of things could not long continue without producing the most unpleasant and sometimes violent altercations between the adherents of the one or the other conference, so that with the Canadian Wesleyans, the British Wesleyans, the Methodist Episcopalians, and the remains of the "Ryanite" secession, all in operation at one and the same time, all presenting conflicting claims, all having friends and supporters, and each branch having its bitter foes, a long-continued scene of turmoil, contention, and strife, characterized the proceedings of our Methodist brethren in Canada, which state of things they no doubt all deplored, but had no remedy to heal the wounds thus made. After enduring this state of things for some time, overtures were made by the Canada Wesleyan Conference to the British Wesleyan Conference, for a cessation of ecclesiastical hostilities, and the re-union of the two bodies, and in 1847 an amicable arrangement was effected in London, through the instrumentality of Messrs. Ryerson and Green, on the part of the Canadian, and a Committee of the British Conference. This arrangement re-united the two branches, and since the period referred to, the Canadian Conference has been presided over by a president annually appointed by the English body. There are about two hundred ministers at present employed in Canada West by the Canada Conference and the Missionary Committee of London, besides twenty in the Eastern Canada district. The Episcopal Methodists have also about an hundred ministers and preachers employed in different sections of the province.

BOOK II.

DOCTRINES OF METHODISM.

ARTICLES OF RELIGION.

INTRODUCTION

The doctrines of the Methodist Episcopal Church are principally embraced in the Twenty-five Articles of Religion, found in the Book of Discipline. These Articles are nearly the same with those of the Church of England, and the Protestant Episcopal Church in the United States. The principal difference between the Articles of the two latter Churches, and those of the Methodist Episcopal Church, consists partly in the number; that of the Church of England being thirty-nine, and of the latter, as above stated, twenty-five; and also in the omission of a few phrases attached to some of the English Articles, with the addition of one in relation to the Rulers of the United States of America.

The Articles of Religion of the Church of England were originally drawn up in the reign of Edward the VI. in the year 1552. They at first consisted of forty-two, but in the reign of Queen Elizabeth, were reduced to the present number of thirty-nine.

When the Rev. John Wesley set apart Dr. Coke to the office of Superintendent of the Societies in America, and instructed him to organize said Societies into an independent Church, he prepared a prayer-book, or Sunday Service, for the use of the infant church, in which prayer-book the Articles of Religion were contained as now found, excepting the one relating to rulers, which was framed at the organization of the church in 1784, and shortly after was printed in the form of Discipline; since which time no change of any importance has been made in any of the articles referred to.

We have stated, in substance, that these articles embrace the *most* of the doctrines of the Methodist Episcopal Church; we do not say that *all* the doctrines of Methodism are clearly set forth in the same; or if all are alluded to, it is only by implication that certain tenets may be inferred; as, for instance—while the doctrine of entire sanctification may be inferred from some of the articles, it is in none of them clearly stated, or plainly taught. Hence, the Articles, while they embody the great fundamental doctrines of the Church, are not, in themselves, a complete body of divinity. Still, what is not clearly stated or taught in the same, is stated and taught in the other standard writings of the Church, such as Wesley's Sermons, and Watson's Institutes.

Objections have been frequently raised against the adoption of articles of faith, as though what is acknowledged to be merely human, must necessarily be unscriptural; and the cry of "man made creeds," has resounded from shore to shore, and from continent to continent. But why all this opposition to a mere statement of the doctrines of the Church, as embraced in articles of faith? Is a merely human opinion in relation to the doctrines of the Bible, any the less human because it is not embodied in an Article of religion? Is an *unwritten* system of belief any the more scriptural because it is taught by the tongue, instead of being taught by the pen? And are the multifarious and contradictory statements of the "no creed" men, in relation to their own doctrines, to be embraced in preference to those which are candidly written, and published for the information of all who choose to read and judge for themselves? When a body of Christians are willing to give a candid, written statement of their religious opinions to the world, so that these opinions may be compared with the letter of Scripture, and be judged of accordingly, if not an evidence of the *correctness* of their faith, is at least a proof of their *sincerity* in maintaining these opinions; while on the other hand, if a body of professed Christians are unwilling to submit their opinions to the public scrutiny, and as an excuse for so refusing, pretend to hold in great abhorrence those who do, the reader may rest assured that there is something wrong about the faith of such professed Christians, which renders them unwilling to bring their opinions to the test of sound criticism. While, therefore, some professed Christians choose to dwell in darkness, and keep others in darkness, the design of the Methodist Episcopal Church is to let her light shine, "that others, seeing her" faith and "good works, may be led to glorify their Father in heaven." Hence the design of embodying in a condensed form the more important doctrines of the Bible, is not for the purpose of *making* a creed, but of *stating* a creed already made, by the great Head of the Church; not for the purpose of leading men astray by giving them an opportunity of knowing and judging of our opinions, but to prevent their being led astray by those who dare not honestly state in writing what are their true sentiments. Besides, a creed may exist as really in an *unwritten* as in a written form. The Constitution of England is unwritten, but it is none the less a Constitution; the Constitution of the United States is a written instrument, and if it is preferable to the former, it is because it is more definite, more easily understood, its positions more clearly defined, and the rights of the people more fully secured. In like manner, a creed may exist without being written, but wants that definiteness, that clearness, that correctness, belonging to the creed which is plainly written, and is confided to the safe keeping of each member of the Church, as a guarantee against false doctrine, and heterodox opinions. Hence, the only valid objection which can be raised against the existence of written articles of religion in the Methodist Episcopal Church, is not that there are such articles in existence, but that they do not express all that the Church believes; not that there are too many, but too few. While, therefore, we claim that the Articles alluded to embrace all that is fundamental to Christianity, we freely admit that there are points of doctrine believed by the Methodist Church, which are not as fully stated in these Articles, as they are in our standard theological works. Our object, therefore, will be, to state the doctrines taught in the Twenty-five Articles, and then speak of the other prominent doctrines which are not embraced in the same, but are believed in, and taught by the Church.

ARTICLE I.

OF FAITH IN THE HOLY TRINITY.

"There is but only one living and true God, everlasting, without body or parts, of infinite power, wisdom and goodness: the maker and preserver of all things visible and invisible. And in unity of this Godhead there are three persons, of one substance, power, and eternity: —the Father, the Son, and the Holy Ghost."

The doctrine embraced in this Article is fundamental, and lies at the foundation of the Christian religion, and teaches the following cardinal truths: 1st. *The existence of God.* 2d. *The Unity of God.* 3d. *The eternity of God.* 4th. *The incorporiety of God.* 5th. *The infinite power of God.* 6th. *The infinite wisdom of God.* 7th. *The infinite goodness of God.* 8th. *The creative and preservative acts of God:* and lastly, *The Trinity in the Unity of the Godhead.* It will not be necessary to enlarge on each of these points, we will allude to but two,—the Incorporeity of God, and the Trinity in Unity.

1. The declaration that God exists "without body or parts" has been objected to by some modern fanatics, who seize on

certain figurative passages of Scripture, wherein God is spoken of as being possessed of hands, eyes, ears, &c., and argue from the same that God possesses both body and parts. This inconsistent and blasphemous doctrine was also taught by an ancient sect of heretics called Antithropomorphites, while it remained for the Mormonites of these "latter days," to assert in the most positive terms, that God has both "body, parts, and passions." This idea, however, is opposed to the infinity of God, who, if possessed of body and parts, must have them in possession as finite parts, or as infinite parts of the great whole. If these parts are finite, the aggregate cannot make an infinite being any more than two and two can form an infinite number; hence God must necessarily be a finite being, which is contrary to reason and Scripture; but if each of these parts is infinite in itself, then every part must be equal to the whole, for the whole cannot be more than infinite; hence, we arrive at the contradictory and absurd conclusion of a plurality of infinites, or in other words, of a plurality of supreme gods! existing in the one living and true God! Besides, it is positively declared that "God is a spirit," which declaration stands diametrically opposed to the doctrine under consideration, for if the meaning of the Saviour in that declaration was merely that God is partly spirit and partly matter, he would have clearly stated the fact by saying "there is a spirit in God," and not as above quoted, declare that "*God is a spirit.*"

2. The doctrine of the Trinity in Unity has also been objected to by ancient as well as modern heretics, who, because they cannot bring their unassisted reason to comprehend the mode or manner of the divine existence, rashly reject the scriptural evidence of such existence as based upon the fact of there being "three persons in one God,—Father, Son, and Holy Ghost." "We cannot," say the objectors, "comprehend how there can exist three persons in the Godhead, each of these persons being distinct and yet forming but one being." Now a mere want of comprehension cannot disprove the existence of any

fact, however incomprehensible that fact may be to us. Let us illustrate; the laws of nature and their mode of operation are in many respects totally incomprehensible; but the *fact* of their existence we dare not deny, or even doubt. If we introduce a single candle into a dark room there is a light, perfect and complete in itself. If we add to the number of burning tapers, there will be a greater intensity of light produced by these several tapers, the light from each being perfect and complete in itself, and yet in the aggregate forming but *one* light. Now an objector might inquire with an air of triumph, "How can there be three distinct and separate lights and yet be but one?" Our answer would be, "The *fact is so;* although we may not be able to explain the manner to your comprehension;" and so in regard to the triune existence of God, the *fact* of such existence is clearly established by Scripture, but the *manner* of such existence may not be explained.

We may illustrate farther by the laws governing the transmission of sound. A public speaker addresses an assemblage of five hundred persons. On the utterance of each syllable by the speaker a certain definite sound is produced, clear and distinct in itself. This sound reaches the ear of each of the auditory as a whole and perfect sound; so perfect and complete, that were there but one person in the room to listen to it, it could not be more complete than it now is, when heard distinctly by five hundred different persons. Now, although there are seemingly *whole* and *perfect* sounds for each of these, yet there is but *one* sound produced by the speaker; and can we comprehend clearly how this one sound may divide and subdivide itself apparently into five hundred or even five thousand distinct parts, and yet remain but a single sound? Again we say, the fact is so; but the precise mode of its being so, may be beyond the comprehension of many, if not of all. Other illustrations of a forcible character might be presented, but as the *fact* is purely a scriptural one, we must seek light and direction on this important subject from the word of God.

3. The existence of a plurality of persons in the Godhead may be clearly inferred from the plural form in which the word "God" is used in the Bible, and that too, in the very beginning of the Sacred History. "In the beginning *Gods* created the heavens and the earth." As far as we know, all Hebrew scholars admit the fact, that in the original, the term which is translated God in the singular number in our version, should be rendered *Gods* in the plural, and so in many other passages where the word occurs. The idea then is, that, according to the Hebrew idiom, a plurality of persons existing as one being, is clearly indicated by the language employed. "Let *us* make man in *our* image, after *our* likeness," clearly indicates the same thing. Nor will it be sufficient to say that God was herein speaking to the angels, and inviting them to assist in the work of creation, for, first, there is no evidence anywhere to be found that angels or other spirits had anything to do with the work of creation, as agents or otherwise. Second, the image in which man was made, was not the image of angels, for we learn that Christ became *man* like unto his brethren; but still, as the apostle plainly declares, "he took not upon him the nature of *angels*, but the seed of Abraham;" hence the nature of men and of angels is totally different and distinct, and consequently the image of God, and of man who was made in the image of God, is different from the image of angels; and as God speaks of an image in the singular form, it is evident that it is not the image of an angel which is spoken of, or to, but the eternal God holding conversation with himself as a Trinity in Unity; or to be more explicit, God the Father sitting in council with the Son and Holy Spirit in relation to the creation of man.

This doctrine is also clearly and beautifully expressed by the prophet Isaiah vi. 8–10; as also in a parallel passage in John xii. 40, compared with Acts xxviii. 25, in which passages the existence of the Trinity is not only expressed, but expressed in such a manner as to leave little room for doubt of there being three persons, and but three in the Godhead. Our limits will not allow us, however, to enlarge our comments on these passages, and we can only refer the reader to a few more passages from the New Testament in support of the doctrine taught in this Article.

In Matt. iii. 18, where the baptism of Christ is recorded, we have first the person of the Son going up from the water; second, the Spirit in the form of a dove descending and lighting upon him; third, the voice of the Father saying, "This is my beloved Son;" and in Matt. xxviii. 19, the disciples were commissioned to baptize "in the name of the Father and of the Son and of the Holy Ghost." The reader will observe that they were not sent to baptize in the *names* of each of these persons, but in the *name* of the Father, &c., an indication that the "THREE ARE ONE." The apostolic benediction also may be adduced as proof of the doctrine of the Trinity, for there would be but little propriety in making a distinction between the persons of the Father, the Lord Jesus Christ, and the Holy Ghost, if so be that a trinity of persons does not exist. In 1 John v. 7, it is asserted, "There are three that bear record in heaven, the Father, the Word, and the Holy Ghost, and these three are one." It is true, that the genuineness of this passage has been disputed by some, but Mr. Wesley and other distinguished biblical critics have unhesitatingly avowed their belief in its authenticity, and if authentic, as we have no doubt it is, it but adds another proof in favor of the doctrine advocated. While then the doctrine of a trinity in unity is set forth in the first Article of religion, and is abundantly supported by Scripture, that of the divinity of Jesus Christ is set forth in the succeeding Article, and like the present, is also supported by the clearest and most substantial proof.

ARTICLE II.

OF THE WORD OR SON OF GOD, WHO WAS MADE VERY MAN.

"The Son, who is the word of the Father, the very and eternal God, of one substance with the Father, took man's nature in the womb of the blessed virgin; so that two whole and perfect natures, that is to say, the Godhead and manhood, were joined together in one person, never to be divided, whereof is one Christ, very God, and very man, who truly suffered, was crucified, dead, and buried, to reconcile his Father to us, and to be a sacrifice not only for original guilt, but also for actual sins of men."

In this Article the deity of Christ is asserted in strong language, as is also the object of his sufferings and death—"to reconcile his Father to us," &c. In relation to the first point, it may be sufficient to present the basis of the Scriptural argument in favor of the doctrine taught. That Christ is God in the proper use of that term, is evident from the following facts:

1. *Divine titles* are given to Christ. Isaiah xl. 3, "Prepare ye the way of the Lord, make straight in the desert a highway for our God;" compared with Matt. iii. 3, "For this is he that was spoken of by the prophet Esaias, saying, 'The voice of one crying in the wilderness, prepare ye the way of the Lord.'" Matt. i. 23, "And they shall call his name Emmanuel—God with us." John i. 1, "In the beginning was the word, and the word was with God, and the word was God." Isa. ix. 6, Christ is called the "Mighty God." 1 Tim. iii. 16, "God manifest in the flesh." Tit. ii. 10, "God our Saviour." 1 John v. 20, "The true God." Acts xx. 28, "God who purchased the Church with his own blood." 1 John iii. 16, "God who laid down his life for us." John xx. 28, "My Lord and my God." Rev. xix. 16, "King of kings, and Lord of Lords." These various titles ascribed to Christ, prove beyond a doubt his divinity, and if it is said that Christ is God, but not the supreme God,

it reduces the advocates of such belief to the necessity of admitting that there are two distinct Gods, a superior and inferior one, which admission would contradict other passages of Holy Writ which declare that there is but "ONE GOD."

2. *Divine attributes* are ascribed to Christ. (1) Eternity. Isa. ix. 6, "The everlasting Father." Rev. i. 11, "Alpha and Omega, the first and the last." (2) Omnipotence. Rev. i. 8, "Almighty." Col. i. 17, "By him all things consist." (3) Omnipresence. Matt. xxviii. 20, "Lo, I am with you alway, even unto the end of the world." Matt. xviii. 20, "For where two or three are gathered together in my name, there am I in the midst."

3. *Divine acts* are ascribed to Christ. "All things were made by him and without him was not anything made that was made. For by him were all things created that are in heaven, and that are in earth, visible and invisible; whether they be thrones, or dominions, or principalities, or powers; all things were created by him and *for* him." The latter clause of this passage is fatal to the opinion that Christ acted as the Creator in a delegated capacity, or that he made the things that are made, as the agent of the Supreme Being. These things were not only "created *by* him," but "FOR him," "and he is *before* all things, and by him all things consist."

4. *Divine worship* was paid to Christ, not only voluntarily, but by express command. "Thou shalt worship the Lord thy God, and him only shalt thou serve," is the command of Jehovah; yet Christ teaches his disciples that, "All men should honor the Son, EVEN AS they honor the Father." Hence Stephen prayed, saying, "Lord Jesus receive my spirit," and on the ascension of Christ the disciples "worshipped him." Not only did Christ on numerous occasions while on earth receive divine worship, but in heaven the angels are represented as worshipping the "first begotten" of the Father.

5. *Jesus Christ forgave sins;* an act which can only be exercised by God himself, for, "Who can forgive sins but God

only?" Yet Christ in many instances forgave sins, not as a delegated agent, or proxy, but as *God;* and unless he was the "very God," he must have usurped the power which belongs to God alone, a supposition at once blasphemous and destructive of Christianity.

The Article under consideration refers to the *manhood* of Christ; but as this is denied by few, if any, at the present day, we pass to notice the nature and design of Christ's sufferings and death, which are in the Article declared to be for the purpose of reconciling the Father to us, and to be a sacrifice not only for original guilt, but for actual sins. Two opinions have been embraced by men in reference to the *nature* of Christ's sufferings, &c. One opinion is, that Christ died merely a martyr's death; and the other, that his sufferings and death were sacrificial in their nature and design. In the former case, Christ appears simply as a man of exalted virtue, suffering persecution and death from his merciless foes, that he might evince the sincerity of his professions, and leave an example for his followers of patience and resignation. In the latter case we see him "bearing our sins in his own body on the tree;" as dying, the just *for* the unjust, that he might bring us to God: as "laying down his life for the sheep"—as being "wounded for our transgressions, bruised for our iniquities, &c."—as having "died for our sins"—as being "made sin (a sin-offering) for us"—as tasting "death for every man." Now, in what sense Christ was a Saviour, we may safely leave to the unbiassed judgment of the reader after he shall have examined the above quotations, and we may simply affirm that if the sacrificial nature of Cnrist's sufferings and death are not taught in the Scriptures, then is nothing taught, and language is without a meaning.

But the article asserts that the object of Christ's death was to "reconcile the Father to us." An objection has been raised to the use of this expression on the ground that it is *man*, and not *God* that is reconciled. Let it be understood, however, that the reconciliation is mutual between the parties, and the objection vanishes. That there is reciprocal hostility between offended Deity and offending man is clearly susceptible of proof. Rom. v. 10, "For if when we were enemies, we were reconciled to God by the death of his Son; much more being reconciled, we shall be saved by his life." Here the reader will observe that the act of reconciling is ascribed to God and not to man; for the reconciliation is effected while men are "*enemies*" to God; that is, while man is in a state of enmity and hostility to God, the latter is reconciled to man by the death of his Son, and man is subsequently reconciled to his Maker by the same means. But to show the propriety of the expression still farther, we may quote the language of the prophet, "God is angry with the wicked every day," and also all those Scriptures which speak of the "wrath of God resting on the children of disobedience," which plainly show that God the Father is reconciled to the sinner as a sinner, while he can be "just and yet the justifier of them that believe." As the extent of the atonement is not clearly expressed in the Article, we will leave this point for future reference in our remarks on Article XX.

ARTICLE III.

OF THE RESURRECTION OF CHRIST.

"Christ did truly rise again from the dead, and took again his body with all things appertaining to the perfection of man's nature, wherewith he ascended into heaven, and there sitteth until he return to judge all men at the last day."

In regard to the resurrection and ascension of Jesus Christ there is no difference of opinion among professed Christians; but the doctrine of the latter part of the Article, which refers to the day of general judgment is denied by some claiming the title of Christians. In support then of the latter doctrine we offer a few scriptural arguments.

1. The Scriptures universally speak of the judgment as being yet in the future. "God *shall* bring every work into judgment." "For we must all stand before the judgment-seat of Christ." "For we must all appear before the judgment-seat of Christ." Those Scriptures evidently show that the judgment of men does not take place at present, or that men are judged *as* they commit good or evil, but that their judgment is in the future.

2. The Scriptures fix the judgment on an appointed day. "He hath appointed a day in the which he will judge the world." "In the day when God shall judge the secrets of men." "The judgment of the great day." "The day of judgment." "The word that I speak shall judge him at the last day." If then the judgment is on an "appointed day"—on the "great day"—on the "last day," it is evident that it cannot be on every day or hour that the sinner may live on earth.

3. The Scriptures represent the judgment of former generations of men as yet in the future. "It shall be more tolerable for the land of Sodom and Gomorrah in the day of judgment than for that city." "And thou, Capernaum, it shall be more tolerable for the land of Sodom in the day of judgment than for thee." "The queen of the south shall rise in the judgment with this generation and condemn it." "The men of Nineveh shall rise up in the judgment with this generation," &c. In these passages we find that generations of men who had died hundreds, yea, thousands of years previously, were still, in our Saviour's time, reserved to the judgment of the great day.

4. The Scriptures speak of the judgment as being after death. "Who shall judge the quick and dead at his appearing." "Who shall give account to him that is ready to judge the quick and dead." "And I saw the dead, small and great, stand before God; and the books were opened, and the dead were judged out of the things which were written in the books according to their works." "It is appointed unto men once to

die, and after this the judgment." No sophistry or misinterpretation can do away the force of these passages as they relate to that great event, the judgment of mankind.

5. The day of judgment is connected with the second coming of Christ, see Matt. xxv. 31–46; and with the end of the world. "But the heavens and the earth that are now, are kept in store, reserved unto fire, against the day of judgment, and perdition of ungodly men." "And I saw a great white throne, and him that sat on it, from whose face the earth and the heavens fled away, and there was found no place for them, and I saw the dead, small and great, stand before God," &c. From these and other considerations we think the doctrine of the Article is clearly established. Remarks in relation to the eternal punishment of the wicked will be reserved for a future Article.

ARTICLE IV.

OF THE HOLY GHOST.

"The Holy Ghost, proceeding from the Father and the Son, is of one substance, majesty, and glory with the Father and the Son, very and eternal God."

Remarks on the doctrine taught in this Article need not be very extended, as the doctrine of a Trinity in Unity, and of the proper and essential divinity of Jesus Christ, have already, to some extent, been treated of in a previous Article. The doctrine of the personality and divinity of the Holy Ghost is intimately connected with the deity of Christ, and the trinity of persons in the Godhead. It has been claimed by Unitarians that the Holy Ghost is but an attribute of God, and that it possesses no distinct personality. The actions and words, however, which are ascribed to the Spirit are evidence that he acts, moves, &c. distinctly from the Father and the Son. "The Spirit of God moved upon the face of the waters." "The Spirit searcheth all things, even the deep things of God." "My Spirit shall not always strive with man." These passages indicate personality; and other passages ascribe divine titles, acts, attributes, and worship to the Spirit of God, which prove that while he is distinct as a person, he is equal in substance, power, and glory with the Father and Son.

1. Divine titles are given to the Holy Ghost. Acts v. 3, 4, "Ananias, why hath Satan filled thine heart to lie to the Holy Ghost? Thou hast not lied unto men but unto God." Here the Spirit is expressly called God, for in lying to the Holy Ghost, Ananias had lied to God.

2. Divine attributes are ascribed to the Holy Ghost. "Eternal Spirit." "Whither shall I go from thy Spirit," &c. "The Spirit searcheth all things," &c. He is also called the "Spirit of truth," "Spirit of grace," "Spirit of holiness," &c.

3. Divine acts are ascribed to the Holy Spirit in Job xxxiii. 4; it is said, "The Spirit of God hath made me, and the breath of the Almighty hath given me life." "It is the Spirit that quickeneth." When Christ rose from the dead he is said to have been "quickened," brought to life "by the Spirit."

4. The form of Christian baptism is an evidence of the personality and divinity of the Holy Ghost. "Go teach all nations, baptizing them in the name of the Father, and of the Son, and of the Holy Ghost." If the Holy Ghost is merely an attribute of deity, what propriety would there be in baptizing first in the name of deity, and then in the name of an attribute of deity? The same reasoning will hold good in regard to the form of the apostolic benediction. When a distinction is drawn between the "love of God" and the "communion of the Holy Ghost," it is evident that the latter person is not to be confounded with the former, but that the Holy Ghost is a distinct person in the Trinity.

ARTICLE V.

THE SUFFICIENCY OF THE HOLY SCRIPTURES FOR SALVATION.

"The Holy Scriptures contain all things necessary to salvation: so that whatsoever is not read therein, nor may be proved thereby, is not to be required of any man that it should be believed as an article of faith, or be thought requisite or necessary to salvation. In the name of the Holy Scriptures we do understand, those canonical books of the Old and New Testament, of whose authority was never any doubt in the Church."

"THE NAMES OF THE CANONICAL BOOKS.

Genesis,	The First Book of Chronicles,
Exodus,	The Second Book of Chronicles,
Leviticus,	The Book of Ezra,
Numbers,	The Book of Nehemiah,
Deuteronomy,	The Book of Esther,
Joshua,	The Book of Job,
Judges,	The Psalms,
Ruth,	The Proverbs,
The First Book of Samuel,	Ecclesiastes or the Preacher,
The Second Book of Samuel,	Canticles or the Songs of Solomon,
The First Book of Kings,	Four Prophets the greater,
The Second Book of Kings,	Twelve Prophets the less.

"All the books of the New Testament as they are commonly received, we do receive, and account canonical."

The Article of religion now under consideration is of great importance to the Christian Church, for as a curse is pronounced against those who add to, or take from the complete canon of Holy Writ, it cannot be a matter of indifference whether we receive *more* than what God has revealed, or whether we receive *less* than he has revealed. On the one hand, it is important to reject mere tradition as a rule of faith and practice, and on the other hand, it is equally important that we reject nothing which God has revealed to man through the inspiration of the Holy Ghost. It is well known that Romanists and Mormonites claim other writings as standards of equal authority with the books of Scripture embraced in the above catalogue. The former not only claim the apocryphal books as a portion of the Canonical Scriptures, but assert also that tradition is equally binding on mankind with the Scriptures of the Old and New Testaments; while the Mormons claim for their golden Bible the same, if not greater authority than they claim for the Word of God, as contained in the books of Moses, the Prophets, and the New Testament. The Methodist Church disclaiming all these, asserts that the books of the Old and New Testaments are the "only rule of faith and practice," and "that whatsoever is not read therein, nor may be proved thereby is not to be required of any man, or be thought necessary to salvation." Thus while care is taken not to "add to" the Word of God, equal care is taken not to take away from the Word of God, as the manner of some is, for it is a well-known fact, that semi-infidelity, under the guise of Christianity, has, and does reject a portion of the Word of God. The books of Job, Songs of Solomon, Ecclesiastes, and Revelation, have all been rejected by these "takers from" the Word of God, and the object of the Article is not only to show to the world what kind of a Bible the Methodists believe in, but to preserve, to all generations, the pure unadulterated Word of God. It may also be added, that while all the *books* of the Old and New Testaments are received as genuine by the Methodist Church, so the common rendering of the Scriptures into the English language by King James's translators is acknowledged to be sufficiently correct. No attempt has ever been made by the Methodist Episcopal Church to form a new Bible, or to modify the old, so as to suit her particular views. Instead of bringing the Bible down to the level of her opinions, her object has been to bring the latter up to the Bible, and she denies the propriety of altering or changing the reading of the sacred text by any man or any body of men for the sake of propagating more rapidly their sectarian views and sentiments.

A few remarks in relation to the uncorrupted preservation

of the books of the Old and New Testaments may not be out of place. In proof of the preservation of the former, the following arguments have been presented by distinguished writers:

1. The Jews were divided into a number of sects, each one being exceedingly jealous of the others, as much or more so than Christian sects are in relation to each other, consequently neither sect could adulterate or mutilate the Old Testament Scriptures without detection and exposure.

2. The Jews, with all their faults, had a great veneration for the Scriptures. Every word and letter in the different books was counted and recorded, so that even the alteration of a single letter could not well escape detection.

3. Our Saviour when upon earth was not slow in reproving the different sects among the Jews for their various faults in relation to faith and practice, but he nowhere accuses them of altering or mutilating the Word of God—an evidence that they had not done so.

4. Since the Christian era, both Jews and Christians have had copies of the Old Testament Scriptures; these, on being now compared together, are found to agree with such exactness as is truly wonderful, and which proves their uncorrupted preservation until the present time.

In relation to the preservation of the New Testament Scriptures in an uncorrupted state we have the following proofs:

1. The number of Christian sects existing since the days of the apostles, each having copies of the New Testament and watching each other with unwearied vigilance, so that had an attempt been made by any one or more sects, to change or alter the commonly received version, the other sects would have immediately sounded an alarm; as may be illustrated by the case of the Baptists in modern times, some of whom, in their zeal for immersion, have translated the Bible, so as to correspond with their opinions in that respect; still it is evident that such translation can never be adopted to any very great extent, and that the alteration of the commonly received ver-

sion of the Bible cannot be made without the fact becoming a matter of public notoriety and exposing the agents in the matter to the reproof of other Christian sects.

2. The earliest copies of the several books of the New Testament were written in the Greek language. Several translations were made at an early period of these several books into other languages. The latter have been compared with the former, and are found to agree.

3. The manuscript copies of the New Testament are very numerous; three hundred of them were compared together by the celebrated Griesbach, and although there were found various readings, as might be expected, yet not a single doctrine or fact is affected by such variety, the difference consisting mostly in the use of different words or phrases to convey the same meaning. From these, and other considerations, the Methodist Episcopal Church, with Protestant denominations generally, believing in the authenticity of the Scriptures of the Old and New Testaments, and of their sufficiency as a rule of faith and practice, practically adopt the motto, "The Bible, the whole Bible, and nothing but the Bible."

ARTICLE VI.

OF THE OLD TESTAMENT.

"The Old Testament is not contrary to the New: for both in the Old and New Testaments everlasting life is offered to mankind by Christ, who is the only mediator between God and man, being both God and man. Wherefore they are not to be heard who feign that the old fathers did look only for transitory promises. Although the law given from God by Moses, as touching ceremonies and rites, doth not bind Christians, nor ought the civil precepts thereof of necessity be received in any commonwealth; yet, notwithstanding, no Christian whatsoever is free from the obedience of the commandments, commonly called moral."

This Article teaches: 1st. The agreement of the Old and New Testaments in relation to the great plan of human redemption by Jesus Christ. 2d. The possibility of salvation for the inhabitants of the Old or Jewish dispensation. 3d. The abrogation of the ceremonial and ritual law of the Jews. 4th. The perpetuity of obligation to the requirements of the moral law. The last clause of the Article is designed to bear a constant testimony against that system of faith called "Antinomianism," which prevailed largely about the middle of the sixteenth, and during the seventeenth centuries in different parts of Europe, and which has been partially revived within the present century by a sect called "Perfectionists." This system of faith teaches in substance, that as Christians are not under law, but under grace, it is not required of them to keep the moral law; hence, the law given by God to Moses, as contained in the two tables, is not, in their opinion, a rule of practice, for those living under the gospel dispensation. The legitimate consequences of such a loose code of morals as this, may be easily imagined, and it is perhaps owing to the latent existence of this kind of belief, that there exists among Christians so called, so little regard for the precepts of the Bible and the pure and wholesome requirements of the moral law.

That the latter has not been abrogated, is evident from the teachings of our Saviour, especially where he says, "Think not that I am come to destroy the law or the prophets; I am not come to destroy but to fulfil. For verily, I say unto you, till heaven and earth pass, one jot or one tittle shall in nowise pass from the law till all be fulfilled. Whosoever therefore shall break one of these least commandments, and shall teach men so, he shall be called the least in the kingdom of heaven." From this quotation it appears evident that any system of religious faith, whether among Catholics or Protestants, which nullifies or abrogates any one of the commandments of the moral law, is not of God, and is to be abhorred and discountenanced by every true Christian.

ARTICLE VII.

ORIGINAL OR BIRTH SIN.

"Original sin standeth not in the following of Adam (as the Pelagians do vainly talk) but it is the corruption of the nature of every man, that naturally is engendered of the offspring of Adam, whereby man is very far gone from original righteousness, and of his own nature inclined to evil, and that continually."

The "Pelagians," referred to in this Article, were a sect who arose about the fifth century, who took their name from Pelagius, a British monk, who lived in Rome, and who taught that mankind are born into the world as pure and unspotted as was Adam, when he first came out of the forming hand of his Creator, and that they have, in themselves, the natural ability independent of the internal workings of the Holy Spirit, to repent of their sins and attain to the highest degrees of piety and virtue. As the latter doctrine is, however, referred to more particularly in the following Article, we will allude here only to the sentiments taught in the one before us.

The doctrine of the Article is, that the nature of every man is corrupt; that he is born unholy and unclean; that he is totally and continually inclined to evil; that as like begets like, and as Adam begat a son in his own image, so all the descendants of Adam partake of the same unholy nature, as naturally and necessarily as a stream partakes of the nature of the fountain from which it flows. Such are the teachings of this Article of the church, and the doctrines herein set forth are abundantly supported by Scripture. In the Epistle to the Romans, Paul asserts that by "one man's disobedience many were made sinners." Reference is here made to Adam's sin, and to the fact that such sin involves all his descendants in guilt and condemnation. A few other passages will be given in support of this doctrine. "The heart is deceitful above all

12

things and desperately wicked." And God saw the wickedness of man that it was great in the earth; and that every imagination of the thoughts of his heart was only evil continually." "Out of it," the heart, "proceed evil thoughts, murders, adulteries, fornications, thefts, false witness, blasphemies." "The carnal mind is enmity against God: for it is not subject to the law of God, neither indeed can be." "Behold I was shapen in iniquity, and in sin did my mother conceive me." "Sin that dwelleth in me." "I know that in me, that is, in my flesh, dwelleth no good thing." These Scriptures abundantly sustain the doctrine of the Article, and we may here remark that the whole gospel economy proceeds on the ground of man's natural depravity, and not merely on the fact that man is a voluntary transgressor.

ARTICLE VIII.

OF FREE WILL.

"The condition of man after the fall of Adam is such that he cannot turn and prepare himself, by his own natural strength and works, to faith and calling upon God; wherefore we have no power to do good works, pleasant and acceptable to God, without the grace of God by Christ preventing us, that we may have a good-will, and working with us, when we have that good-will."

This Article of religion stands opposed to the doctrine advocated by the Pelagians and semi-Pelagians, who teach that man has power in, and of himself, independently of the workings of the Spirit of God, to repent, believe, and obey the gospel; and that as a free moral agent, he has power to comply with all the requirements of the law and gospel, without the aid of the Holy Spirit. While, therefore, the doctrine of free moral agency is by no means repudiated or denied by this Article, neither is denied by the commentators and ministers of the

Methodist Church, yet it is not adopted as an Article of belief, involving the natural ability of man to repent and turn to God, unaided by the Holy Spirit. The light which lighteneth every man which cometh into the world, is, however, vouchsafed to every man, so that while destitute of the Spirit's influence, man might well be considered as dispossessed of a free moral power to do good, yet with such influence imparted, his free moral agency remains unimpaired.

The doctrine that man may convert himself, or change his own heart, is certainly not the doctrine of the Bible. The work of regeneration is purely and solely the work of God by his Spirit, and if men are ever "born again," it will not be the result of their own purpose or determination to become pious, uninfluenced by the Spirit of God, but the Spirit "working in them to will and to do of his own good pleasure," will lead them—if they obey its directions and yield to its influences—into the paths of obedience and holy enjoyment. Thus the "grace of God by Christ" must prevent, that is, go before us, "that we may have a good-will," and when that good-will is possessed, the same grace must work with, and in us, that we may "do good works."

The views thus expressed are clearly taught in the word of God. Our Saviour said to his disciples and others, "Without me ye can do nothing." And again: "No man can come unto me, except the Father which sent me draw him." The apostle also declares, "By grace are ye saved through faith; and that not of *yourselves;* it is the gift of God." Man, also, in many portions of Scripture, is represented as being "dead," "asleep," &c., which expressions convey an idea of utter helplessness and natural inability, while the exhortations, commands, warnings, threatenings, and promises, all prove, that notwithstanding man's *natural inability* to repent, and obey, a *gracious ability* is imparted to all men for that purpose.

ARTICLE IX.

OF THE JUSTIFICATION OF MAN.

"We are accounted righteous before God only for the merit of our Lord and Saviour Jesus Christ by faith, and not for our own works or deservings: wherefore, that we are justified by faith only, is a most wholesome doctrine, and very full of comfort."

The doctrine of justification by faith alone, was the great point of contention between Martin Luther and his Romish brethren. It was in fact the great distinguishing doctrine of the Reformation from Popery; and while popery still maintains its position, and a portion of the protestant church are hasting with rapid strides to "Rome," it is well for us that the doctrine of justification by faith is not only taught in our Articles of Faith, but sincerely believed and plainly advocated from our pulpit and our press.

It is well known that the Roman Catholic Church discards the above doctrine, and maintains in the most pointed manner the merit of good works, and our justification by such works.*

* "I see," said Luther, on a certain occasion, "that the devil, by the means of his teachers and doctors, is incessantly attacking this fundamental article, and that he cannot rest to cease from this object. Well then, I, Doctor Martin Luther, an unworthy evangelist of our Lord Jesus Christ, do confess this article, 'that faith alone, without works, justifies in the sight of God,' and I declare that in spite of the Emperor of the Romans, the Emperor of the Turks, the Emperor of the Tartars, the Emperor of the Persians, the Pope, and all the cardinals, bishops, priests, monks, nuns, kings, princes, nobles, all the world, and all the devils, this doctrine shall stand unshaken forever! that if they will persist in opposing this truth, they will draw upon their heads the flames of hell. This is the true and holy gospel, and the declaration of me, Doctor Martin Luther, according to the light given unto me by the Holy Spirit." "I repeat it once more: let all the evil spirits of earth and hell foam and rage as they will, this is nevertheless true."—*History of Reformation*, page 172.

Hence, baptism, penance, indulgences, &c., are made, not only requisite to salvation, but in their view, entitle a person to salvation, so much so, that the Council of Trent declares, that "if any one shall say that a wicked man is justified by faith alone, let him be accursed." Such is the Roman system of justification, which stands diametrically opposed to the plainest declarations of Scripture. "Being justified by *faith*, we have peace with God." "By grace are ye saved, through *faith;* and that not of yourselves, it is the gift of God." And our Saviour taught his disciples, after they had done all that they could, to say, "We are unprofitable servants."

ARTICLE X.

OF GOOD WORKS

"Although good works, which are the fruits of faith, and follow after justification, cannot put away our sins, and endure the severity of God's judgments, yet are they pleasing and acceptable to God in Christ, and spring out of a true and lively faith, insomuch that by them a lively faith may be as evidently known, as a tree is discerned by its fruit."

Lest any should suppose that the doctrine of justification by faith alone precludes the necessity of good works, the above Article very properly follows the preceding, for the purpose of showing, that as *before* justification, good works are impossible, so, *after* justification, they are indispensable to the existence of a lively faith. It may therefore be considered as a settled doctrine of the Methodist Church, that a man in a state of enmity to God, and while under the condemnation of the law, cannot perform works pleasing and acceptable to God; and why? because "whatsoever is not of faith," a lively, saving, operative faith, "is sin," and because, that "without faith it is impossible to please God," and because the "carnal" or unrenewed "mind is not subject to the law of God, neither indeed can be;" and because "they that are in the flesh cannot please God." These plain and pointed texts of Scripture conclusively prove, that before justification, or reconciliation to God, the works of the sinner are evil, and only evil, and that continually. But it may be objected, "that a work may in itself be good, even while performed by a rebel against God; that a wicked man may sacrifice his life for the sake of saving from death a fellow-creature." This may be so; but it should be remembered that the quality of a moral action depends not so much on the act itself, as on the motive which governs the act. Thus, "Two men went up into the temple to pray, the one a pharisee, and the other a publican"—both prayed, both worshipped God, but that there was a great difference in the quality or character of their acts, we need not state to the biblical reader. Men may, in the performance of the most praiseworthy acts, be governed and influenced solely by motives of pride, vain-glory, self-interest, regard to character, compliance with custom, &c., &c., without being at all influenced by love to God and man, while the true child of God, "whether he eat or drink, or whatsoever he does, he does all to the glory of God."

"Good works," therefore, in the language of the Article, "are the *fruits* of faith;" they are also the *evidence* of faith in a collateral sense. Where these works are not performed, no evidence is given of the existence or exercise of faith in the heart. "By their fruits ye shall know them." He that committeth sin is of the devil." "Whosoever is born of God doth not commit sin," "and he cannot sin because he is born of God." These passages show conclusively that holiness and purity of life are the necessary results of faith in God, and an evidence of being God's children.

ARTICLE XI.

OF WORKS OF SUPEREROGATION.

"Voluntary works, besides, over and above God's commandments, which are called works of supererogation, cannot be taught without arrogancy and impiety. For by them men do declare that they do not only render unto God as much as they are bound to do, but that they do more for his sake than of bounden duty is required: whereas Christ saith plainly, When ye have done all that is commanded of you, say, we are unprofitable servants."

The doctrine of this Article is at variance with the faith and pretensions of the Romish Church, in relation to works of merit and of supererogation. The idea that man can do more than God requires, and that there is absolute merit in such *overwork*, is at once preposterous and unreasonable. How can a man who owes all he has and all he is to God, whose time, talents, influence, obedience, all belong unreservedly to his Maker—who is required to keep the whole law in every point, and who, if he does so, is after all an unprofitable servant—how can such an one do more than God requires? The thing is absolutely impossible, and the doctrine of works of supererogation is clearly the "doctrine of devils," invented for the sake of the "price of indulgences," the "thirty pieces of silver," by which Christ is daily betrayed, and God is hourly robbed of his glory.

ARTICLE XII.

OF SIN AFTER JUSTIFICATION.

"Not every sin willingly committed after justification is the sin against the Holy Ghost, and unpardonable. Wherefore, the grant of repentance is not to be denied to such as fall into sin after justification: after we receive the Holy Ghost, we may depart from grace given, and fall into sin, and by the grace of God rise again, and amend our lives.

And therefore they are to be condemned who say they can no more sin as long as they live here: or deny the peace of forgiveness to such as truly repent."

Our Saviour, when on earth, spoke of the "sin against the Holy Ghost" as being unpardonable; as neither being entitled to forgiveness "in this world or in the world to come." A difference of opinion has obtained among commentators in relation to what constituted the sin against the Holy Ghost, and whether such sin can now be committed by any man. Without entering into a discussion of the subject, we may simply state, that the strong probability is, that this sin consists in attributing the miracles wrought by Jesus Christ to the agency of the devil; as in the case of those who accused the Saviour of "casting out devils through Beelzebub, the prince of the devils." That the possibility of committing the unpardonable sin was not confined to the life-time of our Saviour on earth, appears evident from the assertion of John, 1 John v. 16, "There is a sin unto death; I do not say that he shall pray for it," and we believe the same idea is intended to be conveyed by the apostle Paul, when, in speaking of those who had been once enlightened, &c., says, "It is impossible to renew them again unto repentance, seeing they crucify to themselves the Son of God afresh, and put him to an open shame." But in the language of the Article, it is not every sin willingly committed after justification which is the sin against the Holy Ghost; a good man may fall into sin, lose his state of justification before God, as in the case of David, and like him may repent and be restored again to the "joys of salvation."

As the question, whether the child of God may so fully and finally fall away as to be forever lost, is not settled by the Article before us, we will reserve our remarks on this particular point for another Article. But before we dismiss this Article, the doctrine taught near the close of the same is worthy of particular notice, "They are to be condemned who say they can no more sin as long as they live here."

The object of this part of the Article is to guard men against the foolish and dangerous doctrine, that after justification a person may do what he pleases and still retain his justification; that he may, as a child of God, commit adultery, fornication, murder, &c., and yet these acts not be considered sinful in the sight of God, because, forsooth, he is a child of God! That such diabolical sentiments have been entertained by many, and are yet entertained by some, there can be no doubt, and hence the manifest propriety of guarding the Church against a doctrine that must prove destructive, wherever it is embraced, to the interests of true religion, virtue, and morality. The text, "he cannot sin because he is born of God," yields no support whatever to this pernicious doctrine, for the design of the apostle evidently is to show that he that is born of God, and would have an abiding evidence of the fact, can have it only by abstaining from the commission of every sin; that he "cannot sin" and retain such evidence, or remain a child of God.

The last clause of the Article is also instructive, as it teaches not only the possibility of obtaining forgiveness at the hand of God when sin is committed after justification, but the importance of extending our forgiveness to our erring brethren, provided that in both cases there is true repentance exercised by the offender.

ARTICLE XIII.

OF THE CHURCH.

"The visible Church of Christ is a congregation of faithful men, in which the pure word of God is preached, and the sacraments duly administered, according to Christ's ordinance in all things, that of necessity are requisite to the same."

This Article teaches, 1. That the visible Church of Christ is a *congregation* or *assemblage* of faithful men; that it does not consist of the pope, or his councils, or the priesthood, nor of any order or body of bishops or ministers exclusively, but of a "congregation of faithful men," embracing the laity as well as the priesthood or ministry of the church.

2. The Church is composed of "*faithful* men," and although the "wheat and tares" are necessarily found together, and will continue so to be found until the "harvest," yet the true Church consists only of those who are faithful; of all others, be they popes, cardinals, archbishops, bishops, priests, deacons, or members, it may be said, as of Simon of old, "they have neither part nor lot in the matter, for their hearts are not right in the sight of God."

3. "The *pure word of God* is preached" in the Church; not the decrees of popes, the decisions of councils, the traditions of the fathers; not some fine system of morality, independent of the gospel, or philosophical disquisitions on abstract questions of science, literature, or art; but the pure word of God,—"Jesus Christ and him crucified,"—is preached and expounded with all due ministerial fidelity.

4. *The Sacraments are duly administered.* The sacrament of baptism and the sacrament of the Lord's Supper are duly administered, not by any and every person choosing to administer the same, but by those who are called by God and his Church to the sacred work of the ministry.

Where all these things are found—a congregation of faithful men, the preaching of the pure word of God, and the due administration of the sacraments—there is a true Church of Jesus Christ, let it be called by what distinctive appellation it may, and let it be organized on what ecclesiastical basis it may—there is, we repeat, a true Church of Christ, against which "the gates of hell cannot prevail."

ARTICLE XIV.

OF PURGATORY.

"The Romish doctrine concerning purgatory, pardon, worshipping, and adoration, as well of images as of relics, and also invocation of saints, is a fond thing vainly invented, and grounded upon no warrant of Scripture, but repugnant to the word of God."

The doctrine of purgatory, it is well known, is one of the distinctive features of the Romish Church, and it is also true that the doctrine is taught, if not in name, yet in fact by modern Restorationists, and some other Protestant sects, and yet such a doctrine is evidently without support from the word of God. In no place in that word do we read of the purgatorial fires of a middle state. On the contrary, mankind are divided by the sacred writers into two great classes—the righteous and the wicked; and their future and eternal destination is heaven or hell. The most important text relied upon by the advocates of purgatory in support of this dogma, is the one in 1 Peter iii. 18, 20, where Christ is represented as preaching "to the spirits in prison, who were disobedient in the days of Noah." It is agreed upon by the best biblical critics, however, that the meaning of the passage simply is, that Christ went and preached, through Noah, to the antediluvians who were disobedient, and who were in the prison of hell at the time in which the apostle wrote the epistle. But, admitting, even, that Christ, after he "was put to death in the flesh, and quickened in the spirit, went and preached to the spirits in prison," what support does this give to the fabled doctrine of purgatory? The term "preach," as found in the original Greek, it is well known, signifies simply "to proclaim, to announce as a herald," &c., and in itself nowhere signifies to preach the gospel, or deliverance from punishment, unless the connection requires such a meaning. John "preached" repentance; Christ "preached" deliverance to captives on earth; the apostle says, "preach the word," and in all these cases the matter of preaching is determined, not by the word *preach*, but by the words used in connection with the same. So that could it be proved that Christ went and preached after his death to the spirits in the prison of hell, what, after all, could be inferred therefrom? Simply a declaration or announcement of the fact of his death, which no doubt had been predicted to the unbelieving antediluvians, and the fulfilment of which prediction would serve only to increase their misery, as the announcement of the same would their guilt and condemnation.

The Romish doctrine of *pardon* is also protested against in the Article. It is a well-established fact that the pope, bishops, and priests of Rome, claim the power to absolve the offender, and pardon the transgressor, but it is also certain that none can forgive sins but God only, so that the Romish doctrine on this point is as false as it is dangerous.

Worshipping images, relics, and the invocation of saints, are also condemned by this article of religion; and it is a gratifying fact that the Methodists have always been at the farthest remove from the introduction of images, pictures, embellishments, &c., into their churches, while it is to be deplored that in some Protestant churches a disposition is manifested to return to the Romish practice of decorating the house of God with pictures and images, crosses and candlesticks, which, if not worshipped, are nevertheless the means of drawing the attention of the worshippers from the only proper object of adoration—God the creator. "Thou shalt worship the Lord thy God, and him only shalt thou serve," is the positive command of Jehovah himself.

ARTICLE XV.

OF SPEAKING IN THE CONGREGATION IN SUCH A TONGUE AS THE PEOPLE UNDERSTAND.

"It is a thing plainly repugnant to the word of God, and the custom of the primitive church, to have public prayers in the church, or to administer the sacraments, in a tongue not understood by the people."

That the practice condemned by this Article is unscriptural there can be but little doubt, if we but examine the language of Paul in 1 Cor. xiv. 16, "Else when thou shalt bless with the spirit, how shall he that occupieth the room of the unlearned, say Amen at thy giving of thanks, seeing he understandeth not what thou sayest?" The practice of speaking in an unknown tongue, or a tongue not understood by the people, is not confined to the Romish Church. Modern sectaries have, in their infatuation, pretended to be endued with the gift of tongues, but for what particular purpose does not appear. The apostles, indeed, were endued with this gift, but it was for the purpose of enabling the inhabitants of different portions of the earth to hear, every man in his own "tongue, the wonderful works of God;" but these modern pretended linguists speak in tongues which no one—we doubt even themselves—can understand. Such solemn mockery ought to be discountenanced by every Christian, and while the church, through her ministers, preaches to, or prays for the people, let it be done in such language as the people may understand and say Amen! "So be it."

ARTICLE XVI.

OF THE SACRAMENTS.

"Sacraments, ordained of Christ, are not only badges, or tokens, of Christian men's professions; but rather they are certain signs of grace and of God's good-will toward us, by the which he doth work invisibly in us, and doth not only quicken but also strengthen and confirm their faith in him.

"There are two sacraments ordained of Christ our Lord in the gospel; that is to say, baptism and the supper of the Lord.

"Those five commonly called sacraments, that is to say, confirmation, penance, orders, matrimony, and extreme unction, are not to be accounted for sacraments of the gospel, being such as have partly grown out of the corrupt following of the apostles, and partly are states of life allowed in the Scriptures, but yet have not the like nature of baptism and the Lord's Supper, because they have not any visible sign or ceremony ordained of God.

"The sacraments were not ordained of Christ to be gazed upon, or carried about, but that we should daily use them. And in such only as worthily receive the same they have a wholesome effect or operation; but they that receive them unworthily, purchase to themselves condemnation, as St. Paul saith in 1 Cor. xi. 29."

The term sacrament is derived from the Latin word *sacramentum*, and means a sacred ceremony, or oath of fidelity. It is not a scriptural term, and is used only by way of accommodation, to signify the solemn engagement into which Christians enter with their Lord whenever they observe the sacraments of the church. "A sacrament," says the learned Burnett, in his Exposition on the Articles, "is an institution of Christ, in which some material thing is sanctified by the use of some form of words, in and by which federal acts of this religion do pass on both sides; on ours, by stipulations, professions, or vows—and on God's, by his secret assistances; by these we are also united to the body of Christ, which is the church."

Mr. Watson observes, in regard to the sacraments, that "they are seals, as well as signs; that they afford pledges on the part of God, of grace and salvation; that as a covenant has two parties, our external acts in receiving the sacraments are indications of certain states and dispositions of our mind with regard to God's covenant, without which none can have a personal participation in its benefits, and so the sacrament is useless where these are not found; that these are words of institution, and a promise also by which the sign and the thing signified are connected together."—(*Watson's Institutes*, vol. ii. p. 611.) With the views of these distinguished men before us, we learn that a sacrament is a sign or pledge between God and man; a covenant into which we solemnly enter with the Almighty, whereby obedience and love are promised on the one part, and the gracious offer of salvation on the other, through the merits of Jesus Christ; that they are badges of a Christian profession, and channels or means of grace.

The Romish Church has seven sacraments, as mentioned in the Article; but of these, five do not partake of the nature of a sacrament, inasmuch as they are wanting in the essential qualities of a federal act, or mutual covenant between God and man. Baptism and the Lord's Supper only are recognized as sacraments in the Methodist Episcopal Church.

ARTICLE XVII.

OF BAPTISM.

"Baptism is not only a sign of profession, and mark of difference, whereby Christians are distinguished from others that are not baptized: but it is also a sign of regeneration, or the new birth. The baptism of young children is to be retained in the church."

As the subject of baptism has created no little controversy among Christians, it may be proper to dwell somewhat at length on the doctrine taught in this Article, and in doing so we would invite the attention of the reader to the origin, nature, subjects, and mode of baptism.

1. Baptism, as an ordinance, was *probably* instituted by God in the earliest period of the history of fallen man; it probably originated at the time when sacrificial offerings were first required by God, but there is no positive scriptural evidence that the rite of baptism was known until the time of

Moses, at which time, and ever since, baptism has been recognized as an ordinance of the Jewish Church. That baptism is of as ancient date as the institution of the Jewish economy, is evident from the fact that reference is continually made in the Levitical law and Mosaic history to the washings and purifications required under that dispensation. It is true, the words *baptize* or *baptism* are not found in the Mosaic scriptures; and why? Because the Jewish scriptures were written in Hebrew, and the words themselves are of Greek etymology; and the earliest translations of the Scriptures from Hebrew into Greek was made about twelve hundred years after they were written by Moses, and only about three hundred years before the Christian era. It is not, therefore, to be wondered at, that the words themselves are not found in the five books of Moses, or indeed, in any of the prophets. But is the *thing* to be found there? That it is so is evident from the fact, that the translators of the earliest Greek copies, made soon after the Greek language came into common use among the Jews, render the Hebrew of *wash*, *purify*, &c. by the term baptize, so that all the washings done under the law were so many acts of baptism performed by the subject, or administered by the priest. In proof of this we give a few examples. Heb.: "He that washeth himself after the touching of a dead body, if he touch it again, what availeth his washing?" Greek: "He that is baptized from a dead body," &c. "what availeth his washing?" Judith "went out in the night and washed (Heb.) baptized (Greek) herself at a fountain in the camp." "And when they came from the market they eat not except they wash (baptize) their hands." These instances are sufficient to show that baptism was not an ordinance unknown to the Hebrews, and that, too, at a very early period in their history.

2. The nature of baptism. (1.) It is a figurative ordinance, symbolical of our death unto sin and our being born again from above; of being purified by the water of regeneration and receiving of the Holy Ghost. This ordinance is not designed

to represent the sufferings, death, and resurrection of Jesus Christ, as some suppose. The ordinance of the Lord's Supper "shows forth the death of Christ until his coming again;" and it is not to be supposed that there would be two distinct ordinances signifying one and the same thing. The phrase "being buried with Christ by baptism," has no reference whatever to the external rite, but to the internal death to sin. So also the phrase "risen with Christ," has no reference to an external rite, but to the life of righteousness, or the life of God in the soul.

(2.) Baptism is a sign of profession; a rite which was instituted under the law, and is retained under the gospel, as the distinguishing mark or sign of a profession of faith. As the generic term to *baptize* means to purify and cleanse, not only is there in baptism a sign of inward moral cleansing, but a sign of outward moral conformity to the law of God and the rules of his church on earth.

(3.) Baptism is also considered as the door or entrance into the visible church. "He that believeth and is baptized shall be saved." "Repent and be baptized." "Then were they baptized, both men and women." "Then Philip baptized him," are passages which clearly show that water-baptism is designed to be an initiatory rite, and that in this way men are generally to be received into the church. We say *generally*, for we dare not say that no person can be a member of the household of faith without water-baptism; for we know not that the apostles even were ever baptized, except in the washing of feet; but as a general rule baptism is, and ought to be the initiatory rite.

(4.) Baptism partakes of the nature of a covenant between God and man, and in this appears its true sacramental character. Under the Abrahamic dispensation God made a covenant with the "father of the faithful," to be a God to him and to his seed after him in all their generations. This covenant was an everlasting one, and the rite of circumcision was instituted

13

as the visible sign or seal of this covenant, which embraced spiritual blessings, designed not only for the future generations of the Jews, as a people, but for all the nations of the earth: "In thee, and in thy seed, shall *all* the nations of the earth be blessed." This covenant remained in force after the introduction of Christianity, as is fully proved by the apostle Paul: "They which are of faith, the same are the children of Abraham," and again, "That the blessings of Abraham might come on the gentiles through Jesus Christ."

Under the gospel, however, the rite of circumcision gave place to the more expressive and simple one of baptism, as the sign or token of the Abrahamic covenant. This is evident from the words of the same apostle: "For as many of you as have been baptized into Christ, have put on Christ." "There is neither Jew nor Greek, for ye are all one in Christ." "And if ye are Christ's, then are ye Abraham's seed, and heirs according to the promise." How positively clear, from this language, is the perpetuity of the covenant, and the institution of baptism as the sign and seal of the same? But, if circumcision under the gospel was done away, and the rite of baptism does not take the place thereof, we ask, what other sign or seal has God instituted in place of circumcision? If none, then is there no visible outward sign of the perpetual covenant made between God and man.

3. The *subjects* of baptism may now be properly considered.

(1.) All admit that *adult believers* are proper subjects of baptism; on this point there is, and can be, no dispute.

(2.) *True penitents* are also proper subjects of baptism. This we learn from the answer of Peter to those who were pricked in their hearts, and asked, "What shall we do?" The reply was, "Repent, and be baptized, every one of you, for the remission of sins, and ye shall receive the gift of the Holy Ghost." Now, it is evident that these persons were not believers in the sense of being regenerate; unless regenerating faith precedes repentance for sin, for they were first to repent, secondly, to be baptized, "for"—in order to—the remission of sins, and, thirdly, as the result of such repentance and baptism they were taught to expect the gift of the Holy Ghost. Another prominent example of the baptism of penitents is given in the case of the apostle Paul. After being arrested by the light and voice from heaven, he fasted and prayed in blindness, natural and spiritual, for three days. In this condition Ananias finds him; his natural sight returns, but spiritual darkness remains, and then Ananias says to him, "Why tarriest thou? Arise, and be baptized, and *wash away* thy sins, calling on the name of the Lord." From this example it appears that baptism is both a *means* and seal of pardon, and consequently that true penitents may, nay, ought to be baptized.

(3.) *Infants* are proper subjects of Christian baptism. This doctrine is fairly taught in the Article: "The baptism of young children is to be retained in the church," and it is scarcely any the less clearly taught in the word of God, excepting that there is not a clear command to that effect in so many words. But the absence of such an express command does not, in our opinion, invalidate the doctrine of infant baptism.

That infants are scriptural subjects of baptism appears from the following considerations:—

1. "The perpetuity of the Abrahamic covenant," which included children as well as adults. The perpetuity of this covenant has already been alluded to in a preceding page, and need not be here repeated.

2. "The eligibility of children to church membership." That infants were members of the Jewish church is evident from the fact of their circumcision, which was the initiatory right or door of admission into the church of God. Can we possibly conceive that the children of Christian parents are entitled to lesser privileges than were the children of Jewish parents? Or would it be any inducement to a pious Jew of the present day to become a Christian to be told that although his children are

members of the Jewish church, yet, on his embracing Christianity and becoming a member of the Christian church, his children must be thrust out until they attain to adult years? Does not our Saviour explicitly say, in regard to young children, "of such is the kingdom of heaven?" The "kingdom of heaven" must mean either the kingdom of glory, the work of grace in the heart, or the church of Christ on earth. Now, in whatever sense it is used in the text, it must include the idea of infant church-membership. Is a young child fit for the kingdom of glory? Then why not for the kingdom of grace? If fit for the church triumphant, why not for the church on earth? And was not the promise of God given to Christian parents, and to their "*children*, and to all that are afar off?" If so, and there can be no reasonable doubt of it, then are infants entitled to the initiatory rite which will formally admit them into the visible church of Christ, and to debar them that privilege is not only unwise but unjust to the "children whom God has given us."

3. "The analogy between circumcision and baptism." Circumcision was a token of the covenant made with Abraham: "And ye shall circumcise the flesh of your foreskin; and it shall be a token of a covenant betwixt me and you." "So baptism is the external sign of internal grace; the seal or token of the covenant."

Again; "Circumcision was a symbol of moral cleansing, 'And the Lord thy God will circumcise thy *heart*, and the *heart* of thy seed, to love the Lord thy God with all thy heart, and with all thy soul, that thou mayest live.'" So, "Baptism is not the putting away the filth of the flesh"—not an external washing or cleansing—but is "the washing of regeneration, and renewing of the Holy Ghost;" that is, is symbolical of an internal work of grace in the heart.

Again, if children were fit subjects of circumcision, they are equally fit subjects of baptism. And if it be inquired, as it sometimes is, What good does it do a young child to baptize it? we might reply, What good it did a young child to circumcise it? In the latter case it admitted the child to church-membership, and in the former case it does the same. What more than this does it do in the case of an adult?

4. "The designation of the subjects of baptism by general terms." "All Jerusalem, and all Judea, and all the country round about Jordan, went out to him—John—and were baptized by him." The term, all Jerusalem, &c., refers, of course, to the people of Jerusalem and the other places named, and must include infants as well as adults, for it is a well-established fact that *infant* proselyte baptism was in use among the Jews from the institution of proselyte baptism, and its propriety never had been called in question. Then why should John reject them? and if John could not reject them, why should Christian ministers take upon themselves the fearful responsibility of rejecting infants from the privileges of Christian baptism? and that too in the absence of any express command to that effect. For my right hand, *I* would not dare to do it. The same general terms are employed in the apostolic commission, "Go disciple all nations, baptizing them," &c. Now, if "nations" includes children, then are children to be baptized.

5. "Baptism of households." We find that under the preaching of the apostles many believed and were baptized. Among those were the heads of families, Lydia, the Philippian jailer, and Stephanus. Now, were these believers baptized and admitted to the privileges of the Christian Church and their families left behind, to grope their way through Jewish formality or pagan superstition? Not so; they were baptized, with their households, and thus parents and children were proselyted to the Christian Church.

6. "Testimony of the early Christian fathers." We allude not to their testimony for the purpose of proving a point of doctrine, but for the purpose of showing what was the practice of the early Christians in regard to infant baptism; and we consider this testimony valuable, so far only, as it proves that

infant baptism was the general practice of the Christian Church from the time of the apostles, and if so, it is morally impossible that it should not have been practised *during* the time of the apostles. Tertullian, born A.D. 150—but a few years after the death of the apostle John—speaks of infant baptism as being the practice of the church. Justin Martyr, born near the close of the first century, speaks of those who were members of the church, sixty years old, who were made disciples to Christ in their *infancy*. Irenæus, Origen, Cyprian, and others, in their writings, all prove the practice of infant baptism in the earliest ages of the church: and can it be supposed that a practice should become so general in the course of a single century after the death of the apostles? if so be, it was something entirely new and unscriptural. The supposition is perfectly unreasonable. From these and other considerations, it appears that the "baptism of young children ought to be retained in the church," according to the Article.

4th. The *mode* of baptism may now be considered; and on this point our remarks must necessarily be brief. In the Discipline of the Church it is ordered that "every adult person, and the parents of every child to be baptized, have the choice either of immersion, sprinkling, or pouring." So that the doctrine of the Methodist Church in regard to the mode of baptism may be summed up in these words: The application of water in any becoming mode, in the name of the Father, Son, and Holy Ghost.

Much that has been said in regard to the *nature* of baptism in preceding pages, will throw light on the *mode* of baptism, and if the Methodist Church admits the validity of immersion, as *a* mode of baptism, it by no means endorses that mode as the only one, for numerous reasons: and, 1st. The mode is not designated in Scripture. The command to be baptized is therein found, and if the meaning of *baptize*, is to cleanse, purify, &c., the mode by which the cleansing shall be performed, is left to the judgment of the administrator.

2d. There is no clear proof of the ordinance having been administered by immersion in a single case during the ministry of Christ and his apostles. Even the baptism of Christ by John, does not appear to have been by immersion, because (1.) It was not the customary mode of administering the rite among the Jews. (2.) This mode did not comport with the design of his baptism. He was baptized "to fulfil all righteousness"—the requirements of the Jewish law. In Lev. viii. 6, 12, 30, we find what was the mode of consecrating priests to the sacred office—"Moses brought Aaron and his sons, and washed them *with* water"—not *in* water. "He *poured* anointing oil upon Aaron's head, to sanctify him;" "He *sprinkled* the anointing oil and blood upon Aaron and his sons." Now, in compliance with this well-known custom among the Jews, Christ was baptized—washed—consecrated—by John, and formally inducted into the office of the Christian priesthood, and we maintain that his being immersed would have been an unmeaning ceremony, so far as the *mode* is concerned, and that only by sprinkling, pouring, or both, could the Saviour "fulfil all righteousness." (3.) The prepositions "into," "out of," and "from," in the Greek Testament, do not convey the idea of immersion, as every school-boy knows, who has studied the Greek language. Christ went up "*into* a mountain"—was he immersed in the mountain? "There came boats *from* Tiberias"—had they been immersed in Tiberias? The strong probability is, that Christ went down to Jordan to wash, in compliance with the Jewish custom of consecration. Having washed his hands, and probably his feet, in the water, John took of the liquid element, and poured and sprinkled it upon his person, and the Holy Ghost then lighted upon him. All this is in keeping with the *design* of his baptism: any other mode would have failed in expressiveness.

(4.) The baptism of the thousands on the day of Pentecost affords an evidence that immersion could not have been physically possible. Three thousand were baptized in the space of a few hours. Now, if each of the twelve apostles baptized - which is not at all certain—there would have been two hundred and fifty for each apostle to baptize, within these few hours; and think you that these three thousand could have been immersed in the small brook of Cedron, the receptacle of all the filth and refuse stuff of a large city like Jerusalem?

(5.) The baptism of the Philippian jailer, with his household, in the house, at midnight, is a proof that immersion could not have been the mode, as is also the baptism of Saul, "who arose,"—stood up—" and was baptized."

(6.) The fact that the "Spirit, the water, and the blood, are said to agree in one," is a proof that immersion cannot be the mode of baptism prescribed by the Holy Scriptures. These three "agree," partly in the design, and partly in the mode: and if we can be assured of the mode in which blood was anciently applied to the person, as a symbol of moral cleansing through the blood of Christ—which was invariably by sprinkling—then have we a criterion by which to judge of the proper mode of applying water to the candidate for baptism; and if we learn that the Spirit is said "to be shed on us," to "fall on us," to be "given" to us, to "descend," &c., then may we infer, that pouring or sprinkling are the authorized and proper modes of administering this important symbolical rite; while it is at the same time cheerfully admitted, that immersion is also valid—for those, who from conscientious motives prefer that mode.

ARTICLE XVIII.

OF THE LORD'S SUPPER.

"The supper of the Lord is not only a sign of the love that Christians ought to have among themselves, one to another, but rather is a sacrament of our redemption by Christ's death: insomuch that to such as rightly, worthily, and with faith receive the same, the bread which we break is a partaking of the body of Christ; and likewise the cup of blessing is a partaking of the blood of Christ.

"Transubstantiation, or the change of the substance of bread and wine in the supper of our Lord, cannot be proved by holy writ, but is repugnant to the plain words of Scripture, overthroweth the nature of a sacrament, and hath given occasion to many superstitions.

"The body of Christ is given, taken, and eaten in the supper, only after a heavenly and spiritual manner. And the means whereby the body of Christ is received and eaten in the supper is faith.

"The sacrament of the Lord's Supper was not by Christ's ordinance reserved, carried about, lifted up, or worshipped."

The former part of this article is designed to show what the Lord's Supper is, and the three latter clauses are designed to guard this sacred institution from the false views of the Roman Church, who believe that the body and blood of Christ are really and literally present in the sacrament; that as soon as the priest blesses the elements of bread and wine, a transubstantiation, or change of substance, takes place in these elements, and that they immediately become changed into flesh and blood, soul and divinity, so that the whole Christ is really and bodily present. The absurdity and blasphemy of this doctrine is so apparent, that we need not attempt to prove to the intelligent reader the falsity of a doctrine as unreasonable as it is monstrous.

The Lord's Supper is designated by different names in the New Testament. It is called the Eucharist—the Communion—the Sacrament—the Paschal feast—the Passover—all of which appellations are used to signify some particular property or design in this solemn ordinance: as a Eucharist it partakes of the nature of a solemn thanksgiving to God; as a communion, it shows the fellowship existing between Christ and his disciples, and between the disciples themselves; as a sacrament, it partakes of the nature of a solemn covenant engagement, entered into between the Saviour and his worshippers; as a Paschal feast, or Passover, it is designed to commemorate the sufferings and death of Christ, and in connection therewith, the deliverance wrought out for us by the same. The phrase

Lord's Supper, it is thought by some, was not applied by the Saviour or his apostles to this sacrament; as however it was used in reference to the last supper which Christ ate with his disciples, and the Eucharist was celebrated immediately after supper, it has grown into common use, and is so designated in the Article before us.

The design of this sacrament has perhaps been sufficiently stated, as above. We wish, however, further to say, that in partaking of the same, in commemoration of the sufferings and death of Christ, it is with strict reference to the *vicarious* nature of the atonement; not to commemorate his death as a martyr, or as the founder of a new dispensation, but as "God in Christ, reconciling the world unto himself," by his own blood. Thus we recognize the proper and essential divinity of our Lord, and for this reason we prefer not to join any, in the act of communing, who deny the vicarious nature of the atonement, or the Godhead of the "Man Christ Jesus." Unitarians, Socinians, and others of every grade or name, who deny these doctrines, or either of them, must excuse us if we refuse to partake with them, or neglect to invite them to partake with us at the Lord's table.

ARTICLE XIX.

OF BOTH KINDS.

"The cup of the Lord is not to be denied to the lay people; for both the parts of the Lord's Supper, by Christ's ordinance and commandment, ought to be administered to all Christians alike."

This Article has reference to the unscriptural and unreasonable practice of the Church of Rome, in withholding the cup from the laity in the administration of the Lord's Supper. Notwithstanding it is expressly and fully admitted by that church, that communion in both kinds was the practice of Christ and his apostles, as also of the primitive Christians, yet, by the decrees of councils, and the bulls of popes, anathemas are hurled against those who shall say that the laity of the church ought not to be denied the cup. Aside from the unscriptural character of the prohibition, is it not evident that the laity of that church are denied the sacrament of the Lord's Supper? If by the Lord's Supper is intended the eating of bread and the drinking of wine, as instituted by Jesus Christ; and if it can be celebrated with nothing less than bread and wine; then is it evident that the sacrament of the Eucharist is a thing unknown to the great body of the Roman Church, while denied the use of the cup, and if the definition of the "Church," as given by a former Article, is correct, namely, "a congregation of faithful men, where the pure word of God is preached, and the sacraments duly administered," then it follows, as a matter of necessity, that the Roman Church is no Church of Christ, because the sacraments are not duly administered, according to Christ's institution; or if a church, the clergy only constitute the same, as *they*, only, receive the communion in both kinds.

ARTICLE XX.

OF THE ONE OBLATION OF CHRIST, FINISHED UPON THE CROSS.

"The offering of Christ, once made, is that perfect redemption, pro pitiation, and satisfaction for all the sins of the whole world, both original and actual: and there is none other satisfaction for sin, but that alone. Wherefore, the sacrifice of masses, in the which it is commonly said, that the priest doth offer Christ, for the quick and the dead to have remission of pain or guilt, is a blasphemous fable, and dangerous deceit."

The former part of this Article endorses an important truth taught in God's holy word, namely, the *General Redemption* of our race, through the death and sufferings of our blessed Saviour.

The Christian world has long been divided in opinion in regard to the extent of the atonement; but as in our examination of this and other controverted points, our space is necessarily limited, we shall only be able to glance at the more prominent arguments which may be adduced in favor of the doctrine above alluded to, and in opposition to the one, taught in the system designated by the name of Calvinism. The latter term is used to signify that system of theology taught by John Calvin, in the sixteenth century, endorsed by the Westminster Assembly of Divines, and adopted by the Presbyterian churches of Scotland, the United States, and some other countries, as the body of divinity on which is founded the Articles of Faith, which distinguish the Calvinistic churches from those denominated Arminian.

The essence of the system called Calvinism, may be found in Calvin's Institutes, Westminster Confession of Faith, Confession of Faith of the Presbyterian Church in the United States, and in the Longer, and Shorter Catechisms. From these various sources may be collected the distinguishing features of the Calvinistic system. From the Confession of Faith of the Presbyterian Church in the United States, we will give a few extracts, that the reader may see the bearing which the Article has upon the doctrine of Particular Redemption.

1. "God, from all eternity, did, by the most wise and holy counsel of his own will, freely and unchangeably ordain whatsoever comes to pass." In this extract we are taught that *whatsoever* comes to pass, has been ordained by God from all eternity. The term "*whatsoever*," can be understood only in its legitimate sense, to mean, everything which comes to pass, whether good or evil, natural or moral, physical or mental; and whether predicated of devils, angels, or men; whether coming to pass in heaven, earth, or hell, all has been ordained of God.

2. "By the decree of God, for the manifestation of his glory, some men and angels are predestinated to everlasting life; and others foreordained to everlasting death." This language is so plain, that it seems impossible to misunderstand it, and by it the extent of the atonement must necessarily be limited to the number predestinated to eternal life.

3. "These angels and men thus predestinated and foreordained, are particularly and unchangeably designed; and their number is so certain, and definite, that it can neither be increased, nor diminished." In this Article, we are taught that the number of those predestinated to life, or foreordained to death, is unchangeably and unalterably fixed.

4. "Those of mankind that are predestinated unto life, God, before the foundation of the world was laid, according to his eternal and immutable purpose, and the secret counsel and good pleasure of his own will, hath chosen, in Christ, unto everlasting glory, out of his mere free grace and love, without any foresight of faith, or good works, or perseverance in either of them, or any other thing in the creature as conditions or causes, moving him thereto, and all to the praise of his glorious grace."

5. "Neither are any other redeemed by Christ, effectually called, justified, adopted, sanctified, and saved, but the elect only."

6. "The rest of mankind, God was pleased, according to the unsearchable counsel of his own will, to pass by, and ordain them to dishonor and wrath, for their sin, to the praise of his glorious justice."

7. "All those whom God has predestinated unto life, and those only, he is pleased effectually to call, by his word and Spirit, to grace and salvation, by Jesus Christ. This effectual call is of God's free and special grace alone; not from anything at all foreseen in man, who is altogether passive therein until quickened and renewed by the Holy Spirit."

8. "Elect infants dying in infancy are regenerated and saved

by Christ, through the Spirit; so also are all other elect persons. Others, not elected, although they may be called by the ministry of the word, and may have some common operations of the Spirit, yet they never truly come to Christ, and, therefore, cannot be saved."

In giving the above extracts to the reader we have selected those portions of the Calvinistic creed which have a bearing on the doctrine taught in the Article now under consideration; and by a comparison of these with the Article itself, the reader cannot fail to perceive a wide and essential difference between the teachings of Calvinism, on the one hand, and those of Methodism on the other. The doctrines taught in the above extracts appear to Methodists, and other Arminians, to be both unscriptural and unreasonable. Unscriptural, because we think them to be in direct opposition to the plainest declarations of Scripture; and unreasonable, because that, aside from Scripture, they stand opposed to a correct idea of the character and attributes of the Almighty, as entertained by the enlightened mind. Is it, we ask, either scriptural or reasonable to suppose that God from all eternity ordained *whatsoever* comes to pass? That every action of men, angels and devils was predetermined by God?

2. Is it scriptural or reasonable to suppose that by the decree of God some men and angels are predestinated to life and others to everlasting death?

3. Is it scriptural or reasonable to suppose that the number of the elect and reprobate are so fixed and definite that it cannot by any possible contingency be either increased or diminished?

4. Is it scriptural or reasonable that we should believe that those predestinated or elected to everlasting life are thus chosen without any foresight of faith or good works as conditions?

5. Is it a scriptural doctrine that none are redeemed by Christ but the elect only, while the "reprobate" are left with-

out any interest whatever in the great work of human redemption?

6. Is it either scriptural or reasonable to think that the reprobate are not only passed by without having any provision made for their salvation by Jesus Christ; but are positively ordained to hell and damnation, to dishonor and wrath, merely because Christ not having died for them their salvation is rendered absolutely impossible, not by any act of their own, but by a decree of God, made from all eternity, and then attribute to them the guilt and "sin" of being thus passed by or ordained to eternal death?

7. Is it in accordance with Scripture and reason to believe that while God in his word calls upon all the nations of the earth to look unto him and be SAVED, and commands *all* men everywhere to repent, believe, and obey, that none are designed to be effectually called but the elect only?

8. Is there any Scripture for dividing the infantile portion of mankind into "elect infants" and "reprobate infants;" and for declaring, that if the one class dies in infancy they are regenerated and saved, and of the other, that they "cannot be saved?"

We design not to answer these several questions argumentatively, but simply to state that the former part of the Article before us discards, in *toto*, the doctrine of particular redemption, and of election and reprobation, with its necessary adjunct *infant damnation.* And it is scarcely necessary to repeat the innumerable passages of Scripture which prove, beyond a doubt, that Christ died for the whole world of mankind, for we can scarcely open the New Testament without having our eyes rest on some passage of Scripture where the general redemption of our race is spoken of in the clearest and fullest manner, and that in fact, "The offering of Christ once made *is* a perfect redemption, propitiation, and satisfaction for *all* the sins of the WHOLE WORLD, both original and actual."

The latter part of the Article is aimed at the doctrine embraced in the sacrifice of the *mass*, in which it is said that as often as mass is celebrated Christ is offered or sacrificed anew for the sins of the people, both living and dead. It is not, of course, necessary to say that the pretensions of the Roman clergy, in this respect, are not only unreasonable and absurd, but are positively injurious to the interests of morals and true religion; for no Protestant can look upon the doctrine of the mass without pain and abhorrence.

ARTICLE XXI.

OF THE MARRIAGE OF MINISTERS.

"The ministers of Christ are not commanded by God's law, either to vow the estate of a single life, or to abstain from marriage: therefore, it is lawful for them, as for all other Christians, to marry at their own discretion, as they shall judge the same to serve best to godliness."

The doctrine of clerical celibacy, as taught and required by the Romish Church, is at war with the teachings of both the Old and New Testaments, and destructive of morals and the best interests of society. It was not until the fourth century that the celibacy of the clergy was required by the church, and since that time it has remained a law of the Roman Church that none of its ecclesiastically ordained priests, or other officers, shall contract marriage. The design of this prohibition is to render the clergy more completely subservient to the will of the Roman See, by preventing, as far as possible, the exercise of the social feelings; and it is a well-established fact, that this rule has been promotive of the worst effects, and proved destructive to the morality of even the highest dignitaries of the church, and hence Luther, well knowing the disastrous effects of such prohibition upon the morals of the clergy, wisely and boldly bid defiance to the pope, and the mandates of a corrupt church, by contracting marriage with a nun.

It may be proper here to observe, that in the British Wesleyan Conference a rule has obtained, by which the preachers of the connection are required to abstain from marriage during the time of their novitiate, or probation as preachers. This rule is designed, partly, to keep the younger preachers free from the cares of the world as much as possible during the four years of trial, so that they may have better opportunities for study, &c.; and partly to keep a sufficient number of single men in connection with the conference to supply those portions of the work with unmarried men where the societies are too small or feeble to support a number of preachers with their families. This rule, however, is not an absolute prohibition of marriage, but merely a deferment of this relation until such time as membership in the conference is secured. In other words, the *candidate* for the ministry may not contract marriage, but when he becomes a minister he is at perfect liberty to do so. In the Methodist Episcopal Church in the United States, no rule exists on the subject, except the one contained in this Article.

ARTICLE XXII.

OF THE RITES AND CEREMONIES OF CHURCHES.

"It is not necessary that rites and ceremonies should in all places be the same, or exactly alike: for they have always been different, and may be changed according to the diversity of countries, times, and men's manners, so that nothing be ordained against God's word. Whosoever, through his private judgment, willingly and purposely doth openly break the rites and ceremonies of the church to which he belongs, which are not repugnant to the word of God, and are ordained and approved by common authority, ought to be rebuked openly, that others may fear to do the like, as one that offendeth against the common order of the church, and woundeth the consciences of weak brethren.

"Every particular church may ordain, change, or abolish rites and ceremonies, so that all things may be done to edification."

The doctrine embraced by, and taught in this Article, is of great importance to the church of Christ in all its various branches, for were it necessary that the rites and ceremonies of the church should be in all places and times alike, inasmuch as a difference has obtained, and does obtain, it would be difficult to prove that Christ has a church on earth at all.

There are two things comprehended in the gospel of Christ in relation to his church. One is, that it *must* have what is essential to its existence and perpetuity; the other, that it may or may not have what is not thus essential. The essential appendages to a church are the Scriptures, a living ministry, and the sacraments; the non-essentials are a liturgy, or prescribed form of worship, with all other means of grace, not positively required by God in his word. We may illustrate this point by saying that baptism and the Lord's Supper are essential to the existence of the church; no church may therefore repudiate these ordinances; while love-feasts, class-meetings, confirmation, &c. &c., not being expressly required by the gospel, may, or may not be repudiated, by any branch of the church. So also in regard to the mode of administering the ordinances. That the ordinances of baptism and the Lord's Supper must be administered, is rendered certain by the plain commands of Christ and his apostles, but whether the former shall be administered by sprinkling, pouring, or immersion; or the latter be received while sitting, standing or kneeling, is nowhere stated, and any branch of the church may lawfully adopt such rules, in relation to such points, as may seem expedient and proper. The same course of reasoning will apply also to the government of the church. That a church should exist, is the revealed will of God; and that his church should have some kind of ecclesiastical government, is also rendered certain; but when we come to inquire into the particular form of church government, instituted by Christ and his apostles, we find ourselves without direct scriptural authority. Whether, therefore, a church shall be governed by an episcopacy, by a presbytery, or by itself, independently of all foreign ecclesiastical control, is a question not fully settled by divine revelation, and may be left to the enlightened judgment of individuals, or associated bodies of Christians, to decide for themselves. But in deciding for themselves, they have no right to decide peremptorily for others; every man having a natural right to decide for himself, in regard to these matters, so that he decides on nothing contrary to the word of God.

When an associated body of Christians, in the absence of an express rule in relation to ecclesiastical government, rites and ceremonies, adopt a form of church government for themselves, and ordain certain rites and ceremonies, to be used in the church, then it is not lawful for any one, through his own private judgment, wilfully and purposely to violate the rules and regulations of the church to which he belongs, provided those rules are not repugnant to the word of God, and provided, also, that his connection with such church is voluntary, and not the result of coercion. In either of the latter cases, we believe that a man would have the right to violate any ecclesiastical requirement, which, in his judgment, contravened the laws of God, or the right of voluntarily connecting himself where conscience and duty point out; but otherwise, it is the duty of every Christian to yield a hearty obedience to the requirements of the church of which he is voluntarily a member; and if, for conscience' sake, he cannot yield such obedience, then is it clearly his duty voluntarily to withdraw from the church—if such withdrawal is possible—and seek a connection with some other branch, whose requirements are more congenial with his views of Christian duty. To remain in the church, and refuse obedience to its wholesome requirements; or to withdraw from the church when such requirements are not repugnant to the word of God, is to involve ourselves in the guilt of schism, a sin which is pointedly condemned by the word of God, and is productive of great and lasting injury to the body of Christ; so that nothing short of imperious necessity should ever induce any person to be a promoter or abettor of division in the church of God, or to become a separatist from the church of his former choice.

There is, consequently, much importance to be attached to the due examination of doctrines and ceremonies of any church, before a person voluntarily connects himself with the same. The examination necessary, may require weeks, and even months, before an enlightened judgment can be formed in relation to these matters, by the young and inexperienced Christian, and we consider it an important feature in the polity of the Methodist Episcopal Church, that at least six months must be given to every candidate for membership, to make such examination, before membership is secured, thus guarding the candidate, on the one hand, against improper haste in forming a judgment, and the church, on the other hand, against the introduction of improper persons, by giving it an opportunity of judging of the correctness of their faith and practice.

ARTICLE XXIII.

OF THE RULERS OF THE UNITED STATES OF AMERICA.

"The President, the Congress, the general assemblies, the governors, and the councils of state, as the delegates of the people, are the rulers of the United States of America, according to the division of power made to them by the Constitution of the United States, and by the constitutions of their respective States. And the said States are a sovereign and independent nation, and ought not to be subject to any foreign jurisdiction."*

The above Article, with the note appended to it, is designed to show the views of the Methodist Episcopal Church in rela-

* "As far as it respects civil affairs, we believe it the duty of Christians, and especially all Christian ministers, to be subject to the supreme authority of the country where they may reside, and to use all laudable means to enjoin obedience to the powers that be; and, therefore, it is expected that all our preachers and people who may be under the British, or any other government, will behave themselves as peaceable and orderly subjects."

tion to the civil government of the United States, and also the duty of American Methodists, who may be residing under the protection of the British, or other foreign governments, to be obedient and peaceable subjects, while they remain under such protection. The Article itself was adopted at the time of the organization of the church in 1784, and the note was appended in the year 1820, " to meet the peculiar case of the brethren in Canada, against whom unfounded suspicions had been created, because the Methodist Episcopal Church, of which they were then a part, was regarded as a foreign ecclesiastical authority."

The doctrine taught, both in the Article, and in the note, is, that civil government is of divine origin, that the " powers that be, are ordained of God," and that " whosoever resisteth the power, resisteth the ordinance of God ;" but the Article does not say what particular form of civil government is ordained of God, or whether any such form is prescribed by the Ruler of the universe. Hence, the divine right of kings, or emperors, to reign and rule, is neither asserted, nor denied, while it is asserted and maintained, that the *delegates of the people* of the United States are the rulers of the same ; and that said States not only form a sovereign and independent nation, but ought not to be subject to any foreign jurisdiction. It will be clearly seen, then, that while the Methodist Church teaches subjection to all who are in authority over us, whether at home or abroad, it meddles not with questions of a purely civil and political character, any further than to require obedience to the laws and requirements of the commonwealth. The question now greatly agitated in the nation, whether obedience to all law is required by the gospel, and whether we are bound to yield such obedience to law, when judged to be unrighteous, is a point, which, not having been discussed by the church in her general councils, has, of course, not been formally decided, one way or the other. On this, as on all other points connected with human authority, there will be a variety of opinions entertained ; and while a Christian may not aid personally in the execution of any law which he honestly believes contravenes the laws and mandates of Jehovah, he may not, on the other hand, forcibly resist the execution of any law which the majority of his fellow-citizens have, by their delegates, thought to be necessary for the well-being of the body politic; while it will be incumbent upon him, as a part of the body politic, to labor, in every proper manner, for the repeal of such laws as he believes are opposed to the "higher law," or rule of right, established by the Creator. Thus far, we presume, there will be a unanimity of opinion among all the ministers and members of the Methodist Church. In the language of one of her sons, "The church, by its moral influence, should countenance and sustain the State; and the State protect the church: both institutions being equally of divine appointment, and equally indispensable to the good of society."*

ARTICLE XXIV.

OF CHRISTIAN MEN'S GOODS.

"The riches and goods of Christians are not common, as touching the right, title, and possession of the same, as some do falsely boast. Notwithstanding every man ought, of such things as he possesseth, liberally to give alms to the poor, according to his ability."

This Article is designed to guard men against the false notion that when a man becomes a Christian he loses his individual right to property, and that all that he has should be merged in one common fund. Whatever might be right under a *perfect social system*, it is very evident, as society is now constituted, a community of goods would do more harm than good; the indolent and improvident would prey upon the fruits of industry and economy, and the result would be the general prevalence of anarchy and confusion. It is maintained

* Comfort's Exposition, page 345.

by the advocates of the community system, that the early Christians, who "had all things in common," set an example which we ought to follow; but it is not certain that their course was designed as an example; the probability, nay, the moral certainty is, that it was not; neither is it certain that they had all things common in the sense of having no individual right to control any part thereof. It is true, that when they sold their possessions and goods, and made an offering thereof to the common stock, they lost the individual right to control it, while it is equally evident that by far the greatest portion of the early Christians retained a part of their goods in their own possession, from the fact that there existed among them a distinction between rich and poor, or those who gave and those who received alms, as in the case of Dorcas, the Hebrew widows, and those for whom collections in the churches were taken. The probability therefore is, that "having all things in common," is to be understood in a limited sense, and that the sale of their goods was a voluntary act, not enjoined by Christ or his apostles.

While, therefore, the principle of socialism is not enforced by the word of God, there is a principle recognized, a duty enforced, of giving to the poor according to our abundance; and this duty is of perpetual obligation, or as long as the distinction between rich and poor may be properly said to exist; and the fact that the State may, in some countries, make provision for its resident poor, does not, in our opinion, relieve the Church entirely, if at all, of the duty of giving alms to those who need. There always will be a class in society who are proper objects of charity, who will not avail themselves of any provision made for them by the civil government; and there are others—members of the church—whom it would be disgraceful to the Church of God to allow to become pensioners upon the bounties of the state designed for the poor; these classes must be cared for, their wants must be supplied, and the rich, out of their abundance, must supply these wants, and woe be to the man who, seeing his brother or sister in need, and who having the means to relieve their necessities, "shuts up his bowels of compassion against them."

ARTICLE XXV.

OF A CHRISTIAN MAN'S OATH.

"As we confess that vain and rash swearing is forbidden Christian men by our Lord Jesus Christ and James his apostle, so we judge that the Christian religion doth not prohibit but that a man may swear when the magistrate requireth, in a cause of faith and charity, so it be done according to the prophet's teaching, in justice, judgment, and truth."

The design of this Article is very apparent,—to discountenance the sin of profanity, and at the same time sanction judicial oaths, or oaths required to be taken in a court of justice, or before a magistrate. These oaths, in some form, are required to be taken by the subjects of all civilized countries, and indeed they may be considered a necessary appendage to the proper administration of justice under the present constitution of society. We say that oaths in some form are required to be taken; for whether we "swear by the ever-living God," to tell the truth, or simply "affirm" that we will tell the truth, the solemnity and binding nature of the asseveration is the same in the eye of human law, and we have no doubt is considered as equally sacred and binding by the great Lawgiver of the universe.

The Quakers and some other conscientious persons, refuse to take judicial oaths, on the ground that all swearing is forbidden by the Saviour. Now, while we honor the conscientious scruples of all men, we cannot but think that an improper view is taken of the meaning of the Saviour in the above prohibition. By reading the context carefully the reader will no doubt perceive that the kind of swearing prohibited by Christ is not that required by the civil magistrate, but that of which the Jews were notoriously guilty, swearing falsely by the temple, by the throne of God, and that too when not required to do it by the civil magistrate. That the latter was the meaning of the Saviour, to us is abundantly evident from the fact that when placed upon his trial before the high-priest, he was sworn by the latter to tell the truth. The practice of swearing criminals was common among the Jews, and the form of oath to them administered was in these words, "I adjure thee by the living God to answer, whether the thing be so or not." Now, this very oath, in substance, was administered to Christ, and had he considered it unlawful to take such an oath, he no doubt would have refrained from answering, but instead of this, he immediately replies to the adjuration of the high-priest, thus showing that while he discountenanced profanity in all its forms, he sanctioned the administration of judicial oaths. That judicial oaths are proper is also evident from what the apostle Paul says in relation to them, "An oath for confirmation is to them an end of all strife." Now, had such oaths been unlawful and forbidden, the apostle, no doubt, would have considered it his duty to have said so when speaking of the subject, but instead of this he uses it as an illustration, and then proceeds to show that "God confirmed his promise to Abraham by an oath." These considerations prove the doctrine in the Article to be correct, and show conclusively that while it is forbidden to swear profanely, it is right to swear when judicially required to do so.

APPENDIX TO THE ARTICLES.

In our Introduction to the Articles of Religion, we intimated that there are certain doctrines of Methodism not clearly stated in the same. The reason for this is not to be traced to an unwillingness on the part of the church to publish to the world all that she believes, but to the simple fact, that with the exception of the one which refers to the "Rulers of the United States," the Articles were all prepared for the church by Mr. Wesley himself. Mr. Wesley being a minister of the Church of England, very naturally and properly selected such Articles from the Common Prayer Book which he judged contained sound and wholesome doctrine; while those which admitted of dispute, as it regards their true meaning, were omitted. But while omitting some of the Articles, he did not feel himself at liberty to supply their place with others of his own making; hence several important doctrines which are taught by the Methodists in all parts of the world, are not even alluded to in the Articles of Religion. While a strong disposition to venerate, just as it is, whatever came from the hand of the founders of Methodism, has hitherto prevented the alteration or the addition of any other Articles to the original twenty-five; and more especially as in the constitution of the church it is expressly said that "the General Conference shall not revoke, alter, or change our Articles of Religion;" and as in the provision made for the alteration of the constitution, whereby every other Article of the same may be changed, the above clause is carefully excepted. While, therefore, it might have been desirable, when the church was organized, that all the important features of Methodist theology should have been embodied in the Articles, and is a matter of regret to some that they were not; yet we have reason to be thankful to the great Head of the Church that there has been no disposition manifested to modify or change the existing Articles. While it is also a matter of thankfulness that in Wesley's sermons, and in other standard writings of the church, the important doctrines which are omitted in the Articles, or are but incidentally alluded to, are in the former clearly taught, and by the present race of Methodist ministers are faithfully preached. Among these important doctrines referred to, are the doctrine of the *Witness of the Spirit;* the *Sanctification of believers; the possibility of falling from Grace;* and the doctrine of *Eternal Rewards and Punishments.*

I.

ON THE WITNESS OF THE SPIRIT.

The witness of the Spirit of God that we are the children of God, is one of the glorious privileges of believers; but to understand this subject fully, as taught by Mr. Wesley, we will make a few extracts from his Sermon on Rom. viii. 16, "The Spirit itself beareth witness with our spirit that we are the children of God."

"I. The witness, or testimony of our own spirit." "With regard to the testimony of a Christian's own spirit, the foundation of this is laid in numerous texts of Scripture, which describe the marks of the children of God, and that very plainly." "This may be still further aided by the ministry of the word, meditation, and religious conversation. And every man, using the understanding which God has given him, and which religion was designed to improve, by applying those Scripture marks to himself, may know whether he is a child of God: For instance, 1 John ii. 3, 5, 29: 'And hereby we do know that we know him, if we keep his commandments.—But whoso keepeth his word, in him verily is the love of God perfected: hereby know we that we are in him.—Ye know that every one that doeth righteousness is born of him.'—iii. 4, 19, 24; iv. 13; v. 18. Probably, from the beginning of the world, none of the children of God were ever farther advanced in the grace of God, and the knowledge of Christ, than the apostle John, and those to whom he wrote at that time. Yet they did not despise these marks of being God's children, but applied them to their own hearts, for the confirmation of their faith. Yet all this testimony is no other than rational; the witness of our own spirit, our reason, or understanding. It all resolves itself into this: those who have these marks, these are God's children; but we have these marks, therefore we are his children. But how does it appear that we have these marks—that we love God and our neighbor, and that we keep God's commandments? The question does not mean, how does it appear to *others*, but to *ourselves*. As easily as you can know whether you are alive, in pain, or in ease, may you know whether you are saved from proud wrath, and have the ease of a meek and quiet spirit; whether you love your neighbor as yourselves; whether you are kindly-affectioned, gentle, and long-suffering; whether you outwardly keep God's commandments, by living godly, righteous, and sober lives. This is properly the testimony of our own spirit. It is a consciousness of our having received in, and by the spirit of adoption, the tempers mentioned in the word of God, as belonging to his adopted children.

"But what is the testimony of God's Spirit, which is superadded to, and conjoined with this? How does he bear witness with our spirit, that we are the children of God? It is hard to find words in the language of men, to explain the *deep things of God.* But perhaps one might say, the testimony of the Spirit is an inward impression on the soul, whereby the Spirit of God directly witnesses to my spirit, that I am a child of God; that Jesus hath loved *me*, and given himself for *me;*

that all my sins are blotted out, and *I*, even *I*, am reconciled to God.

"This testimony of the Spirit of God must, in the very nature of things, go before the testimony of our own spirit. We must be holy in heart and life, before we can be conscious that we are so. But we must love God before we can be holy at all; this being the root of all holiness. Now we cannot love God till we know he loves us. And we cannot know his pardoning love to us, till his Spirit witness it to our spirit. Since, therefore, this testimony of his Spirit must precede the love of God, and all holiness, of consequence it must precede our inward consciousness thereof, or the testimony of our own spirit concerning them.

"He that loves God, and delights and rejoices in him with an humble joy, a holy delight, and an obedient love, is a child of God; but I thus love, delight, and rejoice in God: therefore I am a child of God: then a Christian cannot doubt of his being a child of God. Of the former proposition he has as full assurance, as he has that the Scriptures are of God; and of his thus loving God, he has an inward proof, which is nothing short of self-evident.

"The *manner* how the divine testimony is manifested to the heart, I do not take upon me to explain. See John iii. 8. But we know the *fact*, namely, that the Spirit of God gives a believer such a testimony of his adoption, that while it is present to the soul, he can no more doubt the reality of his sonship, than he can doubt of the shining of the sun, while he stands in the full blaze of heaven. But,

"II. How may this joint testimony of God's Spirit and of our own spirit, be clearly distinguished from presumption of mind, and the delusions of Satan? (1.) The Holy Scriptures abound with marks, distinguishing the one from the other. They describe repentance as constantly going before this witness of pardon. (2.) The Scriptures describe the being born of God, which must precede the witness that we are his children, as a change no less than from darkness to light, as well as from the power of Satan unto God. And (3.) The Scriptures describe the joy accompanying the witness of the Spirit, as tending to promote humility. In the presumptuous, deceived man, it is the contrary. Instead of being humble, meek, gentle, teachable, slow to hear, and slow to wrath, he is haughty, assuming, quick to hear, and swift to speak, fiery, vehement, and eager in his conversation: yea, sometimes there is a fierceness in his air and manner of speaking, as well as of his whole deportment, as if he were going to take the matter out of God's hands, and himself to devour his adversaries. (4.) The Scriptures teach, 'This is the love of God—the sure mark thereof—that we keep his commandments.' The genuine lover of God will do his will. But with the presumptuous pretender to the love of God, it is otherwise. He is not zealous, watchful over his tongue, and heart, nor anxious to deny himself, and take up his cross. It follows, from undeniable evidence, that he cannot have the true testimony of his own spirit. He cannot be conscious of having those marks which he has not, nor can the Spirit of God bear witness to a lie; or testify that he is a child of God, when he is manifestly a child of the devil.

"III. What is the witness of the Spirit? The original word may be rendered either *the witness*, or (less ambiguously), *the testimony*, or *the record.* 1 John v. 11. I do not mean to say, that the Spirit of God testifies this by an outward voice; no, nor always by an inward voice, although he may do this sometimes. Neither do I suppose that he always applies some Scripture to the heart, though he often may do this. But he so works upon the soul by his immediate influence, and by a strong though inexplicable operation, that the stormy winds and troubled waves subside, and there is a sweet calm: the heart resting in the arms of Jesus, and the sinner being clearly satisfied that God is reconciled, and that all his *iniquities are forgiven, and his sins covered.* That there is a testimony of the Spirit, is acknowledged by all parties. And it is not questioned whether there is an *indirect* witness or testimony that we are the children of God. This is nearly, if not exactly the same with the testimony of a good conscience towards God. Nor do we assert there can be any real testimony of the Spirit, without the fruit of the Spirit. We assert, on the contrary, that the fruit of the Spirit immediately springs from this testimony. But the point in question is, whether there be any direct testimony of the Spirit at all? Whether there be any other testimony of the Spirit than that which arises from a consciousness of the fruit—I believe there is.

"IV. 'The Spirit itself beareth witness with our spirit, that we are the children of God.' It is manifest that there are two witnesses mentioned, who together testify the same thing—the Spirit of God, and our own spirit. But what is the witness of the Spirit? See verse 15—'Ye have received the Spirit of adoption, whereby we cry, Abba, Father,' and Gal. iv. 6, 'And because ye are sons, God hath sent forth the Spirit of his Son into your hearts, crying, Abba, Father.' And experience agrees with the Scripture testimonies. It has been confirmed by a cloud of living and dying witnesses. It is confirmed by the experience of many at the present day. And it is sanctioned by this additional consideration, that all those who are awakened out of the sleep of sin, cannot be satisfied with anything short of the direct witness of God's Spirit that they are pardoned."

We might enlarge our extracts from the valuable writings of Mr. Wesley on this subject, but we have probably quoted enough to show the views of the Methodist Church on this important branch of Christian doctrine. From these extracts we learn that the order of operation is, (1.) Repentance. (2.) Faith. (3.) Pardon. (4.) The witness of God's Spirit. (5.) The fruits of the Spirit. (6.) The witness of our own spirits; and that this is the scriptural arrangement, or order of operation, there can be no doubt, any more than that the direct witness of the Spirit is given to the children of God. A few scriptural quotations bearing on the latter point, will close this Article. "We *know* that we have passed from death unto life, because we love the brethren." "Beloved, now are we the sons of God, and it doth not yet appear what we shall be, but we *know* that when he shall appear, we shall be like him, for we shall see him as he is." 1 John iii. 2, &c. "For God hath revealed them to us, by his Spirit; for the Spirit searcheth all things, yea, the deep things of God." 1 Cor. ii. 12. Many other passages might be given, but the above must suffice.

II.

OF THE SANCTIFICATION OF BELIEVERS.

The doctrine of entire sanctification is one of the important and distinguishing doctrines of the Methodist Church. The *thing* intended by the term *entire sanctification*, is frequently called by other names equally expressive and comprehensive: as, *Christian perfection*, *perfect love*, *holiness of heart*, *supreme love to God*, &c. In the statement of this doctrine, we feel it important to abide by the old landmarks, and will accordingly give the views of the church, in Mr. Wesley's own language, as found in his sermon on Christian Perfection. In this sermon he inquires, "(1.) In what sense Christians are not; (2.) in what sense they are perfect."

"(1.) In what sense they are not. They are not perfect in knowledge. They are not free from ignorance—no, nor from mistake. We are no more to expect any living man to be infallible, than to be omniscient. They are not free from infirmities, such as weakness, and slowness of understanding, irregular quickness or heaviness of imagination. Such, in another kind, are impropriety of language, ungracefulness of pronunciation; to which one might add a thousand nameless defects either in conversation or behavior. From such infirmities as these, none are perfectly freed, till their spirits return to God; neither can we expect, till then, to be wholly freed from temptation; for 'the servant is not above his master.' But neither in this sense is there any absolute perfection upon earth. There is no perfection of degrees, none which does not admit of a continual increase.

"(2.) In what sense they are perfect. Observe, we are not now speaking of babes in Christ, but adult Christians. But even babes in Christ are so far perfect as not to commit sin. This, St. John affirms expressly; and it cannot be disproved by the examples of the Old Testament. For what if the holiest of the ancient Jews did commit sin? We cannot infer from hence, that 'all Christians do, and must commit sin, as long as they live.'

"But does not the Scripture say, 'A just man sinneth seven times a day?' It does not. Indeed, it says, 'A just man falleth seven times;' but this is quite another thing; for, First, the words 'a day' are not in the text. Secondly, here is no mention of falling into sin at all. What is here mentioned, is, falling into temporal affliction.

"But elsewhere Solomon says, 'There is no man that sinneth not.' Doubtless thus it was in the days of Solomon; yea, and from Solomon to Christ there was then no man that sinned not. But whatever was the case with those under the law, we may safely affirm, with St. John, that since the Gospel was given, 'he that is born of God, sinneth not.'

"The privileges of Christians are in no wise to be measured by what the Old Testament records concerning those who were under the Jewish dispensation; seeing the fulness of time is now come, the Holy Ghost is now given, the great salvation of God is now brought to men, by the revelation of Jesus Christ. The kingdom of heaven is now set up on earth, concerning which the Spirit of God declared of old time (so far is David from being the standard or pattern of Christian perfection,) 'He that is feeble among them at that day, shall be as David;

and the house of David shall be as the angel of the Lord before them.'

"'But the apostles committed sin; Peter, by dissembling, Paul, by his sharp contention with Barnabas.' Suppose they did, will you argue thus—'If two of the apostles once committed sin, then all other Christians, in all ages, do, and must commit sin, as long as they live?' Nay, God forbid we should thus speak. No necessity for sin was laid upon them; the grace of God was surely sufficient for them. And it is sufficient for us at this day.

"But St. James says, 'In many things we offend all.' True, but who are the persons here spoken of? Why, those many masters or teachers whom God had not sent; not the apostle himself, nor any real Christian. That in the word *we*, used by a figure of speech common in all other as well as the inspired writings, the apostle could not possibly include himself, or any other true believer, appears, first, from the ninth verse, 'Therewith bless *we* God, and therewith curse *we* men.' Surely not *we* apostles! not *we* believers! Secondly, from the words preceding the text: 'My brethren, be not many masters—or teachers—knowing that we shall receive the greater condemnation. For in many things we offend all.' We! Who? Not the apostles, nor true believers, but they who were to receive the 'greater condemnation,' because of those many offences. Nay, thirdly, the verse itself proves that 'we offend all,' cannot be spoken either of all men, or of all Christians; for in it immediately follows the mention of a man who offends not as the *we* first mentioned did; from whom, therefore, he is professedly contradistinguished and pronounced a 'perfect man.'

"But St. John himself says, 'If we say that we have no sin we deceive ourselves;' and 'if we say we have not sinned, we make him a liar, and his word is not in us.'

"I answer, (1.) The tenth verse fixes the sense of the eighth: 'If we say we have no sin,' in the former, being explained by,

'If we say we have not sinned' in the latter verse. (2.) The point under consideration is not whether we have, or have not sinned heretofore; and neither of these verses asserts that we do sin or commit sin now. (3.) The ninth verse explains both the eighth and tenth: 'If we confess our sins, he is faithful and just,' not only to forgive us our sins, but also to cleanse us from all unrighteousness, that we may 'go and sin no more.' In conformity, therefore, both to the doctrine of St. John and the whole tenor of the New Testament, we fix this conclusion: a Christian is so far perfect as not to commit sin.

"This is the glorious privilege of every Christian, yea, though he be but a babe in Christ. But it is only of grown Christians it can be affirmed they are in such a sense perfect, as, secondly, to be freed from evil thoughts and evil tempers. From sinful or evil thoughts. Indeed, whence should they spring? 'Out of the heart of man,' if at all, 'proceed evil thoughts.' If, therefore, the heart be no longer evil, then evil thoughts no longer proceed out of it; for, 'a good tree cannot bring forth evil fruit.'

"And as they are freed from evil thoughts, so likewise from evil tempers. Every one of these can say, with St. Paul, 'I am crucified with Jesus; nevertheless I live; yet not I, but Christ liveth in me;' words that manifestly describe a deliverance from inward, as well as from outward sin. 'For what communion hath light with darkness, or Christ with Belial!'

"He, therefore, who liveth in these Christians, hath 'purified their hearts by faith,' insomuch that every one who has 'Christ in him the hope of glory,' 'purifieth himself even as he is pure.' He is purified from pride, for Christ was lowly in heart; he is pure from desire and self-will, for Christ desired only to do the will of his Father; and he is pure from anger in the common sense of the word, for Christ was meek and gentle.

"Thus doth 'Jesus save his people from their sins;' not only outward sins, but from the sins of their hearts. 'True,' says some, 'but not till death, not in this world.' Nay, St. John says, 'Herein is our love made perfect that we may have boldness in the day of judgment; because as he is so are we *in this world.*' 'If we walk in the light, as he is in the light, we *have* fellowship one with another, and the blood of Jesus Christ, his Son, *cleanseth* us from ALL SIN!' Now, it is evident that the apostle speaks of a deliverance wrought in this world, for he saith not the blood of Christ *will* cleanse at the hour of death, or in the day of judgment, but it *cleanseth* at the time present us living Christians from all sin."

Much more might be added from the excellent sermon in which the above extracts are found, but we have stated enough to show what were the views of Mr. Wesley in regard to the doctrine of sanctification, or Christian perfection. And we may here remark that precisely the same views are entertained by the Methodist ministry of the present day in regard to this important branch of Christian theology, as are above taught by the venerated founder of Methodism; and what is still more pleasing, hundreds of them, as well as thousands of the laity, have the abiding witness that they love God with all the heart, and their lives and deportment evince the correctness of the testimony.

III.

OF THE POSSIBILITY OF FALLING FROM GRACE.

The question "May a child of God totally and finally fall from grace, so as to be eternally lost?" is purely a scriptural question, or rather a question which Scripture only can answer; and when thus answered, reason and common sense must unite in pronouncing the decision of Scripture correct. It is well known that the Methodist Church considers the answer of Scripture to be in the affirmative, and only in the affirmative of this question, and consequently that she repudiates the doctrine of the saints' *necessary* final perseverance. But to the law and to the testimony on this point; and—

1. The Old Testament plainly teaches the possibility of total and final apostasy. In Ezek. xviii. 24, it is said, "When the righteous turneth away from his righteousness and committeth iniquity; in his trespass that he hath trespassed, and in his sin that he hath sinned, shall he die." On this passage it may be remarked, (1.) That turning away from righteousness is predicated of the *righteous man*, which can only refer to a child of God. (2.) That the righteous man is supposed to *turn away* from his righteousness. (3.) That, having turned away from his righteousness, he *commits iniquity*. (4.) That having turned away and committed iniquity, IN *the iniquity* that he hath committed, and IN *the sin* he hath sinned, he shall die. (5.) That the iniquity and sin here alluded to is that which involves final and total apostasy, as is evident from the fact, that were it only a partial fall which is intended, then every act of religious dereliction would involve the transgressor in death. Hence, Moses, David, and Peter, all of whom sinned after having become the children of God, must necessarily have perished. (6.) The *death* alluded to in the passage is not the death of the body, for whether the righteous sin or no, they must die temporally; neither is it spiritual death which is alluded to, because the latter is the *consequence*, and not the concomitant of transgression; thus, "when lust hath conceived it bringeth forth sin; and sin when it is *finished* bringeth forth death;" and for yet another reason: in a succeeding verse it is said, "When a righteous man turneth away from his righteousness and committeth iniquity and *dieth in them;* FOR his iniquity that he hath done shall he die;" giving us plainly to understand, that if the backslider from God *dies in* his iniquity, that is, dies temporally, then *for* his iniquity he shall also die, that is, suffer the pains of eternal death. Other passages of the Old Testament might be adduced in support of the doctrine under consideration, but the above are sufficient to prove what

was Jewish theology on that point, as taught by the prophet of God.

2. Let us now inquire what the New Testament says in reference to the same thing.

Paul, in 1 Tim. i. 18, 19, says, "War a good warfare; holding faith and a good conscience; which some having put away, concerning faith have made shipwreck." From these words it is evident, (1.) That Hymenius and Alexander—to whom the apostle refers—had once been in possession of faith, otherwise they could not have put it away. (2.) Their faith was of the right kind; it was possessed in connection with a *good conscience*, and both were of the kind which Paul exhorted Timothy to hold, or retain. (3.) These men, possessing faith and a good conscience, had put them away. (4.) They had made shipwreck of the same, implying that their faith and good conscience were irretrievably lost. (5.) Their final end is predicted by the apostle in another verse, "The Lord shall reward him—Alexander—according to his works;" his evil works, so that in the case of one, at least, of these backsliders the loss of the soul is surely predicated of one who had once saving faith.

In Rom. xi. 11, 17, and subsequent verses, Paul, in addressing his brethren, says, " Some of the branches are broken off, and thou art grafted in among them, and with them partakest of the root and fatness of the olive-tree. Be not high-minded, but fear: if God spared not the natural branches, take heed lest he spare not thee. Behold the goodness and severity of God: on them which fell severity, but toward thee goodness, if thou continue in his goodness, otherwise thou shalt be cut off." On this passage we remark, (1.) That the Roman believers are said to be grafted into the olive-tree, and to partake of the root and fatness thereof. (2.) Paul asserts in the 16th verse, that if the " root be holy so are the branches;" consequently these branches were holy. (3.) If these branches continued not in the goodness of God, they were to be cut off as were the natural branches—the Jews. (4.) When a branch is broken off from the parent tree it must die, unless grafted in again. (5.) No promise or intimation is given that when cut off those branches should ever be restored.

A similar figure is employed by our Saviour when discoursing with his disciples, as recorded in John xv. 2, "Every branch in me that beareth not fruit he—the Father—taketh away;" and again, in verse 5, "If a man abide not in me he is cast forth as a branch, and is withered." Here observe, (1.) That Christ represents his disciples as branches of the true vine: "I am the true vine," verse 1. (2.) That if any of the branches abide not in Christ, the Father taketh them away. (3.) That when cast forth as a branch they are withered—become dry, dead, and fit only for fuel. (4.) That while in this dry and withered state they are, as the figure shows, "gathered and burned;" a fearful evidence that those who are *in* Christ Jesus, if they abide not in him, they shall necessarily perish.

Another evidence of the possibility of total and final apostasy is found in John xvii. 17, and the following verses: "Holy Father, keep through thy name those whom thou hast given me, that they may be one, as we are;" "those that thou gavest me I have kept, and none of them is lost, but the son of perdition." We here observe, (1.) That the persons spoken of were given to Christ by the Father. (2.) That the object of thus giving them to Christ was, that they might be one with him as he was one with the Father. (3.) That this unity or oneness implied a sameness of spirit, of interests, and of enjoyments; in other words, those given to Christ were really and truly his, as adopted sons. (4.) That, notwithstanding this unity and adoption, one of them was lost—the son of perdition. (5.) That this loss was total and final, is abundantly proved by the Scriptures which record his fall, his violent death, and the forfeiture of his privileges as a Christian and Christian minister. From these privileges "Judas, by transgression, *fell*." Acts i.

25. Now, how could he fall if he never had stood? How could Christ have lost him if he never had him?

In Matt. xxv. 1–12, is recorded the parable of the Ten Virgins, five of whom had evidently grace in their hearts, but who, through carelessness and improvidence, neglected to keep in store a good supply against the evil day, and who in consequence of such neglect were shut out in outer darkness. But not to detain the reader with a critical examination of this passage, we pass to notice another of great importance in the settlement of this controverted point.

Heb. vi. 4, 5, 6, "For it is impossible for those who were once enlightened, and have tasted of the heavenly gift, and were made partakers of the Holy Ghost, and have tasted the good word of God, and the powers of the world to come, if they shall fall away, to renew them again unto repentance; seeing they crucify to themselves the Son of God afresh, and put him to an open shame." It is generally admitted that the persons spoken of in this passage are true believers. Should any doubt this fact they will observe, (1.) That the persons spoken of were *once enlightened.* (2.) They had *tasted* of the heavenly gift. (3.) They *were made partakers of the Holy Ghost,* in its regenerating and sanctifying influences. (4.) They had tasted of the good word of God; and, (5.) Of the powers of the world to come. An expression significant of a very high degree of grace, similar to that enjoyed by the apostle Paul, who in his state of rapture was borne aloft to the third heavens, and saw things and heard words that it was "not lawful for man to utter;" a state where the body becomes the temple of the Holy Ghost, and heaven the scene of the soul's rapturous delight. All these considerations prove that the persons spoken of in the text were true believers, and that too of the most exalted character. But these believers might fall away.

"If they shall fall away," has been rendered by good biblical critics, "*have fallen away;*" but, not to insist on this ren dering, the fearful possibility of apostasy is as plainly and clearly taught in the text as it is possible for language to teach it; for, were it impossible that these should fall, it would be not only improper but dishonest in the apostle to predicate the opposite of what is true in the matter. Paul was not in the habit, we opine, of trifling with the feelings of his Christian brethren, nor of "handling the word of God deceitfully." Admitting, then, the possibility of their falling away, the question occurs, "How far could they fall?" (1.) This falling away is not a mere partial declension in religious feeling, or a mere temporary alienation from God, but a total and final apostasy from the faith of the gospel; a falling away so far and so low, that the wretched apostate "crucifies the Son of God afresh and puts him to an open shame"—not only sins against his Saviour openly and wickedly, and of set purpose exposes his Lord to the jeers and taunts of the ungodly; but actually glories in his shame. Would to God that we could believe that the present age afforded no examples of this kind of apostasy; but our own observation and knowledge in regard to what some men have been, and what they are now, constrains us to believe, that in the middle of the nineteenth century, there are many living, fearful examples of this kind of apostasy.

(2.) The impossibility of renewing such apostates to repentance is plainly asserted in the text. It is impossible to renew the grace of repentance in their hearts. Such has been the magnitude of their crimes against their Saviour, and the stubbornness and wickedness of their hearts, that it is not in the power of divine grace to renew them to repentance.

(3.) If it is impossible to renew the grace of repentance in the hearts of such apostates, then their doom is unalterably fixed, and their "damnation is sure."

In Heb. x. 26–29, we have another proof of the possibility of falling from grace, and of being finally lost. "If we sin wilfully after we have received the knowledge of the truth, there remaineth no more sacrifice for sin; but a certain fearful looking for of judgment and fiery indignation which shall devour the adversaries. He that despised Moses' law died without mercy: of how much sorer punishment shall he be thought worthy who hath trodden under foot the Son of God, and hath counted the blood of the covenant wherewith he was sanctified an unholy thing, and hath done despite to the Spirit of grace." This passage is fearfully pregnant with meaning. It teaches, (1.) That it is possible to sin wilfully after we have received the knowledge of the truth. (2.) That this sin may consist in wilfully treading under foot the Son of God; and in counting—esteeming—the blood of the covenant wherewith he was SANCTIFIED an unholy thing—a sin very similar in its nature and results to the sin against the Holy Ghost. (3.) That those who commit the above sin are worthy of a much sorer punishment than those who died under Moses' law, and as no punishment in time can be greater or sorer than the death of the body, so the *sorer* punishment reserved for these apostates from sanctifying grace is the eternal death of the soul.

In closing this Article, it may be proper to state a few reasonable objections against the doctrine of the necessary final perseverance of the saints.

1. We object to it because it is an essential link in the chain of Calvinism; a system which teaches that God has foreordained *whatsoever* comes to pass; that God has elected some men to eternal life, and doomed others to eternal death, without any foresight of the faith and good works of the one, or unbelief and evil works of the other; a system which teaches the possibility of the damnation of infants, and enforces the doctrines of the "horrible decrees."

2. We object to it because it effectually destroys man's free moral agency. Once converted, no will or power that man has in himself, can prevent his entrance into heaven. If he is as wicked as the devil, he must go to heaven, and he cannot help it if he would.

3. We object to this doctrine, because it tends to beget indifference and coldness on the part of Christians, and gives license to crime and immorality on the part of backsliders. The syren song of "once in grace, always in grace," has no doubt lured many to destruction.

4. We object to it again, because it draws an unwarrantable distinction between the sins of the believer, so called, and those of the unbeliever; to the latter it says, "sin, and you shall be lost;" to the former, "sin, and you must be saved," while God says to all—saints or sinners—"The soul that sinneth, it shall die."

5. We object to it, because it stands diametrically opposed to all those warnings, threatenings, expostulations, and declarations, made in the word of God in reference to the unfaithful. What do these warnings mean? does God trifle with the feelings and fears of his children? If not, these children may fall from grace, and be lost forever.

6. We object to the doctrine of necessary perseverance, finally, because it is opposed to all the conditional promises of the gospel. "Be thou faithful unto death," says Christ, "and I will give thee a crown of life." This doctrine, in substance, tells Christ not to be alarmed about his children, that they cannot possibly be otherwise than faithful; while to the latter it says, "If you fall into the most beastly, and accursed sins, you will have a 'little spark of grace' remaining, and the crown of life shall, and must be yours!"

IV.

OF ETERNAL REWARDS AND PUNISHMENTS.

The Methodists believe, as all know, that the rewards of the righteous, and the punishment of the wicked, in the future state, will be endless in duration. In reference to the eternal rewards of the righteous, it will not be necessary, in this Article, to make any remarks, as no believer in the Bible disputes this point of Christian theology. In reference to the eternal punishment of the wicked, it may be proper to state our views as briefly as possible, as we have already transcended our prescribed limits in this part of the work.

The doctrine, then, of the Methodist Church, is, that the punishment of the impenitent and incorrigible sinner, extends to a future state, and is endless in duration.

1. That sinners are punished after the death of the body, is evident, because some sins cannot possibly be punished in this life. Witness the suicide, and the inebriate, who dies in a fit of drunkenness; witness the highway robber and murderer, who falls by the hand of his victim. Now, either these receive no punishment at all; or they receive their punishment before the commission of their crimes, or they receive such punishment in a future state. Which is the most reasonable conclusion, we leave our readers to infer.

2. That there is future punishment in reserve for the wicked appears farther evident from the fact that virtue and vice, righteousness and wickedness, must affect men in the coming state of being. What! are all to share alike in the joys of heaven? The idea is absurd. "If there be any virtue," it will have its future reward, and if there be unrepented wickedness, it must have its punishment; Scripture and reason demand it.

3. The Scriptures abundantly teach the doctrine of future punishment. We read of the "lake of fire," of "outer darkness," of "hell," "torment," &c. &c., all of which are applied to the state or condition of sinners in the spirit world.

4. The fact of there being a day of general judgement, which we have elsewhere shown in our remarks on Article III., is proof of the future punishment of the wicked. If the day of judgment is future, then, of course, the punishment of the wicked is future, for it is after the judgment that the wicked

are said to "go away into everlasting punishment;" and "as it is appointed unto men once to die, and *after* this the judgment," so is it evident that the punishment of the wicked will be after death.

5. The phrases which are used to denote the entire period of man's earthly existence, and those which are employed to denote his punishment as a sinner, are so dissimilar as to render it morally certain that his punishment shall extend to a future state. On the one hand, his stay on earth is likened to a shadow, to vapor, to grass, to a weaver's shuttle; as being short, few, &c.; on the other hand, his punishment is represented as being of unlimited duration, as being forever and ever.

These considerations abundantly prove that the punishment of the wicked will extend beyond time. Another important question is, Will the punishment of the wicked be eternal? Universalism says no, the Bible and the Methodist Church say yes! which will the reader believe? That the Bible teaches the doctrine of endless punishment, must be evident to the candid and sincere inquirer after truth.

1. The terms employed to denote the duration of future punishment, prove its eternity. Everlasting, eternal, forever, forever and ever, unquenchable, dieth not, are all employed to signify the duration of punishment. These words literally mean endless, and any person who will take the trouble to examine a Greek or Hebrew lexicon, will find that the original, as well as the rendering, mean nothing more, and nothing less, literally, than perpetual, immortal, unintermitted, &c.

2. No stronger terms are used, nor can be used—for the good reason that there are no stronger ones—to denote the duration of the rewards of the righteous, than those employed to signify the duration of the punishment of the wicked. If this then is so, is it not clear that such punishment will be unlimited, or else that the happiness of the righteous will come to an end?

3. The free moral agency of man, and the conditionality of salvation, prove the eternity of punishment. As a moral agent, man is the subject of moral government; as a free moral agent, we contend—Universalism and Calvinism to the contrary notwithstanding—that man cannot be saved without the consent of his own will. Now, as salvation depends on his own choice, it must, in the nature of things, be conditional, and if conditional, then salvation may be lost; and if there is one truth more plainly revealed than another, in the word of God, it is the conditionality of salvation. Obey and live; disobey and die, is the substance of Scripture doctrine on this point.

4. Those Scriptures which contain warnings and threatenings of future, eternal wrath, prove the possibility of coming short of eternal salvation. These are so numerous, and so well known, that it seems unnecessary to repeat them. We will quote a few, and leave the entire subject with the reader. "He that believeth not, shall be damned." "These shall go away into everlasting punishment." "Let us therefore fear, lest a promise being left us of entering into his rest, any of you should seem to come short of it." "Depart, ye cursed, into everlasting fire, prepared for the devil and his angels." "Where their worm dieth not, and the fire is not quenched."

We have thus endeavored, as comprehensively as possible, to state in our remarks on the Articles of Religion, and in the Appendix thereto, the leading doctrines of the Methodist Episcopal Church. Our circumscribed limits have not allowed us to enlarge upon these as much as we should have done, had the work been entirely devoted to that subject. As it is, we believe that sufficient has been said to show the scriptural character of our doctrines, and to prove the fact that in deducing articles of religious faith from the Holy Scriptures, the church has not followed "cunningly devised fables," nor adopted the inventions of men as a standard of Christian theology in opposition to the express warrant of Scripture.

BOOK III.

POLITY OF EPISCOPAL METHODISM.

CHAPTER I

SECTION I.

INTRODUCTION.

As Mr. Wesley, under God, was the founder of the Methodist Societies, and the expounder of Methodist theology, so was he the originator of much that is peculiar to the ecclesiastical polity of all the different branches of the great Methodist body in all parts of the world.

While all these branches agree in regard to doctrines and mode of worship, it is well known that they differ somewhat from each other in relation to questions of church government. This difference of opinion might reasonably be expected, and while it is an admitted fact that Mr. Wesley and the Methodists generally, agree that there is no particular form of church government prescribed in the New Testament, and that "it is not necessary that rites and ceremonies should in all places be the same or exactly alike,"—Article of Religion XXII.—it remains but for each branch to adopt such a form of ecclesiastical polity as they believe will be most conducive to the well-being of the church, and which will better promote the glory of God. By such views and feelings, Mr. Wesley was no doubt governed in the establishment of the prudential rules peculiar to the Methodists, and with such design he instituted forms of government for his societies in Europe and America; and if these forms differ, it is because the circumstances and condition of the people in these different countries required a difference to be made: hence, while in England we find one form of government instituted for the Methodists by Mr. Wesley in his deed of declaration; by the appointment of Dr. Coke to the superintendency of the Methodist Societies in America, and the provision made for the ordination of ministers of different grades, we find a different form for the latter. In the one case we find a purely Presbyterian form of church government, and in the other, a form partaking partly of the Presbyterian and partly of the Episcopalian.

That Mr. Wesley did design to establish a moderate Episcopacy for the Methodist Church in America we have no more doubt than that such an Episcopacy was actually established. The enemies of our church organization have, it is true, called in question the correctness of this position, and a Methodist Episcopal writer, in his work on "The Genius and Mission of Methodism,"—recently published,—has ventured the opinion, that "the idea of ordaining a bishop for the infant church in America never entered Wesley's mind," and that "he never conceived the idea of organizing through him (Dr. Coke) an Episcopal Church in America, in the strict and proper sense of that term."* Yet, notwithstanding the above expressed doubts, after a careful investigation of the whole subject, we are "more than ever convinced" that Mr. Wesley did design the establishment of an Episcopal Church in the "strict and proper sense of that term." Among the reasons which incline us to this opinion are the following:—

1. The preparation, by Mr. Wesley, of the Liturgy, or "Sunday Service of the Methodists in North America; with other occasional Services. London: 1784." This liturgy contained, among other things, "the form and manner of making and ordaining, of superintendents, elders, and deacons."† Now,

* Strickland on Methodism, page 35.
† History of the Discipline, page 25.

in view of the above facts, it may well be asked, what meant Mr. Wesley by his threefold form of ordination, if he intended simply the organization of a Presbyterian Church? Why require the ordination of ministers, first, as deacons, then as presbyters; and, in case of superintendency, a third and distinct ordination to that office? That ordination to the latter office was not merely an *appointment* thereto, is evident from the fact, that Coke and Asbury were both *appointed* joint superintendents by Mr. Wesley, while the former, as an *ordained* superintendent, was directed to *set apart* the latter—who had been already *appointed*—to the same same sacred office.

2. In the Discipline of the Methodist Episcopal Church, chap. i. sec. 1, we read, that Mr. Wesley, "preferring the *Episcopal* mode of church government to any other, set apart Thomas Coke—for the *Episcopal* office; and directed him to set apart Francis Asbury for the *same office.*" These words are found in the edition of the Discipline published in 1789, or two years previously to the death of Mr. Wesley, and the question very naturally arises, whether it is probable that such a barefaced falsehood would appear on the page of Discipline, subject to the inspection of Mr. Wesley, if so be it was and is a falsehood—and that Mr. Wesley did not conceive the idea of organizing, through Dr. Coke, an Episcopal Church in America? Common respect for the memory of the fathers and founders of Episcopal Methodism forbids us even to harbor the thought of deception on this point, and we regret that any Episcopal Methodist minister should, even by implication, throw disrespect and distrust upon the motives and character of the illustrious dead, or virtually accuse the church of perpetuating on the very first page of its Book of Discipline a falsehood as gross as the above must be, if so be that no Episcopal form of government was intended by Mr. Wesley.

Having felt it our duty to make these preliminary remarks in relation to the origin of Methodist Episcopacy, we are now more fully prepared to speak of the nature of such Episcopacy, as well as of the different grades in the ministry and laity of the church.

In what sense is the Methodist Episcopal Church in the United States an Episcopal Church? In attempting a reply to this question, such as shall be understood by the general reader, it will be necessary to show in what sense it is not Episcopal, as well as in what sense it is. And, first, the Methodist Church is not Episcopal in the *Roman Catholic* sense of that term.

In an early day Christianity was planted in the imperial city of Rome, through the labors of the apostle Paul. After a lapse of time, the inhabitants became Christians, and during the reign of Constantine, Christianity became the established religion of the Roman Empire. At this period the empire contained about one hundred and twenty provinces, each province embracing many cities, towns and villages. In the course of time each village and town had its Christian minister, and the cities had several of these. It was soon found convenient to exercise an oversight of the more obscure clergy, and, as might naturally be supposed, the more prominent of the city ministers were selected for that purpose. It was necessary that some one should preside as moderators in the assemblies of the clergy appertaining to a city or province, the most distinguished were selected to that office; and what at first was merely an office, became in due time a separate order in the church; hence the origin of diocesan bishops. Soon it was found convenient to have an overseer of the bishops, hence arose archbishops. As these multiplied, it was thought necessary to have some one who should be superior to all others in ecclesiastical authority and dignity, hence arose the papacy; and what with the increase of worldly wealth, and the prevalence of worldly splendor, the church in the course of a few centuries became awfully corrupt; popes, bishops, and the inferior clergy became the subjects of the vilest passions that ever disgraced fallen human nature; the pope claimed to exercise prerogatives which can only belong to God, even that of forgiving sins; and the priests claimed the power, not only of creating from day to day the real body and blood, soul and divinity, of Jesus Christ, but, in consideration of a few paltry pence, claimed the power to pardon, as the representatives of Christ, deeds of the most atrocious character. As it is a doctrine of the Roman Church that she never changes, we are obliged to infer that the same powers are still claimed by her bishops and clergy, and it becomes scarcely necessary to repeat that the Methodist Church is not Episcopal in the Roman Catholic sense of the word. Secondly, The Methodist Episcopal Church is not Episcopal in the Church of England, or Protestant Episcopal sense of the term.

The Church of England claims to have derived a succession of bishops from the apostles—that is, that there always have been bishops who were ordained by other bishops, and that each bishop had been previously ordained deacon, and then priest, and that this triple consecration is absolutely necessary to the perpetuation of the church of Christ, and that all churches which have not such an Episcopacy, are without the ministry, without the sacraments, and are, in fact, no church at all, but only schismatics and pretenders. Now, while it is known that the Church of England received her ordinations from Rome, and that in the Roman chain there are several important links wanting, it is no great wonder that the Methodist Church, with its founder, Mr. Wesley, and some of the highest dignitaries of the Church of England, should pronounce the dogma of uninterrupted apostolical succession to be a cunningly devised fable, which no man has proved, or can prove. By virtue of this pretended regular succession, the bishops of the Church of England, and the Protestant Episcopal Church, claim the sole right of ordination, and of admitting persons to membership in the church by confirmation, and each parish minister claims and exercises the prerogative of governing his own flock, of deciding all questions in controversy, of trying and expelling members, without the advice or judgment of any ecclesiastical court but himself, and from his decision there is no appeal, but to the bishop in person. Now, in neither of the above senses is the Methodist Church episcopal, as will be more clearly shown hereafter.

Thirdly: The Methodist Church is episcopal only in the sense of having a class of officers appointed to take a general superintendence of the affairs of the church, including both its ministry and membership, and in this sense, we maintain that it is not only "strictly and properly" an episcopal church, but what is more, a church which is based upon a scriptural foundation, as nearly as we can judge in relation to such matters. The Episcopacy of Methodism is of that moderate character, which, while it imparts power and efficiency to the office, makes the office itself, and the incumbent of the same, entirely dependent upon the will of the eldership, or presbytery of the church, the one for its perpetuity, the other for his election to, and continuance in, the same. And it is a matter of rejoicing, that the Methodist Church has never, but in a single instance—and that in relation to a disputed point arising from slavery—had cause to mourn the defection of any of its Superintendents, or to distrust their purity of character and singleness of heart.

SECTION II.

APOSTOLIC SUCCESSION.

THE Christian world has been divided for centuries on the subject referred to in the title to this section. Much might be said on the subject of such divisions and sub-divisions of sentiment, but we must at this time confine ourselves to the great questions which now agitate the Christian Church: whether an Episcopacy, or the existence of bishops, made such by a triple consecration, is necessary to the perpetuation of the church of Jesus Christ? And whether such bishops must be able to trace their episcopal descent in an uninterrupted line of personal succession from the apostles? It is important to observe here, what is involved in assuming to answer the above questions in the affirmative. The following results follow an admission of the truth of the above: that bishops are, by divine right and appointment, an order superior to presbyters; that they have powers, privileges, and authority, by the same divine appointment, which the presbyters have not; that *they* only, as the successors of the apostles, can ordain the bishops and other clergy; that such succession from the apostles is *personal*, and may be traced through a series of bishops, from the youngest member of the prelacy, to Peter, the first pope or bishop of Rome; that no ministerial act is valid, that all ordinations, and administration of ordinances and sacraments, are void, unless performed personally, or by the permission and sanction of episcopally ordained successors of the apostles; consequently, that all other churches, admitting the validity of presbyterian ordination, and denying practically the necessity of such prelatical succession, are not in fact churches, but mere voluntary associations, sects, schismatics, &c.; that their ministers are nothing more than *teachers*, *usurpers*, *interlopers*, *blasphemers*, and *impostors*.

Now, before admitting such monstrous absurdities, and

adopting such uncharitable conclusions, as would unchurch and anathematize the fairest and loveliest portion of God's heritage, and would, by implication, consign the holiest men that ever lived, to the blackness and darkness of the bottomless pit, we feel disposed to examine these high pretensions to apostolical authority, as candidly and critically as our narrow limits will allow.

And first, are bishops, by divine right and appointment, and in the sense of being the successors of the apostles, an order *superior* to presbyters? In answering this question, we naturally inquire—What was there peculiar in the office and functions of an apostle of Jesus Christ?

One peculiarity is, that they were directly and personally called by Jesus Christ, without any other call; and without having previously passed through the lower grades in the ministry. Are modern bishops thus called?

Another thing peculiar to the apostolic office, was the manner in which they were *taught* and *fitted* for the work of the ministry. They received all their knowledge of the gospel from Christ himself, and by direct inspiration of the Holy Ghost. Are bishops of the present day taught in this manner?

Another thing true of the apostles is, that they were *infallible* in their teachings. Do their modern "successors" lay claim to infallibility?

Another important fact that should be noticed in reference to the apostles is, that their ministerial commissions gave them universal authority to administer their functions in every part of the world. "Go ye into *all* the world, and preach the gospel to *every* creature." Have modern bishops this universal authority? Are they not, by virtue of their commissions, confined to their own diocese, however small in extent?

No bishop, claiming to be such by divine right, pretends to lay claim to universal authority, excepting his holiness, the bishop of Rome, who, as the only successor of Peter and Paul, calls himself "universal bishop."

Another apostolic peculiarity, was the power of working miracles. This power was given in their commissions, "heal the sick; raise the dead." Is this power included among the others given to our modern "successionists?" The apostles had also the authority to communicate to others the power of working miracles, and the gift of prophesying, and speaking in other tongues, by laying on of their hands. (See Acts xix. 6.) Does the modern episcopate (rather apostolate) possess the same power?

Again, the apostles had the power to remit sins; "Whosesoever sins ye remit, they are remitted." Have their successors been commissioned and authorized to remit sins in any given case? The only power they *claim* or *can* claim in this respect, is, to declare a mere truism: that "God pardoneth and absolveth *all* those who truly repent;" a declaration which any Sunday-school scholar can make, with as much authority as a right reverend prelate.

These are some of the peculiarities pertaining to the apostolic office, and if modern bishops can give evidence that they are in the regular succession in these respects, we will be better prepared to admit their claims on other points. Besides, if regularly descended bishops are successors of the apostles in fact, and the *name* "apostle" is most significant of their high office, why not make use of the name at once? Why so modest and unassuming as to refuse what justly belongs to them? If the reason is not to be found in the exercise of a "voluntary humility," perhaps it might be traced to the fact, that the common sense of mankind would repudiate the idea of appropriating such a title as apostle, to those who are so unlike the real apostles of our Saviour, as the foregoing facts clearly demonstrate.

The real apostles were not backward in appropriating this title to themselves, and what may appear a little remarkable is, that when they selected any other title, they never called themselves *bishops*, but simply *presbyters* or *elder*•

While modern bishops do not claim to be successors of the apostles in the particulars before mentioned, they nevertheless maintain that they are *sole successors*, so far as it relates to the power of ordaining ministers, confirming believers, and governing the churches.

In the examination of the validity of these high claims, it is freely granted that modern bishops have a scriptural and conventional right to ordain, confirm, and rule over the church of God, not as lords, but as ministers of Jesus Christ; but that the *sole* power of government in the church, and sending forth ministers, *exclusively* belongs to them, we most solemnly deny, while we maintain that the apostles themselves did not lay claim to such exclusive powers; neither did their immediate successors, in the first ages of the church. That such powers are to be exercised only by a third superior order in the ministry, is an assumption without warrant or proof, either scriptural or historical.

To make this matter plain, it will be only necessary to show that *presbyters*, as such, had a right to ordain ministers, and govern the church of God; that they are spoken of in the Scriptures as possessing the same qualifications with bishops; as having precisely the same duties to perform; and while there is at least a nominal distinction made between apostles and bishops, there is no such distinction made between bishops and presbyters. This being the case, the exclusive claims of the high church episcopacy must fall to the ground.

In regard to the power of ordination by the presbytery or body of elders, while there is not the shadow of a proof in the New Testament that *bishops*, as such, ever ordained, there is clear demonstrative evidence that *presbyters* did ordain others, hence—1 Tim. iv. 14—"Neglect not the gift that is in thee, which was given thee by the laying on of the hands of the *presbytery*." Here it is plain that the ministerial gift or power which Timothy possessed, was given him *by* the laying on of the hands of the body of the elders who ordained him. And in regard to the *government* of the church, it is equally plain that *bishops*, in distinction from *presbyters*, were not charged with the oversight thereof, for it is said—Acts xx. 17, 28, that Paul "called the elders (not the bishops) of the Church of Ephesus, and said unto them, 'Take heed therefore to yourselves, and to all the flock over the which the Holy Ghost hath made you overseers,' feed the church of God." On this passage we remark, 1st, that the original Greek term for the word "overseer" is "episcopos," the very word from which our term "bishop" is derived, and which is generally translated "bishop" in the English version of the New Testament. Now this term episcopos, overseer, or bishop, is applied to the *identical* persons called *elders* in the 17th verse, and to none other. Consequently, Paul must have considered elders and bishops as one, not only in office, but in order also; and so the Ephesian ministers undoubtedly understood him. But we remark, 2dly, that these episcopal presbyters had the *oversight* of *all* the flock; so that if there was a class in the church at Ephesus who were called bishops, as distinct from elders, these presbyters had the oversight and government of them also. We remark, 3dly, that these bishops, overseers, or elders, in the Ephesian church, are found in the plural number, and *that* not only in a single city, but in a single *church*, and that church probably a small one. Now, if by the term "episcopos," we are to understand necessarily a diocesan bishop, or the "pastor of pastors," we are led to inquire why, in the name of wonder and consistency, they needed so many lordly prelates in that small church? One would almost fancy that *one* bishop of modern dimensions would be amply sufficient for a single congregation. The truth is, there were several elders in the above church, and *every one of them was in fact a New Testament bishop.* This leads us to remark, 4thly, that the government in said church was exercised in common by *all* the elders, there is no intimation that they had a superior officer by divine warrant, to whom any portion of the government had been delegated. The *Holy*

Ghost had made them *all* overseers, and if they had a presiding presbyter or bishop among them, it must have been a mere human arrangement, perfectly proper, no doubt, and justifiable, but a human arrangement after all.

That the terms "presbyter" and "bishop" are, in the New Testament, applied to the same persons, will further appear from Tit. i. 5, 7, where Paul says to Titus—"For this cause left I thee in Crete, that thou shouldest ordain *elders* in every city: if any be blameless, the husband of one wife; for a *bishop* must be blameless as the steward of God." For Paul to request Titus to ordain *elders*, if he could find any suitable persons of a blameless moral character, and assign as a reason for such selection, that a *bishop* must be blameless, would be complete nonsense on the supposition, that bishops were superior to, or distinct from the order of presbyters. It would be like saying, "Appoint a brave man for a *captain*, for a *general* must be brave!" Or more apropos, "Appoint no man for *Justice* of the *Peace*, who is not well acquainted with the law, for a *Justice* of the Supreme Court must be well versed in legal lore!" Such are some of the absurdities that follow the claim that bishops were superior to elders.

But if Scripture is opposed to modern high church claims and pretensions, so is *history*, on which successionists appear to lay so much stress.

Clemens Romanus, who flourished and wrote between the years 70 and 92, speaks of bishops and presbyters as being the same in order.

Ignatius, who wrote A. D. 101, says: "The presbyters preside in the place of the council of the apostles;" and again, "Be ye subject to your presbyters as to the apostles of Jesus Christ." And again: "Let all reverence the presbyters, as the Sanhedrim of God, and the college of the apostles." And again: "See that ye follow the presbyters as the apostles." Now such advice to be subject to, and reverence the elders of the church, as supplying the place of the departed apostles; as being in fact the "College of the Apostles," is hardly compatible with the idea, that bishops, as distinct from presbyters, are the successors of the apostles.* To our own mind, the above quotations show as clearly as a sunbeam, that *presbyters* are, and were, the true apostolic successors.

Polycarp, a disciple of John the apostle, and who wrote during the beginning of the 2d century, has left an epistle which is still extant, in which he speaks of "presbyters" and "deacons;" but says not a word about a *third* order of bishops; which is at least an inferential proof that no such order existed.

Justin Martyn, who wrote about the middle of the 2d century, speaks in his works of "presiding presbyters," a proof that elders did, even then, preside over and govern the church of God.

Irenæus, who wrote about the year 184, uses the terms "bishop" and "presbyter" as synonymous, and speaks of the "*succession of presbyters*." He speaks, also, of several of the earlier pastors of the church at Rome, as "presbyters" simply; and that he referred to the higher order of pastors, is evident from the fact, that he calls them "the presiding presbyters of the church." Now if these first pastors, or bishops of the church of Rome, were superior in order to the eldership of the church, would it have been proper for Justin to have addressed them merely as *presiding presbyters?* Let a modern priest or deacon of the Church of England, or of the Protestant Episcopal Church in America, or of the Roman Catholic Church, address the Right Reverend Father in God, his diocesan bishop, as a presiding *presbyter* merely, and the incongruity between the title and the claims of said bishop, would at once be apparent.

Tertullian, who flourished at the close of the 2d century, and who is claimed by high church writers as the best authority in such matters, proves incidentally that during his time the ruling, or presiding presbyters in the church, began to appropriate the title "bishop" to themselves, and to claim superior power and authority over the body of the clergy; he says, "Bishops have a right to baptize; *afterwards*, the presbyters and deacons." He gives, also, the reason why this distinction was allowed: "Because of the honor of the church;" and declares, that "were it not for the honor and peace of the church, the right of administering baptism, belongs even to laymen." Here, then, we perceive the beginning of episcopal pretensions; the embryo of modern prelacy; and the reason why this superiority was claimed and granted; not because of any divine right, on the part of the bishop, but "because of the honor and peace of the church." Yet even Tertullian denominates the "bishops," elders, and says: "Approved elders preside among us, having received that honor by the suffrages of the brethren." And in another passage he speaks of the "churches over which the apostolical chairs preside." Now if anything can be inferred from these statements, it is, that although in Tertullian's day, a superiority of office was given to presiding presbyters, and they began by way of distinction to be called bishops; yet, they were in *order* presbyters only, and *as presbyters* filled the "apostolic chairs."

Clemens Alexandrinus flourished and wrote a few years after Tertullian. He speaks of but two orders of ministers, superior and inferior. The superior ministers, were presbyters; and the inferior, deacons. He speaks of these two orders, as conducting the worship of God, and makes no allusion to bishops, as such, taking any part in the services.

Origen, a presbyter about the year 230, writes as follows to the church: "We of the clerical order, who *preside* over you." And he further speaks of bishops, simply as occupying a "higher chair," that is, they were *presiding presbyters.*

Twenty years after Origen's time, flourished the great and good Cyprian, bishop of Carthage, who afterwards became a martyr to the truth. As this holy man sustained the highest office in the church, it becomes a matter of importance to know what his views were, on the matter of episcopacy by divine right; and whether he considered a simple presbyter, as having the authority and qualifications to perform all the duties of a bishop. During his absence from his church, he writes to the presbyters who remained, and says to them: "I beseech you, that you perform your own duties, and also those that belong to me; so that nothing may be wanting, either in doctrine or diligence." "I exhort; and commit the charge to you, that you would discharge *my* duty, act in *my* place, and perform *all* those things, which the administration of the church requires." We might multiply quotations from Cyprian, to prove that in his day, bishops and presbyters were equal in order and power, by divine right; that elders could and did discharge *all* the functions of the bishop, or presiding presbyter, without being specially set apart, or ordained thereto, as a third, and higher order of ministers, but the above extracts must suffice.

FIRMILLIAN, who was contemporary with Cyprian, and who was also a bishop, being the presiding minister of the church of Cesarea, remarks, that "in the church, presbyters preside, and have the power of baptizing, *confirming*, and ORDAINING." This is very high authority for ministerial parity. Firmillian was held in deservedly high repute as a bishop. He was chosen president of the council of Antioch; and the evidence he thus leaves is more valuable, as it relates simply to the practice of the church, (*viz.*) that elders baptized, *confirmed*, and ORDAINED.

We have thus glanced at the history of the church, and the testimony of the "fathers" for the first three centuries; and we find ourselves strongly fortified in the position, that primitive bishops were merely elders at the first; that the name signified the presiding presbyter; and that not until the church began to be corrupt, did the bishops claim to be an order superior to, and distinct from presbyters.

AMBROSE, who wrote toward the close of the 4th century,

and after the presiding officers of churches had succeeded in laying claim to superior power and authority, remarks: "The apostles' writings are not altogether agreeable to the order of things, as now practised in the church; because (he adds) the first or chief presbyters were then called bishops." "The bishops were constituted such, by the judgment of a number of the presbyters." He says further, that "the presbyters and bishops had *one* and the *same ordination*." Now if Ambrose spoke the truth in relation to the identity of presbyterian and episcopal ordination, how ridiculous for modern pretenders to lay claim to a spiritual descent from the apostles, through an unbroken chain of episcopal links, constituted such by a triple consecration, first, as deacons; then, as presbyters; and thirdly as bishops!

In addition to these testimonies already adduced, it is a well-authenticated fact, that in the church at Alexandria, from the time of Mark the evangelist to the time of Dionysius, about the year 250, it was the invariable practice for the elders of that church to elect one from among themselves, place him in the episcopal chair, and give him the name of bishop. This being placed in the chair, was all the episcopal ordination he had, and this was performed *exclusively* by the elders. If, then, there was anything equivalent to an ordination in the case, it furnishes a proof that bishops, as superior ministers in the church, derived their powers from the eldership alone.

CHRYSOSTOM, who wrote about the close of the 4th, and beginning of the 5th centuries, at which time the bishops claimed undue authority over the elders of the church, rebukes them sharply by saying: "The bishops being above the presbyters *solely* by their suffrages, and by this alone, they seem to assume an unjust superiority over the presbyters." Mark here, that the bishops were such, not by *divine right*, not by *triple consecration*, but *solely* by the suffrages of the elders.

SAINT AUGUSTINE, in writing to his brethren, tells them, "By a presbyter you must understand a bishop; for what is a bishop (he inquires) but the first presbyter?" He also addresses the bishops as "fellow-presbyters," and asserts, that "in Alexandria, and throughout the whole of Egypt, the presbyters consecrate, when the bishop is not present."

Having given these authorities, from the early Christian fathers, we will quote one or two from the canons of councils. The council of Ancyra met in the year 315. In the 13th canon of said council, it is said: "It is not allowed for *village bishops* to ordain presbyters or deacons, nor is it allowed *even* to city presbyters to do this, in another diocese, without the license of the bishop." From this canon three things are evident, 1st, that *city presbyters* were considered superior to *village bishops.* 2d, that the mere fact of a man's being a bishop gave him no right to ordain. 3d, that a city presbyter could ordain in his own diocese without a license from the bishop, while a village bishop could not ordain, either in his own or another diocese, without a license from the city bishop. Now, in view of such evidence, we may inquire what becomes of the claim that "bishops, by divine right, have the sole power of ordination;" when a simple presbyter could do what a bishop was forbidden to do?

Ten years after the council of Ancyra, sat the famous council of Nice, which addressed an epistle to the church at Alexandria, in which epistle, express permission is given to presbyters to ordain; and which further sanctions the ancient usages of said church, in allowing their presbyters to ordain others.

Having thus proven that bishops and elders were, in the earlier and purer days of the church, one in order, and that elders, as such, had the power of ordaining, and presiding in the church, we pass to notice the several links in the chain of episcopal succession, which are said to connect modern prelates, of the 19th century, with Peter, Paul, and John, of the first. And in the examination of this point, as far as Scripture or history throw light upon this subject, if we discover a want of connection between the several links of this celebrated chain;

or a want of proof that such connection exists, or ever existed, as claimed by the "apostolic successors," we will of course be at liberty to form our own opinion of the modesty and propriety of the claims of such as bear the name and title of "Right Reverend Bishops of the only true Church."

It is important here to remark, that however numerous the streams through which the succession *might* have flowed, yet the "successors" claim to trace with certainty their "succession" through *one channel only;* and that channel at the beginning is the *Roman.* It is true, they claim that before the Romish Church became corrupt, and impure, the episcopal stream was introduced into Britain; and that said stream has flowed on, century after century, disconnected from, and uncontaminated by, the rottenness and corruption of the Roman Church. We will, however, show hereafter, that England received her bishops and archbishops from Rome, during the *darkest, foulest,* and *bloodiest* days of the latter. But let us now return to the unbroken chain.

Who was the first bishop of Rome? The "successionists" say, that the apostle Peter was the first link in the chain. But hold! Peter, as we have shown already, was not a *bishop* (in name at least), but an *apostle,* and *presbyter.* How then could he be bishop of Rome, or any other place, when he was not—at least did not claim to be—bishop at all? How does it happen that the New Testament, especially the Acts of the Apostles, and the Epistles of Peter and Paul, are entirely silent on such a vitally important point? How does it happen that early ecclesiastical writers differ on the question; and that some even deny that Peter ever was in Rome? How is it, we repeat, that the most learned prelates and ministers of the Church of England, and even of Rome, find it so difficult to prove this fact, as to oblige them to acknowledge their doubts, whether Peter ever was in Rome? Indeed, the strong probability is—nay, it is almost certain—that Peter never saw Rome; and that if either of the apostles was bishop of the church there, *Paul* must have been the person. Paul we *know* was in Rome, but we have no evidence that he was there in any other capacity, than as an *apostle*, and *prisoner*. Neither is there the smallest degree of evidence to show that he ever ordained a successor in Rome, even allowing that he was the first bishop; and the same is true also of Peter. Admitting then, for the sake of argument, that Peter, or Paul was the first pope, who succeeded to the episcopal or papal chair? who, that being first ordained deacon, then elder, was, by a triple consecration, regularly installed second Bishop of Rome? It is indeed an easy matter to suppose, and then to *assert*, that *Linus* was the favored person, as is supposed and asserted by successionist divines; but supposition and assertion are not proof; and especially in a case like this, where proof is everything, supposition, and assertion nothing; and where, too, ecclesiastical history is opposed to such conjecture; for Eusebius, one of the earlier historians of the church, who wrote about the year 320, and during the reign of Constantine, declares, in reference to the point under consideration, "How many, and what sincere followers of them (Peter and Paul) have been approved to take the charge of those churches by them founded, it is not easy to say, except such, and so many, as may be collected from the words of St. Paul?" Now where do we find from Paul's writings, that either he or Peter consecrated Linus as the second bishop of Rome? If the subject of apostolic succession, at its very source or commencement, was a matter of doubt and perplexity to an accredited historian like Eusebius, over 1500 years ago, what can we think of the barefaced assertions of the writers of the present day, who pompously connect Linus with Peter, and link with link, and then confidently exclaim, "here is our chain! here is the list! look at it, and judge for yourselves!" Well; we feel disposed to look at this subject a little further, before we dismiss it.

In examining the testimony of the ancient fathers, who admit that Peter was bishop of Rome, we find them divided in sentiment, as to who was the successor of Peter. Three of them assert, that CLEMENT succeeded Peter. Four others suppose that LINUS succeeded Peter. But from the testimony of others it is proved conclusively, that *Linus* died some years before the death of the apostle, so that he could not have succeeded the latter. Others of the fathers give it as their opinion, that neither *Linus* nor *Clement* succeeded Peter, but that CLETUS was the successor. In view of these conflicting testimonies, how supremely ridiculous, nay, how wicked, for professed ministers of the gospel of Jesus Christ to palm off upon ignorant men and women a long list of episcopal successors, while not only the second link in this unbroken chain, but even the *first*, fails them ?

If we admit, however, that LINUS, or CLEMENT, or CLETUS, was the second bishop, who, we inquire, was the third ? Oh ! the *list* says " CLETUS !" Well, who ordained Cletus deacon ? who an elder ? who a bishop ? And was he the successor of *Linus ?* or the successor of *Clement ?* or the successor of *himself ?* A catalogue of bishops, carefully preserved in the Romish Church, which ought to be very high authority with high churchmen, makes Cletus succeed Linus, as the *third* bishop of Rome, Clement as the fourth, and Anacletus as the fifth ; but it is provable that *Cletus* and *Anacletus* were one and the same person, " Cletus" being merely an abbreviation of " Anacletus." How then could he be third and fifth bishop of Rome ? And what became of the unfortunate *Clement*, the fourth bishop, compressed between the third and fifth bishops ? Does the compression crush him into nothing, if, indeed, he ever had a being ? From the contradictory statements of the " fathers," and other ecclesiastical writers, one would almost suppose that the existence of these first bishops was purely fabulous. For instance, PLATINA, the great biographer of the popes, says that Peter made *Clement* bishop of Rome ; while it is certain that the apostle had been dead for *twenty years* before Clement was a bishop at all ! Here, then, is darkness ! Here is confusion! Here we have the unbroken and unbreakable chain of apostolic succession, which is not capable of supporting itself with five links, nor four, nor three, nor two, nor even one!

We might thus follow the length of this fabulous chain, from link to link, till we arrive at the beginning of the fifth century, and from this period to that of the glorious reformation under Luther, the bishops of Rome appear to have been generally selected from among the most abandoned and profligate wretches that ever cursed the earth! Men guilty of drunkenness, whoredom, incest, murder, and other unspeakable crimes, were elevated to the so-called St. Peter's seat. Not only were the successors corrupt, but two, sometimes three, occupied the papal throne at the same time. Pope anathematized pope, and hurled thunderbolts of wrath at the souls of their predecessors, declaring former ordinations null and void, and requiring the re-ordination of those ministers already ordained. What a beautiful list!

But we must pass over a portion of this history, that we may examine particularly one link in the chain. We refer to pope John VIII. If any credit is to be given to history, this pope was nothing else than a disguised female, who, by concealing her sex, was admitted to the priesthood, and by her art and address, subsequently became the successor of Leo IV., in the year 854. She filled the chair, and performed the functions of the pope of Rome, for the space of one year, one month, and four days; and indelicate as the allusion may seem, truth requires us to add, that her death was caused by giving birth to an illegitimate child, while walking in procession to the Lateran church, in Rome. After her death, she was succeeded by pope Benedict III.

We have been thus careful in giving names and dates, because this link in the chain is not a very pleasing one, even to protestant "successors" of the apostles, knowing as they do, that a spurious link is no link at all: hence the sticklers for an unbroken chain have pretended to have doubts as to the truth of this historical fact. But we assure the reader, that if the correctness of the fact were not fully established by unimpeachable testimony, we would not have noticed it at all.

PLATINA, a Romish historian, who wrote the history of the church, affirms it to have been a "*generally admitted fact.*" PRIDEAUX, another ecclesiastical historian of celebrity, declares that " there are *fifty authorities belonging to the church in favor of it.*" FLAVIUS ILLYRICUS, another historian, gives a large number of authorities, and proves from the testimony of authors who wrote soon after the events transpired, that they were not even doubted, but spoken of by said authors as *well-authenticated historical facts.* MOSHEIM, the celebrated and popular historian, who is frequently referred to by high church writers as evidence in proof of some of their claims, asserts that "*during the five succeeding centuries, the facts were generally believed ; and that a vast number of writers bore testimony to the truth of the same.*" He even asserts that " before the reformation, the fact referred to was not considered incredible in itself, nor ignominious to the church." He further states : " It is not at all credible from any principles of moral evidence, that an event should be believed and related in the same manner, by a multitude of historians, during five centuries immediately succeeding its supposed date, had that event been destitute of all foundation."

Now, when we remember that all the authorities referred to by the above named historians, were members of the Romish church, and that they could not possibly have been prompted by sectarian prejudice to record these shameful, yet painful facts ; when we consider, too, that these authorities wrote soon after the events took place, it would be the height of incredulity to disbelieve what they assert on the subject. Indeed some, if not all the authorities referred to, in proof of the unbroken succession, have this very link included in the list. Now, we ask in the name of candor and of decency, could this abandoned female transmit the true apostolic virtue to her successors, or spiritual descendants? We will not insult the reader's understanding by attempting a reply.

Suffer us now for a moment, to take a glance at the moral character and proceedings of a few of the succeeding popes. Stephen VI. is called the most wicked of men. Clement II. was poisoned by pope Damasos II. Sergius III. rescinded the acts of his predecessor pope Farmosus, beheaded his dead body, and threw it into the Tiber. Pope John IX., the illegitimate son of Sergius III., is said to have been the blackest monster that ever lived. Pope John XIII. was killed in the act of adultery. Sixtus IV. licensed brothels in Rome, for the sake of the income. Pope Alexander VI. was guilty of incest with his own daughter. But to end this horrible list of incarnate devils, let it be sufficient to say, that PRIDEAUX—himself an episcopalian divine of high standing—enumerates among the popes, thirty-eight usurpers, forty sodomites, forty magicians or jugglers, forty-one devourers (as he calls them), and twenty incurable babylonians. And, he might have added, one prostitute!

Here, then, is a chain with no less than *one hundred and eighty links;* a pretty long one, it is true, but whether such a one as to excite admiration, and cause men to glory that they are regularly connected with it, and that the "succession" may be traced through it, is a matter which we must leave for the "apostolic" descendants to decide.

SECTION III.

SAME SUBJECT CONTINUED.

We are sometimes met by the assertion, "that the English and American episcopacy are not indebted to, nor dependent upon, this Romish chain for their succession; that long before the Church of Rome had become corrupt, the Church of England had obtained its episcopacy; and that the stream thus obtained from a pure fountain, has retained its original purity, uncorrupted by, and independent of, the Church of Rome."

Now this is certainly a strange assertion. Strange! because it is notoriously untrue; contradicted not only by ecclesiastical, but also by profane history. The Romish succession of bishops was introduced into England in the person of Augustine, a monk, who was ordained by the pope's authority. Augustine, on his arrival in England, accompanied by forty other monks, found bishops in the church; but these English bishops had only presbyterian ordination. Augustine, anxious to bring them into the succession, insisted on their re-ordination, by the imposition of his hands, to which many submitted. The above fact proves that till nearly the close of the 6th century, the English clergy had by some means got along without the popish succession, and that they appear to have been satisfied till then, with the ancient order of things, namely, presbyterian ordination; but the popish succession having been now obtained, or imposed upon them, it was not long before the clergy, as a general thing, became decidedly popish, not only in doctrine, but in practice also. Subsequent history proves also that the clergy, instead of preserving themselves and the church from contact with the "mother of abominations," had recourse, again and again, to the pope, for the ordination of their bishops, so that in the archepiscopal see of Canterbury, from the time of Theodore, A. D. 668, till the year 1414, no less than FOURTEEN BISHOPS and ARCHBISHOPS obtained their appointment and ordination at the hands of the pope, or the pope's legate.

In the Archbishopric of York, during a space of a little over two hundred years—from 1119 to 1342—no less than TEN BISHOPS were ordained by the pope or his orders. In the See of Durham, FOUR of its bishops were ordained at Rome during the same period. In the See of Winchester, during nearly the same period, SIX of the bishops were ordained by the pope.

Thus we might go on from one diocese to another, through the whole of England, and we should find that all of them received more or less of their bishops from Rome. And why not? Was not popery the established religion of the kingdom? And where should the church look for its "bishops and other clergy" but to the fountain-head, however corrupt that fountain might be? It should also be remembered that the prelates above alluded to, were given by Rome to England, during the darkest and bloodiest days of the popedom.

We can thus trace the succession of the present race of English bishops, and also of the American bishops, back to bloody Rome; for Bishop White, the first bishop of the Protestant Episcopal Church, received his ordination from the archbishop of Canterbury, and he from his fellow-bishops, who received theirs indirectly and remotely from the pope himself.

Having thus examined the claim of apostolic succession, having followed the length of the chain from beginning to end, we are prepared to ask in all sincerity, what think ye of this claim? Is it well founded? Does it commend itself to our sober judgment and enlightened reason? Are we prepared to admit, that those who have this spurious and corrupt succession, constitute the *only true church* of Jesus Christ, and that all other Christians are schismatics and heretics?

But it is maintained that even allowing the stream along which the succession has flowed to have been impure, yet "bishops as a third order, and as the successors of the apostles, are the *only* persons who may lawfully ordain, because that presbyters or elders have not this authority expressly given them in their commission." In reply we remark, that in the commission given to the apostles, there is no *express* authority given *them* to ordain and send forth ministers. Their commission directed them to teach, preach and baptize, but said not a word about ordaining; yet it is evident that in the absence of express authority, they did ordain ministers. We beg you also to remember a fact already referred to, namely, that although exercising the functions of ordination, the apostles were never called bishops; that they never called themselves bishops; nor ever claimed to be such. But while they did not claim to be bishops, they did claim to be elders, or presbyters; hence Peter, in writing to his brethren, says: "The elders who are among you I exhort, who am also an ELDER." The apostle John, also, in two of his epistles, introduces himself not as a bishop, but as an elder, thus: "The *elder* to the elect lady." "The *elder* to the well-beloved Gaius." From these passages we infer that the apostles were in fact elders; that elders were the highest order of ministers known in the church; and that the apostles exercised the right of ordination, by virtue of their ministerial standing as elders in the church of God. It may be proper here also to observe, that in the description given of the glories of the church triumphant by the apostle John, in the book of Revelation, there is nothing said about either apostles or bishops being recognized as such in the kingdom of heaven, while *elders* are not only named, but referred to as occupying the highest rank among the blood-washed throng; an evidence to our own mind, that whatever may be the relative order of elders as ministers in the church on earth, in heaven they have no superior order among the redeemed. If, then, the apostles were in fact elders, and elders only so far as order is concerned, it will of course follow that their successors can be nothing more, and that the power of ordination should be retained and exercised by the eldership of the church, they being the only representatives of the Lord Jesus Christ on earth; while bishops are such, not because they are *bishops*, but because that being bishops they are elders also; and, as elders, are the true successors of the apostles, in common with their brethren of the presbytery.

But the question may arise in some minds, "How came this third order to be recognized in the church as a *distinct and superior order?*" In reply, we need simply state that, like all other corruptions and abuses, this one fastened itself upon the church almost imperceptibly, and by slow degrees. At an early age after the apostles, it was thought best that the power of ordination should not be used indiscriminately by the elders of the church, but for the sake of greater unity, and to prevent as far as possible the abuse of this power by individual presbyters, its exercise should be limited in most cases to the presiding presbyter or elder, whose station as president—added to his greater wisdom and experience—better qualified him to judge of the expediency of exercising the power of ordination in any given case. This arrangement was no doubt called for, and was perfectly proper; indeed, we can discover marks of wisdom and Christian prudence in the same: but it was a mere human arrangement after all, without divine warrant or authority; without even apostolic example to recommend it; and when once introduced into, and entailed upon the church as a fixed usage, it is easy to comprehend how new powers might be added to that of ordination, until at length the presiding presbyter or bishop claimed the exclusive privilege of conferring orders as a divine right belonging only to the bishop.*

From these remarks, it can be seen that bishops have no more Scriptural or divine right to ordain, than any simple presbyter in the church; yet for the sake of peace, harmony, and greater unity, it may be proper for the presbyters to enter

* Occasion has been taken from a knowledge of the above facts to oppose the episcopal office as unnecessary and even dangerous to the liberties of the church. We should, however, carefully distinguish between the proper use and abuse of a thing. All good things may be abused, and all blessings may be perverted; so with the episcopacy: good in its design and operations, when properly checked. No genuine protestant doubts the fact of the Roman priesthood, or presbytery, as such, being a curse instead of a blessing to the world; but surely it would be wrong to discard the entire body of Christian elders on that account, or to seek the annihilation of either the order or office.

into a human arrangement, by which the power or privilege of granting orders may be delegated to some one or more of their number. But this delegation of power for the time being, cannot alienate even for a moment the divine right of presbyters to set apart proper persons to the ministry, when circumstances seem imperiously to demand it. To make this matter plain, we will suppose that the sovereign of Great Britain, being the fountain of all power and honor in her own dominions, should authorize her cabinet ministers, or either of them, to confer titles of nobility on whomsoever she should previously select. And suppose, further, that for the sake of greater convenience, the cabinet should select one of their number as their agent or representative in this matter, who *alone* should have a conventional right officially to confer these titles. And suppose, further, that this arrangement should become fixed usage without any further instructio from the Queen than those before stated, and that wher tain changes took place in the cabinet, the succeeding min for good reasons, refused to abide by the above arrangem would they not be competent to rescind the rule which had hitherto governed the cabinet, and use the authority given them by their sovereign in conferring these titles? Nay! under certain circumstances, might it not be their imperative duty to resume the exercise of their common powers, especially if the minister previously appointed for the purpose had abused his authority, either by refusing to confer titles upon the persons selected, or by conferring them upon persons not selected, or by exacting exorbitant sums of money from those on whom titles were conferred? Might it not, I ask, be the solemn duty of the members of the cabinet to resume their delegated powers? It certainly might. Just so in reference to presbyters. Jesus Christ, who selects whom he will as his ministers, has conferred upon the elders of his church, or either of them, the power of conferring orders upon those previously selected by him. These elders may, for the sake of unity and convenience, waive the *personal* exercise of this power, and delegate the same to one or more of their number, and may denominate the persons thus delegated their bishops, presidents, superintendents, chairmen, moderators, presiding elders, or anything else they choose; but the persons thus selected remain elders still, the same in *order* with their brother elders, but superior in *office*. And if, as has been the case with modern bishops, improper and even ungodly persons have been ordained by them to the office of the ministry; and if, as can also be clearly shown, persons properly qualified and selected to that office by the Head of the Church himself, have by these same prelates been denied ordination, as in the case of the Rev. Joseph Benson and others: ought not the presbytery of the church over which these unfaithful bishops preside, to resume the power of ordination, and not only withhold it from improper persons, but confer it where the God of heaven has clearly indicated that it should be conferred? Should they not confer the power to ordain and send forth ministers, upon persons who will faithfully discharge the duties they owe to God, to his church, and to its divinely commissioned ministers?

Such is the episcopacy of the Methodist Episcopal Church in these United States. Such, also, is the Presidency of the British Wesleyan Church, and other Methodist Churches in Europe and America. Such, also, is the prevailing sentiment and practice of every protestant church in the world, excepting, of course, that branch of the church which is governed not by its immediate pastors, but by a hierarchy, a spiritual aristocracy, an episcopal nobility, as far elevated above the eldership, as the latter are above the laity; an order of ministers claiming the exclusive possession and use of the "keys of the kingdom of heaven," and exercising the sole right of admitting persons to the ministry, and even to the bosom of the church. From such an exclusive, monopolizing episcopacy as this, we earnestly pray to be delivered; and we pity the minister, who, supposing there is a divine warrant for such claims, suffers himself to be so far blinded by error as to withhold from ministers and members of other churches, an acknowledgment of their true relation to the body of Christ.

We are however happy to know, that while many allow themselves to indulge in uncharitable feelings toward other churches, there are hundreds of other ministers, who although in the "succession," so called, willingly acknowledge the validity of presbyterian ordination, and the propriety of its administration under certain circumstances. It was with such views as these, that the "apostle of Methodism," himself a "presbyter," and as high in order by divine right, as his Grace the Archbishop of Canterbury, set apart certain persons to the work of the ministry;—persons who had given indubitable evidence of their being previously called to the work by the Holy Ghost, but who were refused ordination by the English hierarchy. On the same principle, Mr. Wesley, while as yet there were no Methodist presbyters in America, appointed a fellow-presbyter, Dr. Coke, to go and confer ordination upon these men of God, who (while other pastors fled, and left their flocks to perish in the wilderness) maintained their ground in the midst of danger, and fed their people with the bread of life. It is true, as before stated, that Mr. Wesley, as a member and minister of the Church of England, preferred an episcopal form of church government, and in accordance with his expressed wish, the early preachers formed themselves and flock into an *episcopal* church, and ordained men as deacons, elders, and superintendents; but in the view of Mr. Wesley, Dr. Coke, and the preachers ordained by him, there was a wide difference between a high-toned, aristocratic, bombastic episcopacy, such as prevailed in England and Rome, and a moderate episcopal superintendency, such as prevailed among the Moravians, Waldenses, and German Lutherans. They knew how to distinguish between an *order* and an *office;* between the abuses of a lordly, purse-proud hierarchy, and the simplicity and utility of an apostolic superintendency, and wisely and prudently—as the history of the past sixty-seven years fully demonstrates—organized in accordance with the wishes of the father of Methodism, a system of church government, which for simplicity, moderation, unity, and efficient moral power, challenges the admiration of the Christian world!

This system of church government might well be denominated a *presbyterian episcopacy*, as it embraces the advantages of both the presbyterian and episcopal forms of government, and rejects whatever is superfluous and unnecessary in either one or the other. A system, in a word, which teaches the validity of presbyterian ordination, with, at the same time, an episcopal superintendency.

But it is said, that the "Methodist Episcopal succession is spurious, because it cannot be traced back further than the time of Wesley." In reply, we may remark that we have no desire to trace it back any further; that even if we could succeed in tracing the same back to the Romish line, the result would by no means add to our honor as a church, or the validity of our ministerial acts. The "succession" is too rotten for us to desire any affinity with it, or dependence on it, or descent from it. Such a succession as we *have*, thank God! is from a pure source, carried down through a pure stream, and destined, we trust, to retain its purity, till time is no longer.

We may further reply, that on the ground of the ministerial parity of bishops and presbyters, we *have* the succession as truly and scripturally as any other episcopal church on earth. But to let this view of the subject pass, it should be remembered by the objectors, that the clergy of the English church and her American daughter cannot trace *their* succession back further than the time of the Reformation under Luther. We have before proved, that prior to the Reformation, the English church received her ordinations from Rome; that in fact, as a church, she was part and parcel of the Church of Rome. All her ecclesiastical authority was derived from the Pope. All her archbishops and bishops were appointed either directly or indirectly by him, or at least with his consent and approbation, and *every one* of said bishops took an oath of obedience to the Pope, as an indispensable prerequisite to consecration.*

Now if the Pope, as universal bishop, and as the vicegerent of Jesus Christ, had a scriptural right to appoint and ordain these bishops, on the sworn promise of their obedience to him as their head; he had also, when their consecration oath was violated by disobedience and opposition, the scriptural right to depose them from their office of bishop, so that in the latter case, the powers of bishops being withdrawn, all their subsequent acts as bishops would be null and void. It is therefore a matter of no little importance to know that such depositions did take place. Bishops and archbishops were not only deposed by the Pope, but excommunicated from the church. What then became of their previous official authority to ordain, and of what value were their acts, subsequent to the period of their deposition and expulsion? And yet these very bishops continued, in spite of the Pope's anathema, to administer the functions of their office. We may well admire their courage and independence, but we must confess that the succession here came to a stand. Here we meet with other assertions, namely: "that the ecclesiastical authorities at Rome,

* The following is the form of oath taken by such bishops: "I, N——, from this hour, will be faithful and obedient to my lord N—— Pope, and to his successors; the counsel that they shall deliver to me, I will reveal to no one to their damage. I will be their helper in retaining the papacy and royalties of St. Peter, and I will defend them against every man. I will be careful to preserve, defend, and promote the rights, honor, privileges, and authority of the pope. I will not be (a party) in any counsel, deed, or treaty, in which may be devised anything sinister against the pope, or prejudicial to his person, rights, or power: and if I shall know any such thing to be under discussion by any parties soever, I will hinder it as far as I am able, and as soon as I know it, I will signify it to my lord the Pope. The apostolic mandates I will observe with all my powers, and I will cause them to be observed by others. HERETICS and REBELS against my *lord the Pope*, I *will persecute and attack*."

who conferred ordination on the English bishops and clergy, had no power to depose them;" "that the episcopal and ministerial power *once given*, can never be taken away;" "that once a bishop, always a bishop; once a priest, always a priest." This is strange logic! If this reasoning is correct, it will follow that Judas Iscariot, after he betrayed his Lord, would, without repentance or contrition, have always remained a true apostle as long as he lived; notwithstanding the apostle Peter asserts, that "from his ministry and apostleship, Judas, by transgression, *fell*." Had Judas lived for many years after his transgression—had he been as wicked and persecuting as Nero himself—had he become an apostate from Christianity—yet would he have been (if the above reasoning is correct) an apostle still. Had all the apostles combined in deposing him, he might have laughed them in the face, and exclaimed—" once a bishop, always a bishop; once an apostle, always an apostle." Who does not see the glaring absurdity of such a doctrine as this? a doctrine so utterly destitute of reason that we wonder that any man "pretending to holy orders," or to any degree of discernment, or common sense, should be found guilty of maintaining it. But let us examine this point a little further. On the principles of high churchmen, the Roman Catholic Church, before the Reformation, *was* either the *true* church of Christ, or it *was not*. If it *was*, its acts of deposition and excommunication must have been equally valid with its acts of admission and ordination, so that every deposed priest, or bishop, became a mere layman; consequently the subsequent pretended official acts of these persons could not be worth a straw. In proof of this, see Matt. xvi. 18, 19—where Christ says to Peter, "Thou art Peter; and upon this rock will I build my church," &c. "And I will give unto thee the keys of the kingdom of heaven; and whatsoever thou shalt bind on earth, shall be bound in heaven; and whatsoever thou shalt loose on earth, shall be loosed in heaven." On the supposition, then, that the Church of Rome was, before the Reformation, the true church, the Pope must have been a legitimate and regular successor of the apostle Peter, to whom was committed the keys of the kingdom, with the original power of binding, and loosing; and as the authority to bind, and loose, was general in its application, it is evident that "*whatsoever*" the Pope "bound" on earth by his bulls, or "loosed" by his excommunications, was bound or loosed in heaven—whether layman, deacon, priest, or bishop. Where then is the English succession? But if the Roman Catholic Church before the Reformation *was not* the *true* church of Jesus Christ, of what virtue were her previous acts of ordination? If she was not the true church, she must have been a spurious one, her official acts spurious, her ordinations spurious, and thus the succession be a spurious succession.

We are not particular which of these horns of a dilemma the successionists may prefer; for our own part, we are thankful that we are not obliged to hang upon either, as we repudiate the whole system of apostolical succession as a humbug, a cheat, a delusion of the devil, wherewith to beguile unstable souls from the true fold of Christ. No! the true test of a gospel ministry and a gospel church is *success*, and not *succession*. Christ says of his true ministers, by their *fruits* ye shall know them; while prelatical usurpers exclaim, by the *succession-list* ye shall know them; "Examine this list," say they, "and if you find a regular series of *names*, from that of the person whose claim you are inquiring into, back to that of the apostle Peter, you may rest assured such a person is in the true succession; no matter what his moral character; no matter what his natural or acquired fitness for the office; no matter what his want of success in calling sinners to repentance; if his name is only on the list, he is a true minister of Jesus Christ. But if his name is not on the list, if he has the piety of John, the eloquence of Apollos, the Christian boldness of Peter, and the success of Paul, yet is he no minister, but an intruder into the sacred office, a mere teacher pretending to holy orders. Yea! if he can appeal, as Paul, to the thousands converted through his instrumentality, and say, 'The seals of my apostleship are ye in the Lord;' and 'ye are our epistles written in our hearts known and read of all men,' yet, if his name is not on the list, he is no minister—the congregations which he serves are without the gospel, without sacraments, without church-membership, and without an interest in the kingdom of God."

Now what high-toned arrogance is this! Nay! what downright impudence to unchristianize nearly every protestant church in the Christian world! Methodists, Baptists, Presbyterians, Lutherans, Protestants of France, Independents, Quakers, &c., must all be contented with the position of heathens, having an interest only in the "uncovenanted mercies of God!"

We are now prepared, by way of recapitulation and inference, to state a few leading objections to the doctrine of apostolic succession, as held by the high church party. And 1st, we object to the claims because they are *without divine warrant.* We defy the most learned prelate to place his finger on the passage of Scripture from which the justice of these claims may be even inferred—Christ says to his true ministers, "Lo I am with you alway, even unto the end of the world;" but he nowhere states that they must be ordained by those who have passed through a triple consecration.

2d. We object to the claims of uninterrupted succession because the history of the Christian church is in direct opposition to them. Even popish historians, and the most accredited writers in the Church of England, prove the falsity of these claims, and show beyond a doubt that this doctrine is a "cunningly devised fable."

3d. We object to these claims again, because the brightest ornaments that ever graced the episcopal chair, in the English and American Episcopal Churches, have denied the validity of the same. We instance only the following Archbishops and Bishops: Cranmer, Whitgift, Grindal, Leighton, Jewel, Whittaker, Reynolds, Tillottson, Burnet, Stillingfleet, Hoadley, Usher, Dowman, Croft, Hall, Bancroft, Andrews, Forbes, Wake, Chillingworth, and White, the latter being the first bishop of the Protestant Episcopal Church in America. These eminent Episcopalian prelates, with hundreds of others, have borne ample testimony in favor of our position, and in opposition to these claims.

4th. We object to these claims, because that to yield to them, would be entailing upon the church a lordly hierarchy, and that, too, under the pretence that it is by divine right; while Jesus taught his disciples to "call no man Master upon earth;" for, saith he, "one is your Master, even Christ, and *all* ye are brethren." Besides: a pretended superiority of this kind requires a corresponding amount of means to sustain it; hence, the Archbishop of Canterbury and his brother prelates, must have from twenty-five thousand to one hundred thousand dollars each, per annum, and the other clergy in proportion to their rank; while the bishops of the Protestant Episcopal Church in America, although not receiving as much, have certainly much larger salaries than are necessary for their comfortable support.

5th. This system, and these claims, have a tendency to foster a spirit of pride and vain-glory. Who has not witnessed with pain and mental distress, the lordly air and haughty bearing of some who profess to be ministers of the meek and lowly Jesus, who said to his disciples, "He that will be the greatest among you, let him be your servant?" And is it not a proper inference, that whatever tends to exalt man in his own eyes, by giving him a fancied superiority over others, cannot be of God?

A 6th objection to these claims is, that they nourish a spirit of bigotry and sectarianism. "The temple of the Lord are we!" and, "We thank thee, O God, that we are not as other men are—without the church, without the ministry, without the sacraments, or even as these poor deluded dissenters." "We are the only true church; all other *professed* Christians are entitled only to the uncovenanted mercies of God, the same as heathens who have no church, no ministry, no sacraments." In perfect keeping with the above pharisaic language, are the official reports of some of the diocesan "successors." When describing their visits to certain places, they speak of the Episcopal "Church," the "Presbyterian meeting-house," the "Baptist house of worship," the "Methodist chapel," &c. Hence, also, while they gladly avail themselves, in cases of necessity of the proffered use of these "meeting-houses" and "places of worship," they never are known to reciprocate the favor, by inviting clergymen of other denominations to the use of their "churches."

7th. A lordly hierarchy, in its legitimate consequences, endangers the stability and perpetuity of republican institutions. James I. of England, with a greater knowledge of human nature than is generally ascribed to him, wittily said, "No Bishop, no King." That is, "Without bishops, monarchy cannot exist." The truth of this remark has been exemplified in every age, proving that it requires the aid of an aristocratic order of the clergy, to sustain the pillars of a monarch's throne; and that without such aid and support, monarchies cannot exist. But the above saying of the king might very well be reversed, "No King, no Bishop," understanding the latter term in the same sense as it is used by "apostolic" pretenders. Who does not see, that, under the pure and genial influences of republican institutions, the high claims before alluded to, never have been, and never can be yielded to, by a free and sovereign people? And although diocesan prelates may ostentatiously style themselves "Bishop of New York," "Bishop of New Jersey," "Bishop of Maryland," and may renew their efforts to have the few thousands of their Israel dignified with the name of the "Church of the United States," yet it will be many long years, we trust, before their ambition is gratified, by the consent of the mass of the population. When such consent is given to these exclusive claims, then farewell to republicanism, liberty, and happiness.

8th. We object, finally, to these claims, that they trifle with the interests of the souls of men; basing, as they do, the salvation of the soul upon a connection with a church in which the "succession" is found; while they deny emphatically the scriptural doctrine of regeneration, and the necessity of "holiness, without which no man shall see the Lord;" and that while they "tithe mint and cummin," and insist on the necessity of a "regular succession," they neglect the "weightier matters of the law, judgment, mercy, and faith."

These objections are urged, not against the *Episcopal Church* as such, but simply against the unwarrantable pretensions of a portion of said church, who stigmatize all others as heretics, schismatics, and heathen.

Having thus examined the claims of those who "say they are apostles," or the exclusive descendants and successors of the apostles; having "tried" them, and proved that they "are not" what they profess to be; having shown that these pretensions are not well founded, it will be unnecessary to remind the reader, that we have brought no railing accusation against the English or American Episcopal Churches. We have not attempted to deny their position as important branches of the Church of Christ. We have not called in question the piety or learning of their ministers; we say nothing against their form of church government, however much we may differ from them in opinion on this point; we have not assailed their doctrines and liturgy; we have not refused to acknowledge them as true successors of the apostles; we have said not a word against their rites and ceremonies; we have not whispered a syllable against their priestly robes or episcopal vestments; on every one of these points, we probably differ from them in opinion; but still, in regard to such secondary matters, our motto is, "Live, and let live." Our only object has been to show the folly of claiming an *exclusive* right to the kingdom of God, by virtue of a mysterious episcopal unction, handed down from generation to generation. What we have written has been merely on the defensive. If high church episcopalians will not unchurch us, we certainly shall not try to unchurch them; and even if they will persist in their wholesale denunciations, we can but pity, and pray for them; knowing, as we do, that it is not the imposition of a bishop's hands that will prepare the soul of either minister or lay member for heaven, but "that, in every nation, he that feareth God and worketh righteousness, is accepted with him;" and that "not every one that saith, Lord, Lord! shall enter into the kingdom of heaven; but he that doeth the will of my Father which is in heaven."

We will close this section by adopting the beautiful language of the episcopal liturgy, which I would to God were written on the tablets of the hearts of those who so frequently repeat it:—

"From all blindness of heart; from pride, vain-glory, and hypocrisy; from envy, hatred, and malice, and all uncharitableness:

"Good Lord deliver us."

Amen.

SECTION IV.

ORIGIN OF METHODIST EPISCOPACY, &C.

In the two former sections we have attempted to show the absurdity of the claims of the high churchmen in relation to an uninterrupted succession from the apostles. The object of the present section is to show the origin and scriptural character of the superintendency of the Methodist Episcopal Church.

We have more than once asserted in this work, that John Wesley was, under God, the father and founder of Methodism. By referring to Book I. of this work, the reader will learn that the rise of Methodism in America in 1766, was owing to the indefatigable exertions of a few local preachers, who, having emigrated from Europe, introduced the doctrines and customs of Methodism into America; that when the Societies and members became more numerous, Mr. Wesley sent over a number of regular travelling preachers; that through the labors of the latter, the cause continued to spread and grow, even amidst all the excitement of the war of the revolution; so that at the close thereof, it was found that a large increase had been made during the continuance of hostilities. We have also adverted to the fact, that in 1784, Mr. Wesley provided a superintendency, or episcopacy, for his Societies in America. As, however, the episcopacy of the Methodist Church has been violently assailed, not only by the successionists before alluded to, but by non-episcopal writers and divines, it seems necessary to make a few additional remarks in the present section, in relation to its origin and true character.

As stated in the first section of this book, not only non-episcopal writers have denied the intention of Mr. Wesley to establish an Episcopal form of church government in America, but by at least one Methodist Episcopal writer, the same denial has been expressed. The proof furnished by such persons is usually the celebrated and often-quoted letter of Mr. Wesley to Bishop Asbury, a copy of which we prefer to give the reader, that he may judge of its contents, and of the validity of the objections founded on the same.

"To THE REV. FRANCIS ASBURY:

"*London*, Sept. 20, 1788.

"There is indeed a wide difference between the relation wherein you stand to the Americans, and the relation wherein I stand to all the Methodists: I am, under God, the father of the whole family. Therefore I naturally care for you all, in a manner no other person can do. Therefore I, in a measure, provide for you all: for the supplies which Dr. Coke provides for you, he would not provide, were it not for me—were it not that I not only permit him to collect, but also support him in so doing.

"But in one point, my dear brother, I am a little afraid both you and the doctor differ from me—I study to be *little*—you study to be *great:* I *creep*—you *strut* along. I found a *school*—you a *college!*—nay, and call it after your own names. O, beware! do not seek to be something. Let me be nothing, and 'Christ be all in all.'

"One instance of this your *greatness*, has given me great concern. How can you—how dare you suffer yourself to be called a *bishop?* I shudder and start at the very thought! Men may call me a knave, and a fool, a rascal, a scoundrel, and I am content: but they shall never, by my consent, call me a *bishop*. For my sake, for God's sake, for Christ's sake, put a full end to this. Let the Presbyterians do what they please—but let the Methodists know their calling better.

"Thus, my dear Franky, I have told you all that is in my heart: and let this, when I am no more seen, bear witness how sincerely I am your affectionate friend and brother,

"J. WESLEY."

To understand the full force and meaning of the above letter, it is necessary to take into consideration the occasion which called for its being written. It will be remembered by the reader, that when Dr. Coke was ordained to the superintendency of the Methodist Episcopal Church by Mr. Wesley himself, the latter directed him to set apart Francis Asbury to the same office. Mr. Asbury was, in an emphatic sense, the *apostle* of American Methodism, and had, many years before his ordination as bishop, been appointed by Mr. Wesley as his General Assistant in America. He was, however, superseded by the appointment of Mr. Rankin, an older and more experienced preacher, who being sent to America by Mr. Wesley, was appointed General Assistant in the place of Mr. Asbury. This appointment does not appear to have given very general satisfaction to the preachers or people in America, inasmuch as they supposed that Mr. Asbury, from his long residence among them, was the better qualified of the two for the office of superintendent. This opinion of the people was well known to Mr. Rankin, and may account, in part, for his rather short stay in America. Upon his return to England, Mr. Asbury was again invested with the honors and responsibilities of the General Superintendency. It was quite natural that Mr. Rankin, under these circumstances, should view Mr. Asbury somewhat in the light of a rival, and that, being prejudiced against him, he should, after his arrival in England, so far operate upon the mind of Mr. Wesley, as to induce the fear that Mr. Asbury was an ambitious and aspiring man. It is evident, however, from the subsequent appointment of Mr. Asbury by Mr. Wesley, that whatever fears the latter might have indulged in, they had greatly subsided; so much so, that Mr. Asbury was entitled to his fullest confidence, as a man, and Christian minister. Hence, in accordance with the wishes of the American preachers and people, that under any system of ecclesiastical government which Mr. Wesley might provide for his Societies in America, Mr. Asbury might be placed at the head of affairs, provision was made by the former to elevate the latter to the joint superintendency of the church that was soon to be organized by his agent Doctor Coke. After the said organization had taken place, and Mr. Asbury had become a joint superintendent, the American preachers, aware that Mr. Wesley had intended the organization of an Episcopal Church, in the proper sense of that word, and if so, that the title bishop was more scriptural and expressive than that of superintendent, began to employ the former term in their addresses to those who filled that office, and the latter, in accordance with the expressed wishes of the people, allowed themselves to be addressed by that title.

The assumption of the title bishop, re-awakened the fears in which Mr. Wesley had before indulged in reference to Mr. Asbury's ambition. He, being accustomed from early life to associate with the title bishop all that is pompous and splendid—

all that is costly and aristocratic, and having been informed that Mr. Asbury had become ambitious, and was thirsting for dominion, and that he could not bear an equal, &c. &c., all of which charges were the offspring of jealousy and disappointed ambition on the part of a rival, led Mr. Wesley to believe that reproof had in fact become necessary, and hence the letter above quoted, from which the opponents of Methodist Episcopacy have drawn the following conclusions. (1.) That Mr. Wesley did not design the establishment of a Methodist *Episcopal* Church in America. (2.) That he did not intend that Dr. Coke and Mr. Asbury should be, in any sense whatever, bishops of the church which he authorized the former to organize. An examination of these two points will therefore demand attention.

On the second day of September, 1784, Mr. Wesley—having had the condition of his American Societies under consideration for a length of time, and believing it to be his imperative duty to provide the ministry and sacraments for these "sheep in the wilderness,"—associated with himself Dr. Coke and the Rev. Mr. Creighton, both of whom, like himself, were presbyters of the Church of England, and proceeded to ordain Thomas Vasey and Richard Whatcoat to the office of elders or presbyters in the church of God; and then, being assisted by Mr. Creighton and the two newly ordained presbyters, proceeded to ordain Dr. Coke to the office of Superintendent of the Methodist Societies in America, and gave him the following credentials:—

"To all to whom these presents shall come, John Wesley, late Fellow of Lincoln College in Oxford, Presbyter of the Church of England, sendeth greeting:

"Whereas many of the people in the southern provinces of North America, who desire to continue under my care, and still adhere to the doctrine and discipline of the Church of England, are greatly distressed for want of ministers to administer the sacraments of baptism and the Lord's Supper, according to the usage of the same church; and whereas there does not appear to be any other way of supplying them with ministers:—

"Know all men, that *I, John Wesley*, think myself to be providentially called, at this time, to set apart some persons for the work of the ministry in America. And therefore, under the protection of Almighty God, and with a single eye to his glory, I have this day set apart as a superintendent, by the imposition of my hands and prayer (being assisted by other ordained ministers), Thomas Coke, doctor of civil law, a presbyter of the Church of England, and a man whom I judge to be well qualified for that great work. And I do hereby recommend him to all whom it may concern, as a fit person to preside over the flock of Christ.

"In testimony whereof, I have hereunto set my hand and seal, this second day of September, in the year of our Lord one thousand seven hundred and eighty-four.

"JOHN WESLEY."

In examining the above testimonial of Dr. Coke's ordination, the reader will observe, that one of Mr. Wesley's declared reasons for the same, is, that his people in North America "still adhere to the doctrines and *discipline* of the Church of England." Now, the inquiry naturally arises, whether, in view of such adherence on the part of the Americans to the discipline of the Church of England, and especially in view of the fact, that Mr. Wesley gives such adherence as a *reason* for his acts in the premises, he would have entailed upon his children a form of church government as unlike the form of the Church of England as it was possible to make it, if so be that he intended a Presbyterian, a Congregational, or any other non-episcopal form? The only reasonable answer is, that such being the desire of the Americans to adhere to the discipline of the Church of England, Mr. Wesley was disposed to meet that desire in the best way he possibly could, by giving them a form of ecclesiastical government, as nearly like that of the Church of England, as circumstances would admit of. For the purpose of throwing still farther light on this subject, we will also favor the reader with the letter which Mr. Wesley gave to Dr. Coke for the brethren in America, and which he wished the doctor to publish as extensively as possible on his arrival:—

"*Bristol, September* 10, 1784.

"To Dr. Coke, Mr. Asbury, and our brethren in North America.

"By a very uncommon train of providences, many of the provinces of North America are totally disjoined from the mother country, and erected into independent states. The English government has no authority over them, either civil or ecclesiastical, any more than over the States of Holland. A civil authority is exercised over them, partly by the Congress, partly by the provincial assemblies. But no one either claims or exercises any ecclesiastical authority at all. In this peculiar situation, thousands of the inhabitants of these States desire my advice; and in compliance with their desire I have drawn up a little sketch. Lord King's Account of the Primitive Church convinced me, many years ago, that bishops and presbyters are the same order, and consequently have the same right to ordain. For many years I have been importuned, from time to time, to exercise this right, by ordaining part of our travelling preachers. But I have still refused, not only for peace' sake, but because I was determined as little as possible to violate the established order of the national church, to which I belonged.

"But the case is widely different between England and North America. Here there are bishops who have a legal jurisdiction. In America there are none, neither any parish ministers; so that, for some hundreds of miles together, there is none either to baptize or to administer the Lord's Supper. Here, therefore, my scruples were at an end; and I conceive myself at full liberty, as I violate no order, and invade no man's right, by appointing and sending laborers into the harvest.

"I have accordingly appointed Dr. Coke and Mr. Francis Asbury to be joint superintendents over our brethren in North America; as also Richard Whatcoat and Thomas Vasey, to act as elders among them, by baptizing and administering the Lord's supper. And I have prepared a liturgy little differing from that of the Church of England (I think the best constituted national church in the world), which I advise all the travelling preachers to use on the Lord's day, in all the congregations, reading the litany only on Wednesdays and Fridays, and praying extempore on all other days. I advise, also, the elders to administer the supper of the Lord, on every Lord's day.

"If any one will point out a more rational and scriptural way of feeding and guiding these poor sheep in the wilderness, I will gladly embrace it. At present, I cannot see any better method than that I have taken.

"It has, indeed, been proposed to desire the English bishops to ordain part of our preachers for America. But to this I object: 1. I desired the bishop of London to ordain one, but could not prevail. 2. If they consented, we know the slowness of their proceedings; but the matter admits of no delay. 3. If they were to ordain them now, they would expect to govern them hereafter. And how grievously would this entangle us! 4. As our American brethren are totally disentangled both from the state and the English hierarchy, we dare not entangle them again, either with the one or the other. They are now at full liberty, simply to follow the Scriptures and the primitive church. And we judge it best that they should stand fast in that liberty wherewith God has so strangely made them free. JOHN WESLEY."

This letter proves: (1.) That the office to which Dr. Coke had been ordained, and Mr. Asbury had been appointed by Mr. Wesley, was superior to the office of a presbyter or elder; else why ordain Dr. Coke, when he had been for years invested with full presbyterial powers by the Church of England? On a contrary view of the case, the ordination of the doctor by Mr. Wesley must have been a mere farce got up for the occasion. (2.) The letter proves that Mr. Wesley esteemed the liturgy of the Church of England above any other form of service; and that, in providing for the wants of an infant connection, he, in fact, prepared the same for the worship and government of said connection. (3.) The "Liturgy"—or Sunday Service, as it is sometimes called—thus prepared by Mr. Wesley, contained three distinct services of ordination, namely, for deacons, elders, and superintendents; and to suppose that he would thus provide for the *three-fold* consecration of the highest officers of the church; and yet not intend the existence of such an office as the *episcopate*, either in name or fact, is a supposition at once so absurd as scarcely to demand notice. If, however, it be objected, that Mr. Wesley did not use the term bishop in said liturgy, but the term superintendent, and therefore he could not mean bishop; we have only to reply, that both the terms mean one and the same thing—an *overseer;* and that if the fact of his dropping the use of the name *bishop*, is evidence that he disapproved of the *office* in the American Church, so the erasure of the term *presbyter*, or its contraction *priest*, from his liturgy, and the substitution of the word *elder*, is evidence that he disapproved of the office of a presbyter in the same church; and yet nothing is more certain than that he provided for the latter office.

It is true that Mr. Wesley disliked the use of the term *presbyter*, when applied to his preachers, and for the same reason he disapproved of the use of the term *bishop*, when applied to the General Superintendents of the Methodist Church. He also disliked the use of the term *College*, as applied to a Methodist literary institution, and preferred the less pretending name of *School;* but can we from these facts infer that John Wesley—himself a presbyter—did not believe in the office of a presbyter? or that he did not believe in the utility or lawfulness of colleges? The idea is perfectly preposterous. The fact is, that Mr. Wesley was opposed to the application of the terms bishop and presbyter to his ministers in America, while he was more than willing that they should fill the offices designated by such titles, under the more unassuming names of superintendent and elder. This, however, was a mere matter of scrupulous taste with Mr. Wesley, rather than anything else —a fault, if fault it was, which certainly may well be forgiven him, in view of the gross abuses of the titles and offices by some of the dignitaries of the Romish Church, and her daughter, the Church of England.

Let it be remembered, too, as stated in Section I. of this chapter, that the Methodist Church in the United States had been organized as an *Episcopal* Church for more than six years prior to the death of Mr. Wesley; that the minutes of the conference which organized the church as an Episcopal church, together with all the facts and circumstances, were well known to him, and submitted to him for his approval by Dr. Coke; and that not a single word of disapprobation, either in reference to the Doctor's action in the premises, or to the name and title of the church, was spoken or written by Mr. Wesley, and we have proof of the most convincing character, that Mr. Wesley did design our form of church government to be *Episcopalian;* and that the fathers and founders of our church polity, did not deceive, when they proclaimed upon the page of the Book of Discipline, that Mr. Wesley, "preferring the Episcopal mode of church government to any other, solemnly set apart Thomas Coke for the Episcopal office, and directed him to set apart Francis Asbury for the same office." These, then, being facts, we are prepared to claim John Wesley as the originator of American Episcopal Methodism.

But aside from these considerations, we claim that even if Mr. Wesley had not provided an Episcopal form of government for the American Methodists, the latter, when constituted an independent church, had a scriptural right to choose such a form of government as was best suited to their circumstances and condition. If it is a fact, according to the XXXIV. Article of the Church of England, and the Protestant Episcopal Church in America, that "Every particular or national church, hath authority to ordain, change, and abolish ceremonies or rites of the church, ordained only by man's authority, so that all things be done to edifying." If it is a fact, in the language of the same Article, that "It is not necessary that traditions and ceremonies be in all places one, or utterly alike; for at all times they have been divers, and may be changed according to the diversity of countries, times, and men's manners, so that nothing be ordained against God's word;" if, we repeat it, these are facts, then had the Methodist Episcopal Church a scriptural, and even canonical right to ordain such rites and ceremonies as seemed good to her. We say she had a *canonical* right to do so; that is, allowing that before her independence she was considered an integral part of the Church of England, the 34th Article of that church gave her the right to ordain, change, and abolish such ceremonies and rites as had been ordained by merely human authority.

That the terms "rites," "traditions," and "ceremonies," do not mean merely the form of church service, which a church at its pleasure may adopt, is evident from the fact that the same Article asserts that he who doth purposely and openly break the same, through private judgment, offends against the common order of the church, and "hurteth the authority of the magistrate." Now it cannot be supposed that a mere deviation on the part of an individual from the prescribed form of church service, would be hurtful to the authority of the magistrate, for, 1st, the magistrate has no scriptural authority in the matter whatsoever, and 2dly, it would be beneath the dignity of the subject to suppose that the Article refers to the authority of the magistrate to prescribe how many and what prayers a man shall repeat in his attempts to worship God. The only reasonable meaning which can be attached to this language is, that when, by common authority, a certain form of ecclesiastical government is established in any church, no individual may, of his own private judgment, purposely violate the rules and requirements of such established order of things, while a body of Christians living in a foreign land, and subject to no ecclesiastical jurisdiction whatsoever, may "ordain, change and abolish" such usages and forms as they please. To illustrate this point clearly: had Mr. Wesley ordained ministers for the Church of England, he would have been a transgressor of the doctrine taught in the Article. Had he made the attempt to ordain Dr. Coke as a bishop of the establishment, he would have exposed himself to the open rebuke of his ecclesiastical superiors. But Mr. Wesley attempted no such thing. He simply made provision for the proper organization of an independent foreign church, and that church, availing itself of the privilege given to establish itself on any basis it chose, adopted such a mode of government as the exigencies of the case demanded, and the above Article allowed. It should be remembered, too, that the Methodist Episcopal Church was duly organized, while as yet there was no other independent Protestant Episcopal Church in America, the body of Christians now bearing that name not having been duly organized, till several years after the Methodist Church had been in being, and was known and acknowledged by the civil authorities of the nation as an independent ecclesiastical body, having its own bishops, its own ministry, its own membership, and all other things requisite to its proper organization. So far, then, as authority could be given by the Articles of Religion of the Church of England, the organization of the Methodist Episcopal Church was not only scriptural, but canonical.

SECTION V.

ADVANTAGES OF THE METHODIST EPISCOPAL FORM OF CHURCH GOVERNMENT WHEN COMPARED WITH OTHER FORMS.

GOVERNMENT of some kind is as necessary for the church of God, as it is essential for nations. There are different forms of civil government—as an absolute, or limited monarchy; an aristocracy, a democracy; a republic, &c. &c. The great object of a good government is, to unite, if possible, the three qualities of strength, permanency, and protection. These will require a good foundation, a proper structure, and an efficient executive. An absolute monarchy is admitted to be the strongest kind of civil government, and a democracy to afford the greatest amount of liberty to the governed. A system of government between these two extremes, is probably the form that is best suited to the wants of man in these latter days. Such a system of mixed government may be found to exist in the limited monarchy of Great Britain, and still more perfectly in the republicanism of the United States of America. In each of these governments, the chief executive power is lodged in the hands of one person, who moves and directs the large number of subordinate officers under him. Such a system is at a proper distance from autocracy on the one hand, and anarchy on the other.

In like manner, ecclesiastical government may be made to exist under different forms, combining more or less strength, and affording more or less protection to the governed. The absolute monarchy of Romanism, with the Pope at its head, is found at one extreme; and a state of complete ecclesiastical independence, may be found at the other extreme. The former system combines more strength with its operations; the latter gives greater latitude in matters of faith and practice. The former is an ecclesiastical despotism—the latter borders on a state of spiritual anarchy and confusion. "There being no king in Israel, every man does that which is right in his own eyes." Between these two extremes, there is, and ought to be, a medium course—a mixed form of church government—which will combine the strength of the one system, and secure the liberty of the other, as far as it is proper to secure it; in a word, a system combining strength and efficiency with a proper degree of security for the rights and privileges of those who are disposed to become the subjects of such ecclesiastical government. And such, we may be allowed to claim, is the government of the Methodist Episcopal Church in these United States.

But in order that the reader may judge of the comparative strength and efficiency of the different systems of church government now prevailing, we may be allowed to refer to them somewhat in detail.

1. Romish Episcopacy.—In this system, as already asserted, we find a purely spiritual despotism. The strength and power of the system centres in one person—the pope—who claims to be the "successor of St. Peter," the "vicegerent of God," "supreme over all mortals," "over all emperors, kings, princes, potentates, and people," "King of kings, and Lord of lords." Such are a few of the titles claimed by his "Holiness." And it should be understood that these titles are not by Romanists considered as mere empty sounds, but that all Roman Catholics, from the higher dignitaries of the Church, down to the lowest private member, acknowledge the validity of such titles, and pay the most obsequious obedience to the pope as universal bishop. To strengthen the power of the pope, all cardinals, archbishops, bishops, priests, deacons, &c. &c., must swear eternal fealty to him and to his government. Hence the pope, with or without his councils, is the fountain of all law, and the source of all ecclesiastical honor. His "bulls" are as authoritative as are the mandates of Jehovah, issued from amidst the thunderings and lightnings of

Sinai's smoking summit. In a word, his will is law, and with his host of titled dignitaries in all parts of Christendom, he has the power to enforce his will, if not by the sharpness of steel, the force of powder, or the fires and tortures of the inquisition, by other means no less effectual, and no less dangerous to the rights and liberties of mankind.

2. English Episcopacy.—In this system of church government may be found less strength than in the Romish system, but a greater degree of freedom for the subjects of its power, and yet not so much as they should be allowed to possess by a professedly Protestant Church. The episcopacy of the Church of England exists in two archbishops and twenty-four bishops, all of whom are *ex officio* lords of Parliament, or peers of the realm. The archbishop of Canterbury, who is "primate of all England," is the first peer of the realm, and takes precedence, not only of all the bishops and clergy, but of all the nobility, consisting of dukes, earls, marquises, &c. &c., the royal family alone excepted. All the bishops of the Church of England are, in fact, the creatures of the crown; that is, the reigning sovereign virtually appoints the bishops to vacant sees, and every subordinate clergyman, or inferior officer, is also, directly or indirectly, the appointee of the civil government. In this system, therefore, we cannot fail to perceive a partial leaning toward the Romish system of government, especially as the lay members of the Church of England have no voice whatever as members in the affairs of the church, but are in all respects, subject to the civil and ecclesiastical "powers that be." Such a system, to say the least, based upon secular patronage, and courtly influence and authority, must be detrimental to the interests of that religion, in reference to which our Saviour said, "My kingdom is not of this world."

3. Protestant Episcopacy.—This system prevails in the United States, as the form of government selected by the adherents of the Church of England, after the war of the Revolution, and the independence of the North American Colonies

The Constitution of the Protestant Episcopal Church was adopted in October, 1789, nearly five years subsequent to the organization of the Methodist Episcopal Church. In the system of Protestant Episcopacy, there is more to admire than in that of English Episcopacy. The bishops in the former are not lords, or spiritual peers of the realm, in a civil sense. Indeed, whatever disposition might exist on their part, or on the part of their adherents, to engraft the English system of governmental patronage into their church polity, it is well known that the Constitution of the United States, and those of the respective States, completely debars them from making any such attempt.

The supreme legislative and judicial power of this church is lodged in the General Convention, which meets triennally, and is composed of an upper and lower house, very similar, in fact, to the Houses of Lords and Commons in England. The upper house consists exclusively of the bishops, who may originate acts, and concur in those of the lower house; and who possess an absolute negative in relation thereto; so that no act can become a law unless the upper house agrees thereto. The lower house consists of clergymen and lay deputies, who may or may not be members of the church, provided they are duly elected by the bodies they represent.

The bishops of this church have their respective dioceses, or episcopal parishes, beyond which they possess no episcopal authority whatever, unless invited in case of vacancy to exercise the functions of their office. Their salaries amount to from two to seven thousand dollars per annum, and they are amenable only to the house of bishops for immorality or gross official dereliction. Such is the Episcopacy of the Protestant Episcopal Church in the United States—an episcopacy which has embraced many worthy men, and yet which has been disgraced by one or more less worthy persons, of doubtful morals.

4. Presbyterianism.—In this system we find a total abandonment of episcopacy in all its forms; the supreme legislative

and judicial power being invested in the body of elders—teaching and ruling—who are delegated by their respective presbyteries to meet in the General Assembly, which body represents the church as a whole. The Presbyterian system embodies much power and efficiency, because of the connectional principle which pervades the entire system. It has, in fact, many excellencies, and but few defects, the latter being owing to the want of a general superintendency of some kind, which would have a tendency to consolidate the different parts of the system more perfectly. The most perfect system of Presbyterianism is that found in the Scottish Churches, as also in the Presbyterian Church of the United States.

5. Congregationalism.—By this system of church government is understood the absolute independence of each local church, in regard to matters of faith and ecclesiastical polity; discarding at once, not only episcopacy in all its forms, but even presbyterianism itself. Under this system, each local church is the supreme legislative and judicial body, in regard to all matters which appertain to the doctrines or practices of its individual members; and no other church council or presbytery has any right whatever to interfere with their independence in these respects, except to give advice when requested.

Congregationalism was the established form of church government in the days of Puritanism, in many of the colonies, and under this system some very sanguinary laws were passed for the hanging of Quakers, witches, &c. &c. The inhabitants of the colonies where this system prevailed, as also in some of the States after independence was secured, were taxed by law for the support of the "*standing order;*" and it rendered itself powerful only as it wielded the sword of the civil magistrate. Since the latter has been taken from it, and it has been left to stand upon its own merits, it has been found that there is a great want of system and efficiency in this form of ecclesiastical polity; so much so, that there has been for many years a gradual advance towards the Presbyterian form.

6. METHODIST EPISCOPACY.—We now proceed to notice the advantages of the polity adopted by the Methodist Episcopal Church. And in doing so, it will be necessary to diverge more or less from the main feature of the system, namely, the episcopacy itself. In the examination of these points, it will, no doubt, be perceived by the reader, that while our church polity secures strength and vitality on the one hand, it also secures the rights and privileges of every member and minister in the church, on the other; that it combines whatever is excellent in other systems, and discards what are acknowledged to be serious defects in those systems.

It should be remembered that Methodism is aggressive in its character and operations. Its great object is not to provide fat parishes for its priests, or rich dioceses for its bishops; not to decorate its ministers and altars with flowing drapery, or splendid vestments, not to minister to the vitiated taste of a cold and heartless congregation; or to sit down in ease and enjoy the good things of this life; but to "spread scriptural holiness" over the world; to wage war with sin, and to carry the battle even to the gates of hell. Its object is to go to the sinner and invite him to Christ; if he accepts the invitation, then to lead him into the audience-chamber of the King of kings; if he finds mercy—as we know he will, if sincere—then lead him into "green pastures, and by the side of still waters," that he may "grow in grace, and in the knowledge of the truth;" to place safeguards around him, that he may not fall a prey to the adversary; to place before him such incentives to piety, and such inducements to holiness, as shall prompt him to make his "calling and election sure." All this is the proper work of the ministry, and instead of waiting until the invitation is given to come and preach in some snug little parish church, the Methodist itinerant receives his commission to "go into all the world;" to "go into the highways and hedges, and compel men to come in." Such is the object of Methodism.

But to accomplish these desirable results, a mode of operation must be pursued, which will be likely to secure the end in view, and such instruments must be employed as shall be willing not only to endure the necessary hardships, and make the necessary sacrifices, but who are otherwise qualified for the great work of saving souls. Such a mode of operation is found in the itinerant system of Methodism, and such instruments are found in the thousands of ministers who have many of them literally "forsaken all for Christ's sake, and the gospel's," and the thousands and millions who have been converted to God through such instrumentalities, afford abundant evidence of the efficiency of the system by which they have been brought into the fold of Christ.

To preserve these sheep, to save these lambs, pastors must be provided, and government must be instituted. How shall these pastors be appointed; and what form of government shall be instituted? Shall we allow each individual sheep to select its own shepherd? Then we might have as many shepherds as there are sheep. Shall we institute a form of government similar to the Romish Episcopacy? This would be both unscriptural and dangerous. Shall we select the English Episcopal form? This certainly could not be tolerated in a land of freedom. Shall we choose the Protestant Episcopal mode of government? This would be to allow persons who are not even communicants of our own, or any other church, to make our laws, and frame our church polity for us—yea, even infidels and avowed skeptics might meet in "solemn conclave," to enact laws for the government of the "body of Christ." Shall we submit to the Presbyterian form of church government? This would destroy at once the aggressive character of the church. Shall we then adopt the congregational mode? This would not only destroy the connectional principle, but would be fatal to the itinerant system. No! we will combine together, if possible, the excellences of each, and discard that which is unfit for the government of Christ's flock. We will have a general superintendency, without the usual pomp and trappings of a lordly hierarchy. We will have a ministry who will fulfil their commission without waiting for a "call" to the more able parishes. We will have a system of government that will preclude the despotism of Rome, and the anarchy of pure independency.

Such is the system of government as adopted in the Methodist Episcopal Church, and the reader who will peruse the succeeding sections of this work, will not fail to be struck with the admirable arrangement of the whole superstructure, and the perfect adaptation of all the parts to each other, so that from the bishop down to the most humble member, the rights of all are fully and perfectly secured.

Objections have been urged against the system thus adopted, because of the absence of lay delegates in the general and annual conferences. In reference, however, to the latter bodies, scarcely any reply need be made to the objection, as it is a well-known fact, that the business transacted by such bodies, is purely ministerial in its character; and what good end could be secured by a lay delegation, we have yet to learn. In relation to a delegation of lay members in the General Conference, it may be necessary to say that the greater part of the business here transacted, relates almost exclusively to the preachers; but besides, the plan of having a lay delegation in the General Conference, would be utterly impracticable. In a church as large as the Methodist Episcopal Church, the number of ministerial delegates must necessarily be large, in order to have a fair representation of the different portions of the church; and indeed the attendance now is so large as to make it a serious tax on the time and hospitality of the inhabitants of the place where the conference is held. Now, if we were to double or treble the number in attendance, it would proportionably increase the burden. These delegates must also come from all parts of the church, thousands of miles distant; to do this, a vast amount of expense must be met, and who will meet such additional outlays? Will the delegates pay their own expenses? Then shall we make rich men necessary to us, while the poor, because of his poverty, will have the privilege of staying at home. Besides, our lay members generally belong to the humbler ranks in society; true, we have some judges, and lawyers, and distinguished statesmen, and physicians, who are worthy members of the church, and who have the pecuniary ability to pay their own expenses, but their time is more properly, and perhaps more profitably spent in attending to the duties of their professions, than in spending weeks, perhaps months, in hearing the appeals of preachers, and listening to the arguments of divines.

There is still another consideration which outweighs all others in relation to lay representation, and that is its absolute impossibility. To have a fair and proportionate number of clerical and lay delegates, would require both classes to be represented in an equal ratio; that is, for instance: one clerical delegate for every twenty-one ministers; and one lay delegate for every twenty-one members. This would give us, according to our present numbers in the church, about two hundred clerical delegates, and over *thirty-three thousand* lay delegates! But suppose we make the ratio of representation one delegate for every thousand ministers and members; then should we have *four* ministerial delegates, to *seven hundred* lay delegates. As we find the delegation to be still rather large, supposing we make the ratio one for every five thousand; then we have of ministerial delegates, NONE! and of lay delegates *one hundred and forty!*

There are still other considerations which might be presented as reasons for rejecting the practice of a lay delegation in the councils of the church; one or two only we will name, and drop the subject. A lay delegation would inevitably produce the spirit and practice of electioneering in the primary bodies of the church, thus keeping the body in a continual state of agitation, producing discord and dissensions among brethren. It would also beget a spirit of vain-glory, by raising one member above another. It would be attended with so much inconvenience, as to be totally impracticable in its operations, and it would tend to secularize the church of God, by appointing men for its legislators and governors, who are purely secular in their calling and profession; and lastly, the practice has been faithfully tried in other Methodist bodies, and has not answered the expectations of its warmest friends. Hence, we had better leave the matter as it is, praying that God may always preserve the councils of the church from adopting any measures that shall not be promotive of his glory, and the good of mankind.

In the further examination of the polity of Episcopal Methodism, we propose to confine ourselves mostly to the matter found in the Book of Discipline, and to select such portions of the same, as will throw light on the subject, while we will purposely omit everything that is not needed for this purpose, and add any explanatory remarks which we may think necessary to a better understanding of the same.

CHAPTER II.

GENERAL RULES, AND RECEPTION AND EXPULSION OF MEMBERS.

SECTION I.

THE NATURE, DESIGN, AND GENERAL RULES OF OUR UNITED SOCIETIES.

"(1.) In the latter end of the year 1739, eight or ten persons came to Mr. Wesley in London, who appeared to be deeply convinced of sin, and earnestly groaning for redemption. They desired, as did two or three more the next day, that he would spend some time with them in prayer, and advise them how to flee from the wrath to come, which they saw continually hanging over their heads. That he might have more time for this great work, he appointed a day when they might all come together, which from thenceforward they did every week, namely, on Thursday, in the evening. To these, and as many more as desired to join with them (for their number increased daily), he gave those advices, from time to time, which he judged most needful for them, and they always concluded their meeting with prayer, suited to their several necessities.

(2.) This was the rise of the United Society, first in *Europe*, and then in *America*. Such a Society is no other than a "company of men having the form, and *seeking the power of godliness*, united in order to pray together, to receive the word of exhortation, and to watch over each other in love, that they may help each other to work out their salvation."

(3.) That it may the more easily be discerned whether they

are indeed working out their own salvation, each Society is divided into smaller companies, called classes, according to their respective places of abode. There are about twelve persons in a class, one of whom is styled *the Leader*. It is his duty,

I. To see each person in his class once a week, at least, in order,

1. To inquire how their souls prosper.

2. To advise, reprove, comfort, or exhort, as occasion may require.

3. To receive what they are willing to give toward the relief of the preachers, church, and poor.*

II. To meet the ministers and the stewards of the Society once a week, in order,

1. To inform the minister of any that are sick, or of any that walk disorderly, and will not be reproved.

2. To pay the stewards what they have received of their several classes during the week preceding.

(4.) There is only one condition previously required of those who desire admission into these Societies—" a desire to flee from the wrath to come, and be saved from their sins." But wherever this is really fixed in the soul, it will be shown by its fruits. It is therefore expected of all who continue therein, that they should continue to evidence their desires for salvation,

First. By doing no harm; by avoiding evil of every kind, especially that which is most generally practised; such as,

The taking of the name of God in vain;

The profaning the day of the Lord, either by doing ordinary work therein, or by buying or selling;

Drunkenness, buying or selling spirituous liquors, or drinking them, unless in cases of extreme necessity;

The buying and selling of men, women, and children, with an intention to enslave them;

* This part refers to towns and cities; where the poor are generally numerous, and church expenses considerable.

Fighting, quarrelling, brawling, brother going to law with brother, returning evil for evil, or railing for railing, the using many words in buying or selling;

The buying or selling goods that have not paid the duty;

The giving or taking things on usury—i. e. unlawful interest;

Uncharitable or unprofitable conversation, particularly speaking evil of magistrates or of ministers;

Doing to others as we would not they should do unto us;

Doing what we know is not for the glory of God; as:

The putting on of gold, and costly apparel;

The taking such diversions as cannot be used in the name of the Lord Jesus;

The singing those songs, or reading those books which do not tend to the knowledge or love of God;

Softness, and needless self-indulgence;

Laying up treasure upon earth;

Borrowing, without a probability of paying, or taking up goods, without a probability of paying for them.

(5.) It is expected of all who continue in these Societies, that they should continue to evidence their desire of salvation,

Secondly. By doing good, by being in every kind merciful after their power, as they have opportunity, doing good of every possible sort, and as far as possible, to all men. To their bodies, of the ability which God giveth, by giving food to the hungry, by clothing the naked, by visiting or helping them that are sick or in prison;

To their souls, by instructing, reproving, or exhorting, all we have any intercourse with; trampling under foot that enthusiastic doctrine, that "we are not to do good, unless our hearts be free to it."

By doing good, especially to them who are of the household of faith, or groaning so to be; employing them preferably to others, buying one of another, helping each other in business; and so much the more, as the world will love its own, and them only;

By all possible diligence and frugality, that the gospel be not blamed;

By running with patience the race which is set before them, denying themselves, and taking up their crosses daily; submitting to bear the reproach of Christ, to be as the filth and offscouring of the world; and looking that men should say all manner of evil of them, falsely, for the Lord's sake.

(6.) It is expected of all who desire to continue in these Societies, that they should continue to evidence their desire of salvation,

Thirdly. By attending upon all the ordinances of God: such are,

The public worship of God;

The ministry of the word, either read or expounded;

The Supper of the Lord;

Family and private prayer;

Searching the Scriptures; and

Fasting, or abstinence.

(7.) These are the general rules of our Societies: all of which we are taught of God to observe, even in his written word, which is the only rule, and the sufficient rule, both of our faith and practice. And all these we know his Spirit writes on truly awakened hearts. If there be any among us who observe them not, who habitually break any of them, let it be known unto them who watch over that soul as they who must give an account. We will admonish him of the error of his ways. We will bear with him for a season. But then, if he repent not, he hath no more place among us. We have delivered our own souls."

We have thus quoted at length the general rules, that the uninformed reader may see at a glance the requirements which the Discipline of the Methodist Church makes of all its ministers and members; and we think that every candid reader will admit that a more scriptural code of morality and religious practice could not well be drawn up by man. Such as they are, we commend them to the prayerful attention of all, and especially of the members of the church.

SECTION II.

OF RECEIVING MEMBERS INTO THE CHURCH.

1. How shall we prevent improper persons from insinuating themselves into the church?

ANS. 1. Let none be received into the church, until they are recommended by a leader with whom they have met six months on trial, and have been baptized; and shall on examination by the minister in charge, give satisfactory assurances, both of the correctness of their faith, and their willingness to observe and keep the rules of the church. Nevertheless, if a member in good standing in any orthodox church shall desire to unite with us, such applicant may, by giving satisfactory answers to the usual inquiries, be received at once into full fellowship.

2. Let none be admitted on trial except they are well recommended by one you know, or until they have met twice or thrice in class.

3. Read the rules to them the first time they meet.

4. The official minister or preacher shall, at every quarterly meeting, read the names of those that are received into the church, and also those that are excluded therefrom.

SECTION III.

ON THE TRIAL AND EXPULSION OF MEMBERS.

1. Probationers in the church may, for neglect of duty, or disorderly conduct, be discontinued at any time, without the usual forms of trial and expulsion. Six months' probation are granted, that every candidate for membership may become

thoroughly acquainted with the doctrines, usages, and discipline of the church; and that the church may have a reasonable length of time to judge of the correctness of his faith and practice. When he fails to give evidence of a desire to abide by the rules of the church, he may be silently dropped from his probationary connection, by the preacher having charge.

2. An accused *member* is brought to trial before the Society of which he is a member, or a select number of them, in the presence of a bishop, elder, deacon, or preacher, in the following manner: Let the accused and accuser be brought face to face; but if this cannot be done, let the next best evidence be procured. If the accused person be found guilty, by the decision of a majority of the members before whom he is brought to trial, and the crime be such as is expressly forbidden in the word of God, sufficient to exclude a person from the kingdom of grace and glory, let the minister, or preacher, who has the charge of the circuit, expel him. If the accused person evade a trial by absenting himself, after sufficient notice given him, and the circumstances of the accusation afford strong presumption of guilt, let him be esteemed as guilty, and be accordingly excluded. Witnesses from without shall not be rejected.

2. But in cases of neglect of duties of any kind, imprudent conduct, indulging sinful tempers, or words, the buying, selling, or using intoxicating liquors as a beverage, or disobedience to the order and discipline of the church: First, let private reproof be given by a preacher or leader; and if there be an acknowledgment of the fault, and proper humiliation, the person may be borne with. On a second offence, the preacher or leader may take one or two faithful friends. On a third offence let the case be brought before the Society, or a select number, and if there be no sign of real humiliation, the offender shall be cut off.

3. If a member shall be clearly convicted of endeavoring to sow dissensions in the Societies, by inveighing against the doctrines and discipline of the church, such person shall be first

reproved by the senior minister, or preacher, and if he persist, he shall be expelled.

4. If a member wilfully and repeatedly neglect to meet in class, the minister or preacher shall visit him whenever practicable, and explain to him the consequence of continued neglect, namely exclusion, and if there be no amendment, the minister or preacher shall bring the case before the Society, or a select number, before whom he shall have been cited to appear, and if found guilty, he shall be laid aside.

5. If, in any case of the trial of a member, the preacher differ in judgment from the Society, or the select number, concerning the guilt or innocence of the accused person, the preacher may refer the whole matter to the next quarterly conference; and if the person excluded complain of injustice having been done in his case, he shall be allowed an appeal to the next quarterly conference, unless he shall have absented himself from trial.

6. If a member who has been excluded complain to an annual conference, after having appealed to a quarterly conference, that there has been incorrect administration of the discipline in his case, and if it shall appear to the annual conference that such complaint is well founded, and the annual conference shall so decide, such decision shall restore the expelled person to membership in the church.

7. On any dispute between two or more members of the church, concerning the payment of debts, or otherwise, which cannot be settled by the parties concerned, the preacher who has the charge of the Society, shall recommend to the parties a reference to one arbiter chosen by the plaintiff, and another chosen by the defendant, and a third chosen by these two, all being members of the church, which board of arbiters shall decide the question. If either party is dissatisfied with the decision given, such party may apply to the ensuing quarterly conference for a second arbitration, and if the quarterly conference see sufficient reason, they shall grant the same, in which

case each party shall choose two arbiters, and the four thus chosen shall select a fifth one, the decision of which board shall be final.

8. When a complaint is made against any member of the church for non-payment of debt, if the amount is ascertained, the preacher having charge shall call the debtor before a committee of three or more, to show cause why he does not make payment. The committee shall determine what further time shall be granted him before making payment, and what security, if any, shall be given for the same.

9. In case of a refusal to comply with the decision of the arbiters, or with the decision of the committee, whether on the part of the plaintiff or defendant, the member so refusing shall be liable to trial for disobedience to the order and discipline of the church ; and if they are found guilty of such refusal, and persist in the same, they shall be expelled.

10. When any member fails in business, or contracts debts which he is not able to pay, the preacher shall appoint two or three judicious members of the church to inspect the accounts, contracts, and circumstances of the supposed delinquent, and if he shall have behaved dishonestly, or fraudulently, or borrowed money without a probability of paying, he shall, after proper trial before the Society, or select number, be expelled.—*Dis.* pp. 54–56.

11. In relation to smuggling, bribery, &c. the following rules are laid down: Extirpate buying or selling goods which have not paid the duty laid on them by government, out of the church. Let none remain with us who will not totally abstain from this evil in every kind and degree. Extirpate bribery, receiving anything directly or indirectly for voting at any election. Show no respect to persons herein, but expel all that touch the accursed thing. And strongly advise our people to discountenance all treats given by candidates before or at elections, and not to be partakers in any respect of such iniquitous practices.—*Dis.* p. 64.

CHAPTER III.

OF THE MINISTERS, PREACHERS, AND OTHER OFFICERS OF THE CHURCH.

SECTION I.

OF THE BISHOPS AND THEIR DUTY; AND TO WHOM RESPONSIBLE.

1. A BISHOP is constituted by the election of the General Conference, and the laying on of the hands of three bishops; or of one bishop and two elders; or, if there are no bishops, by the laying on of the hands of three elders appointed for that purpose by the General Conference.

2. The duties of the bishop are to preside in the General and Annual Conferences; to fix the appointments of the presiding elders and preachers for the several districts, circuits and stations; to appoint missionaries among the colored people and Indians, and to destitute portions of our own land, and to foreign lands; in the intervals of conference to change, receive and suspend preachers, as necessity may require, and as the Discipline directs; to travel through the connection at large; to ordain bishops, elders, and deacons, when properly elected by the General or Annual Conferences; to decide questions of law, when presiding in an annual conference, subject to an appeal to the General Conference; to prepare a course of reading and study for candidates for the ministry, and to oversee the spiritual and temporal interests of the church.

3. The following limitations are placed upon the power of the bishops: They shall not allow any preacher to remain in the same station more than two years at a time; nor reappoint

them to the same station till after an absence of four years, excepting agents, editors, chaplains, missionaries, and teachers in colleges or seminaries of learning. They shall not allow a preacher to remain in the same city more than four years in succession, nor return him to it till he shall have been absent four years. They shall not appoint a presiding elder to the same district for more than four years in ten.

4. The power with which the bishops are invested was formerly much greater than it is now. In 1784, no person could be ordained to any ministerial office without the consent of the bishop. The preachers were prohibited from printing any book without the approbation of one of the bishops. The bishop was also—as is now the case in the Protestant Episcopal Church—authorized to receive appeals from the preachers and people, and decide them. In these and some other respects, their powers have become very much modified, and the authority originally vested in them has reverted to the General Conference, or been given to the annual and quarterly conferences.

5. The bishops have no right to originate a motion in the General or Annual Conferences. Neither have they a right to vote on any question pending before these bodies.

6. They are held rigidly responsible to the body of elders represented in the General Conference, for all their acts, both official and private; and they may be expelled for any conduct which may be improper in a bishop, even though not immoral, and when so expelled they can have no appeal.

6. In the interval of the General Conference a bishop, if accused of crime or immorality, shall be cited to appear before two presiding elders and seven other elders; or before two presiding elders, five travelling elders, and two travelling deacons; these nine shall form a court of inquiry, and if two thirds of the number believe him guilty they shall have authority to suspend him until the next General Conference.

From the above it will be readily perceived that the Episcopacy of the Methodist Episcopal Church is indeed a moderate one; that the bishops are the creatures of the eldership, and constantly amenable to it; and may at any time, for cause, be deposed from their high office and authority; that, in fact, with the exception of appointing the preachers to their respective fields of labor, they possess but little more power—if indeed as much—than is possessed by the humblest and most obscure travelling preacher.

SECTION II.

OF THE PRESIDING ELDERS AND THEIR DUTY

1. The presiding elders, as shown in the preceding section, are chosen and stationed by the bishops, and like all other travelling ministers, are amenable to the annual conference of which they are members, for their private and official acts.

2. It is the duty of the presiding elder to take charge of all the elders, deacons, travelling and local preachers and exhorters in his district; to change, receive, and suspend preachers in his district during the intervals of the conferences, and in the absence of the bishop; to preside also, in the absence of the bishop—if appointed by the latter—in the annual conference; to be present, as far as practicable, at all the quarterly conferences, and preside therein; to oversee the spiritual and temporal business of the church in his district; to promote the cause of Missions, Sunday Schools, and the circulation of religious books; to decide all questions of law in a quarterly conference, subject to an appeal to the president of the next annual conference; to attend the bishops when present in his district, and advise them of the state of his district when absent.

3. From the above it will be seen that the presiding elder is properly the representative of the bishop, and that such office is not only a responsible one, but is absolutely necessary to the proper government of the church, more especially as, by virtue

of his office and by common consent, the presiding elder is made the adviser of the bishop in fixing the appointments of the preachers, and in arranging the boundaries of the districts, circuits, and stations.

SECTION III.

OF THE ELECTION AND ORDINATION OF TRAVELLING ELDERS AND THEIR DUTY, AND OF THE MODE OF TRYING THEM.

1. A travelling elder is constituted by the election of an annual conference, and the laying on of the hands of a bishop and some of the elders who are present.

2. The duty of a travelling elder is to administer baptism and the Lord's Supper, and to perform the office of matrimony, and all parts of divine worship, and to do all the duties of a travelling preacher.

3. A travelling elder is eligible to an election as delegate to the General Conference, and also to the Episcopacy even although he never has been a presiding elder; he may assist in the ordination of other elders, and even of bishops, if through death, resignation, or otherwise, there are no bishops.

4. A travelling elder is responsible to his conference for all his private and official acts, and by his conference may be tried, suspended, deposed, or expelled from the church. In the intervals of an annual conference, if reported guilty of some crime, the presiding elder, in the absence of the bishop, shall call a committee of at least three travelling ministers, and investigate the truth of the report. If the elder be clearly convicted of unchristian conduct, he shall be suspended from all ministerial services and church privileges until the next session of the annual conference. If the charge is not preferred until the session of the conference, the case may be referred to a committee, who shall keep a faithful record of the proceedings and

testimony, and lay the same before the conference, on which, with such other evidence as may be admitted, the case shall be decided.

5. In cases of improper words, tempers, and actions, the person offending shall be reprehended by his senior in office. On a second transgression, two or three ministers or preachers are to be taken as witnesses. If not then cured, he shall be tried at the next annual conference, and if guilty and impenitent shall be expelled from the connection.

6. When a travelling elder, or other member of an annual conference, fails in business, or is unable to pay his debts, the presiding elder shall appoint three judicious members of the church to examine into the state of his affairs, and if, in the opinion of such members, the minister has behaved dishonestly, or has contracted debts without the probability of paying, the presiding elder shall then bring him before a committee of at least three ministers, who may suspend him until the ensuing conference.

7. When a travelling elder, or other member of an annual conference, disseminates, publicly or privately, doctrines which are contrary to our Articles of Religion, the same process is to be observed as in cases of gross immorality, unless the offending minister shall engage not to disseminate such doctrines, in which case the offender may be borne with until the next annual conference.

8. When a travelling minister is accused of being so unacceptable, inefficient, or secular, as to be no longer useful as a travelling preacher, the annual conference shall investigate the case, and if the complaint is well founded, and the accused will not voluntarily retire, the conference may locate him without his consent.

9. Provided, that in all the above cases, the minister so suspended, deposed, located, or expelled, shall be allowed an appeal to the next General Conference, if he signify his intention to appeal at the time of his condemnation, or as soon thereafter

as he is informed of the same, and when the General Conference shall have heard both sides of the question, they shall finally decide the whole matter.

10. When any travelling elder, or other minister, shall be deprived of his credentials, they shall be filed with the papers of the annual conference of which he was a member; and should he, at any future time, give satisfactory evidence of his amendment, and procures a recommendation from a quarterly or other annual conference, for the restoration of his credentials, the same may be restored to him, by vote of the conference of which he was a member.

SECTION IV.

OF THE ELECTION AND ORDINATION OF TRAVELLING DEACONS, AND THEIR DUTY.

1. A travelling deacon is constituted by the election of an annual conference, and by the laying on of the hands of the bishop.

2. It is the duty of the travelling deacon to baptize, and perform the office of matrimony, in the absence of the elder; to assist the elder in the administration of the Lord's Supper, and to do all the duties of a travelling preacher.

3. A travelling deacon is eligible to the office of an elder, after having travelled two years as a deacon, and has qualified himself in the course of study prescribed by the bishops.

4. An accused travelling deacon is brought to trial in the same manner as an accused travelling elder; for information in regard to which, we refer the reader to the preceding section.

SECTION V.

OF SUPERNUMERARY AND SUPERANNUATED PREACHERS.

1. A supernumerary preacher is one so worn out in the itinerant service, as to be rendered incapable of preaching constantly, but at the same time is willing to do any work which the conference may direct, and his strength enable him to perform.

2. A superannuated preacher is one so worn out in the itinerant service, as to be considered incapable of doing any efficient work as a minister, and consequently receives no appointment from the bishop, but is at liberty to go where he pleases, and improve his time and remaining strength as best he may.

3. None but regular travelling preachers, or members of an annual conference, or bishops, can be supernumerary or superannuated, and while sustaining either of the above relations, they are entitled to a portion of the conference funds, and are subject, like all other effective preachers, to the conference of which they are members.

SECTION VI.

OF TRAVELLING PREACHERS, AND THEIR DUTY.

1. The term travelling preacher is frequently used to designate all who belong to the conference, whether presiding elders, elders, deacons, or licentiates, but in its proper and technical sense, it includes only the latter class, and in this sense it is used in this section—to denote those, who, not having been received into full connection in the conference, nor been ordained, are on trial, and are candidates for the ministerial office.

2. A travelling preacher is received on trial by the annual

conference, after having been recommended as a proper person by the quarterly conference of which he is a member.

3. While on trial in an annual conference, a travelling preacher may be discontinued by such conference, but if accused of crime, the presiding elder shall call a committee of three local preachers, who may suspend him, and the quarterly conference may expel him from the church, nevertheless, he shall have an appeal to the ensuing annual conference.

4. The duty of a travelling preacher is to preach, visit from house to house, meet the Societies, classes, and bands, visit the sick, and in all respects show himself to be a laborer in the vineyard of the Lord.

5. A travelling preacher is eligible to full connection in the annual conference, and to deacon's orders, after he shall have travelled two successive years on trial, and has qualified himself in the course of study prescribed by the bishops.

SECTION VII.

OF PREACHERS IN CHARGE, AND THEIR DUTY.

1. A preacher in charge is one who has the pastoral care of a circuit or station. He may be either an elder, deacon, or preacher, in connection with the conference; or he may be a local preacher or minister, employed by the presiding elder to fill some vacancy.

2. The duties of a preacher in charge are, to oversee the junior preachers on his circuit, should there be any; to renew the tickets for the admission of members into love-feast, quarterly; to meet the stewards and leaders as often as possible; to appoint all the leaders, and change them when he sees it necessary; to receive, try, and expel members, according to the form of discipline; to hold watch-nights and love-feasts; to hold quarterly meetings in the absence of the presiding

elder; to take care that every Society be duly supplied with books; to take an exact account of the number of members in each Society, and report the same to the conference; to give an account of his circuit or station once a quarter, to his presiding elder; to meet the men and women apart, in the large Societies, wherever it is practicable; to overlook the accounts of the stewards; to appoint a person to receive the quarterly collection in the classes; to see that public collections be made quarterly, if need be; to encourage the support of missions and Sunday-schools, and the circulation of bibles, tracts, and Sunday-school books, form Societies, and make collections for those objects. It is his duty, also, to give certificates of membership to those about to remove; to enforce all the rules of the Society; to read those rules once a year in each congregation, and once a quarter in each Society; to recommend arbitrations in cases of dispute; to appoint committees for the trial of members, and to preside at such trials; to appoint prayer-meetings whenever he can, on his charge; to license proper persons to exhort, provided he obtains the consent of the class, of which the person is a member, or of the leaders' meeting.

3. A preacher in charge, if a member of an annual conference, is responsible to such conference for all his official acts, and if a local preacher, to the quarterly conference of which he is a member.

SECTION VIII.

OF LOCAL ELDERS, DEACONS, AND PREACHERS.

1. A local elder is one, who, having filled the office of a local deacon for four successive years, has been ordained to the eldership by the election of an annual conference, and the laying on of the hands of the bishop and other elders. Before such election and ordination, it is necessary that he be recom-

mended by the quarterly conference of which he is a member. Provided, always, that no slaveholder shall be eligible to the office of an elder, where the laws will allow him to emancipate his slaves.

2. A local deacon is one, who, having filled the office of a local preacher for four successive years, has been elected by an annual conference—after proper recommendation—and been ordained by the laying on of the hands of the bishop. No slaveholder is eligible to this office who can manumit his slaves.

3. A local preacher is one who has received license to preach from the quarterly conference. Said license must be renewed once a year, at least, in order to be valid.

4. All local elders, deacons, or preachers, must have their names recorded in a class-book, and must meet in class, and when they remove from one circuit or station to another, they must obtain certificates of their standing at the time of their removal, before they can be received as members or preachers in other places.

5. When a travelling preacher is located or discontinued, he becomes a member of the quarterly conference where he resides, or where he has had his last appointment.

6. It is the duty of local elders to preach, and administer the sacraments, especially in those places not visited by the travelling elders; of the local deacons, to assist in the administration of the Lord's Supper, and to baptize, &c., and of the local preachers, to preach wherever, and whenever practicable. It is expected of all local ministers that they preach at least once every Sabbath-day.

7. The difference between travelling and local preachers and ministers, consists chiefly in the fact that the former give themselves wholly to the work of the ministry, while the latter pursue some secular calling in connection with the sacred office—the former might properly be called regular ministers, and the latter secular ministers.

8. Local ministers and preachers are amenable to the quar-

terly conference for their private and official conduct, and if suspended or expelled they have an appeal to the annual conference, whose decision in their case is final.*

SECTION IX.

OF EXHORTERS, STEWARDS, CLASS-LEADERS, AND TRUSTEES.

1. Exhorters are licensed by the preachers in charge, after having been recommended by the class or leader's meeting. They are subject, like local preachers, to an annual examination of character in the quarterly conference, and to have their licenses renewed by the presiding elder, if approved by the quarterly conference. It is the duty of exhorters to hold meetings in the absence of a preacher, and to call sinners to repentance whenever opportunity offers. If accused of crime, an exhorter is to be tried by the Society, or select number, and if guilty may be expelled by the preacher in charge, he having an appeal to the quarterly conference.

2. Stewards are nominated by the preacher in charge, and appointed by the quarterly conference. On every circuit or station there must not be less than three nor more than seven stewards. It is their duty to take an exact account of all the money or other provision collected for the support of the preachers on the circuit or station; to seek out the poor and needy, and relieve them; to inform the preachers of any sick or disorderly persons; to tell the preachers what they think wrong in them; to attend the quarterly meetings, and give advice when required in planning the circuit; to give counsel in matters of arbitration; provide elements for the Lord's Supper;

* Ministers of the Methodist Church coming from Europe or America, may be received according to their credentials, by an annual conference, and ministers from other evangelical churches may be received without reordination by taking upon them our ordination vows.

to write circular letters to the Societies to be more liberal, if need be; to register baptisms and marriages; and be subject to the bishops and other ministers of the circuit or station. The stewards are amenable to the quarterly conference for their official conduct, but they can only be tried by the Society, or a select number, and if expelled have an appeal to the quarterly conference.

3. *Class-leaders* are appointed by the preacher in charge, and are responsible to him for the proper discharge of their duties. It is their duty to meet their class once a week, in order to inquire into the spiritual state of each member of the same, and to advise, reprove, comfort, or exhort them as occasion may require; to receive what they are willing to give toward the relief of the preachers, church and poor, and to pay the same over to the stewards; to meet the ministers and stewards once a week, when practicable, and inform them of any that are sick, or that walk disorderly and will not be reproved; to meet in quarterly conferences, and be the spiritual assistants of the minister and preachers on the circuits and stations. The usual number of members committed to the special charge of a class-leader is about twelve, although there are frequently found as many as twenty or thirty in one class. Class-leaders are responsible to the Society for their moral and Christian conduct.

4. *Trustees.* These are appointed for the purpose of holding in trust for the benefit of the Society in any given place, all real and personal estate which may belong to such Society, such as churches, burying-grounds, parsonages, parsonage furniture, &c. According to the laws of most states and territories, they form a body corporate, and are the legal representatives of the Society whose property they hold in trust, and as such may sue and be sued. Except where the statutes of the states and territories otherwise provide, a new board of trustees is appointed by the preacher in charge, or presiding elder of the district, and afterwards, in case of vacancy, the preacher in charge shall nominate

persons to supply such vacancy, and the remaining trustees shall proceed to elect and confirm such nomination.

In most states and territories, however, statutes are made by which the election of all trustees is to be governed. They are generally divided into three classes, each class holding office for three years, and alternately going out of office every year. It is also provided that the church, society, or congregation, by a majority of votes of the male members thereof, of twenty-one years of age, shall elect the necessary number of trustees.

The Discipline requires that all trustees shall have been members of the church for the space of one year previous to their election, and that they shall be at least twenty-one years of age. They are responsible to the quarterly conference for their official acts, and are required to present a report annually to said quarterly conference, of their acts as a board during the preceding year.

It is the duty of trustees to hold sacredly in trust for the purposes specified in the deed of conveyance, all property committed to their charge, and to allow it to be diverted to no other use or purpose whatsoever. In case of official misconduct, a trustee may be removed and restrained by application to the proper civil court.

CHAPTER IV.

OF THE GENERAL, ANNUAL, AND QUARTERLY CONFERENCES, AND OTHER COLLECTIVE BODIES IN THE CHURCH.

SECTION I.

OF THE GENERAL CONFERENCE.

1. THE General Conference is composed of one member for every twenty-one members of an annual conference, and if there should be a fraction of two thirds that number—fourteen —such fraction shall entitle the conference to an additional delegate. Provided always that no conference shall be denied the privilege of two delegates.

2. The general conference is required to meet on the first day of May, quadrennially, in such places as it shall at previous conferences fix upon: but the bishops, with the advice of all the annual conferences, may call a special session of the general conference at any time; or if there be no bishop, the annual conferences may call such a session.

3. The bishops shall preside in the general conference, but if there is no bishop the conference shall choose a president, *pro tem.* No person can be a member of the general conference who has not travelled four full calendar years, and is in full connection in an annual conference at the time of his election. Two thirds of all the members elected shall form a quorum for the transaction of business.

4. The general conference has full power to make rules and

regulations for the church, under certain restrictions and limitations; (1.) They shall not revoke, alter, or change our Articles of Religion, nor establish any new standards or rules of doctrine contrary to our present existing and established standards of doctrine. (2.) They shall not allow of more than one representative for every fourteen members of an annual conference, nor less than one for every thirty. (3.) They shall not change or alter any part or rule of our government so as to do away Episcopacy, or destroy the plan of our itinerant general superintendency. (4.) They shall not revoke or change the general rules of the Society. (5.) They shall not do away the privileges of our ministers and preachers, of trial by a committee and of an appeal; nor the privileges of our members, of trial before the Society or by a committee, and of an appeal. (6.) They shall not appropriate the produce of the book concern and chartered fund to any purpose other than for the benefit of the travelling, supernumerary, superannuated, and worn-out preachers, their wives, widows, and children.

Provided, nevertheless, that when three fourths of all the members of the several annual conferences present and voting shall concur in recommending any change in the above restrictions, then a majority of two thirds of the general conference shall suffice to alter the same, excepting the first Article, relating to doctrine; or when a majority of two thirds of the general conference shall by vote recommend such alteration, as soon as three fourths of the members of all the annual conferences shall have concurred therein, such alteration shall take effect.

5. The general conference, according to the present ratio of representation, consists of about one hundred and sixty members. It appoints its own secretaries, elects the book agents, editors, and missionary secretaries; tries appeals from travelling ministers, and examines strictly the character and official acts of the bishops; it examines the journals of the several annual conferences, and either approves or disapproves of the same; it creates new annual conferences, and fixes their bounds, and ap-

points the place of its next meeting. After remaining in session for from four to six weeks, it adjourns to the first day of May in four years thereafter.

SECTION II.

OF THE ANNUAL CONFERENCE.

1. The Annual Conference is composed of all the travelling preachers in full connection, within its bounds, each of whom has an equal voice in the transaction of business. A bishop, by virtue of his office, is the president of the conference, but in case of necessary absence, he may appoint a substitute from among the presiding elders, or if he fails to do so, the conference may appoint its own president from among the same.

2. The bishops appoint the *time* of holding the conferences, and must allow each conference to sit a week, at least; the conference appoints the *place* of its session, which is usually done by accepting some one of the numerous applications sent up by Societies, and quarterly conferences.

3. The business of an annual conference is, to admit preachers on trial; receive preachers into full connection; elect travelling and local preachers to deacons' and elders' orders; grant locations; and supernumerary and superannuated relations to those who apply; examine the character of each preacher by calling their names over before the conference, and inquiring if there are any objections to them; to try and expel preachers, if need be, and hear appeals from suspended or expelled local preachers; to receive reports from all the preachers, of the amounts raised for their salaries, and of the amount of money raised for the worn-out preachers, widows, and orphans; for the cause of missions, tracts, the American Bible Society, the Sunday School Union of the Methodist Episcopal Church, or any other purpose for which collections have been ordered by the conference, or for which the Discipline provides.

4. The session of an annual conference extends from five to ten days, according to the number of members belonging to it, and the amount of business to be transacted. The largest number in any one conference is two hundred and eighty-three, and the smallest number is fifty-one.

SECTION III.

OF THE QUARTERLY CONFERENCE.

1. A Quarterly Conference is composed of all the travelling and local preachers, exhorters, stewards, and leaders on any circuit or station. There are usually one or two travelling preachers, from one to six or eight local preachers, one or more exhorters, seven stewards, and from five to twenty or more class-leaders, belonging to each quarterly conference. The presiding elder of the district is the president thereof, or, in case of absence, the preacher in charge is the responsible president.

2. The quarterly conference meets four times in each year, and may adjourn from day to day till its business is finished, but cannot adjourn to a distant day for that purpose. The presiding elder appoints the *time* of holding the quarterly conference, but the conference appoints the place of its own sittings. The business of the conference is ordinarily despatched in the course of a few hours.

3. It is the business of the quarterly conference to hear complaints against local preachers, and to receive and try appeals from expelled members; to superintend the interests of Sunday Schools within its bounds; to estimate by a committee the amount necessary to be raised for fuel and the table expenses of the travelling preacher or preachers of the circuit or station; to take cognizance of all the local preachers and exhorters; to appoint stewards, the preacher in charge having the right to nominate; to grant licenses to preach; to recommend the re-

newal of exhorters' licenses; to recommend to the annual conference suitable persons for admission on trial in the annual conference; to recommend suitable persons to be ordained as local deacons and elders; to recommend the re-admission of located elders and deacons to an annual conference; to appoint a recording steward to keep all the records of the quarterly conference; to appoint a district steward to meet in convention and estimate the amount necessary to be raised for the fuel and table expenses, house-rent, &c., of the presiding elder; to advise the action of trustees, and take all such steps for the well-being of the church or churches within its bounds, as shall be deemed expedient and right.

4. In all questions of law, the presiding elder shall be the judge, subject to an appeal to the president of the next annual conference, but the application of law shall remain with the quarterly conference.

SECTION IV.

OF LEADERS', OR OFFICIAL MEETINGS.

1. These meetings originally embraced only the leaders of classes, but by common consent, and as a matter of utility, they now embrace all the members of the quarterly conference, the preacher in charge being the chairman thereof.

2. The official board, or leaders' meeting, usually meets once in each month, when convenient, or oftener when necessary and is subject at all times to the call of the preacher in charge.

3. It is the business of the leaders' meeting to recommend suitable persons to the preacher in charge, for license to exhort; otherwise, the duties of the same are not very clearly defined in the Discipline; common usage, however, makes it the business of such meeting to advise and assist the preacher in charge in the administration of discipline; to recommend suit-

able persons, whose term of probation has expired for membership in the church; to attend to the financial interests of the church, and devise ways and means for raising the allowance of the preachers, and to do all other business of an ecclesiastical nature, which may properly come before them.

SECTION V.

OF SOCIETY AND CLASS-MEETINGS.

1. These meetings are frequently held for the purpose of spiritual improvement; to hear complaints against members, and to judge of the guilt or innocence of the accused; to judge of the qualifications of probationers as to faith and doctrine, who apply for membership in the church, and to transact such other business as may be referred to them, either by the pastor, or official board. The preacher in charge always presides in such meetings.

2. In this section may be noticed also the fact that a single class has power to recommend suitable persons to the preacher in charge for license to exhort, and to do such other business as properly belongs to it as a class. A preacher or leader may preside over the class in its business deliberations; and either the preacher or leader may call a meeting of the class at any time, although the members of the class are not obliged to attend such a call more than once a week.

CHAPTER V.

OF THE PUBLIC AND SOCIAL MEANS OF GRACE.

SECTION I.

OF PUBLIC WORSHIP.

1. PUBLIC worship on the Lord's day consists of singing, prayer—concluding with the Lord's prayer—reading the Scriptures of the Old and New Testaments, singing, preaching, singing, prayer, and the benediction.

2. On the evening of the Lord's day, and on other days of the week, the same order is observed, excepting the reading of the Scriptures.

3. In administering the ordinances of baptism and the Lord's Supper, the forms prescribed in the Discipline, and prepared by Mr. Wesley, are invariably used. These forms are short but comprehensive, and are merely abbreviations of those found in the Book of Common Prayer of the Church of England. It is thought by many, that the form relating to baptism needs revision, as it seems to endorse the dogma of baptismal regeneration, which is certainly not the doctrine of the Methodist Episcopal Church. In the burial of the dead, and the solemnization of matrimony, the forms prescribed in the Discipline are generally but not always used.

4. Public worship is usually held each Sabbath on stations, once in two weeks on circuits, and occasionally on week evenings. Preaching at four or five o'clock in the morning—sc

much the practice in Mr. Wesley's time, and in the earlier days of Methodism—has, in the United States, very generally fallen into disuse.

5. The rule of discipline requiring the men and women to sit apart in all our churches, is fast becoming obsolete, especially in such churches as are built with pews or slips, to sell or rent. It is found most convenient, in large places, for families to be seated together, and we may express the hope that a rule which cannot be enforced, and which has no scriptural warrant nor precedent, will be expunged from the page of disci-

SECTION II.

OF CLASS-MEETINGS.

1. These, according to discipline, are required to be held weekly, in every place. The object of class-meetings is to inquire into the spiritual state of each member of the class, and to advise, reprove, comfort, and exhort, as occasion may require. There are usually about twelve persons in a class, although there are frequently found twenty, thirty, or more.

2. The exercises of class-meeting consist of singing, prayer, and the relation of Christian experience. These meetings are of immense importance to the church, and cannot be neglected without detriment to its spiritual interests, but whether Mr. Wesley ever designed to establish class-meetings as a term or condition of *church-membership*, is a question which has not been largely discussed, nor finally settled. One thing appears to be certain, namely; that all Methodists who enjoy a sense of the pardoning favor of God, love class-meetings, even though they are but a prudential means of grace, and on the other hand, a wilful neglect of class-meetings is an almost certain indication of a low state of religious enjoyment.

3. Strangers—that is, persons not members of the church or

Society—may be admitted to the privileges of class-meeting twice or thrice, but not oftener, without violating the rules of the Society. This rule may be considered by many as savoring too much of a spirit of sectarianism, but when the nature and design of a class-meeting is duly considered, we feel persuaded that none but the bigoted and uncharitable will object to them on that account. Indeed, the design of class-meetings would be completely frustrated if all of every class, whether pious or ungodly, were admitted thereto. Even members of the Methodist Church have no ecclesiastical or conventional right to meet in any class but their own, without the permission of the leader.

4. Leaders are required frequently to meet each other's classes. The object of this rule is to give the members of the different classes the benefit of the advice and counsel of the various leaders, and to prevent as far as possible a spirit of formality.

SECTION III.

OF BAND MEETINGS.

1. Two, three, or four true believers, who have confidence in each other, form a band; and in each band all must be men, or all women; and all must be married, or all single. The bands meet once a week to converse on purely spiritual matters, and to help each other in the way to heaven, by complying with that command of God, expressed by the apostle James, "Confess your faults one to another, and pray one for another, that ye may be healed." The members of the band pledge themselves to abstain from all sin, and zealously to maintain good works.

2. Belonging to a band is perfectly voluntary on the part of all the members. Indeed, none but the decidedly pious and devoted can have any desire to meet therein. The band meet-

ings differ much in their nature and design from the auricular confessionals of the Church of Rome; the latter being composed of the priest and a single supposed penitent, the former of a few believers.

3. These band meetings are frequent in large Societies, but it is deeply to be regretted that they have fallen so much into disuse in most places; as all who have belonged to them can testify to their utility as a prudential means of grace.

SECTION IV.

OF PRAYER-MEETINGS.

1. These are held semi-weekly, or oftener, in nearly every place where Societies are established. Sunday and Thursday evenings are usually selected for the above meetings in the Methodist Church. These meetings are nearly, if not quite as important to the interests of true religion in the Methodist Church as class-meetings, and should not be dispensed with for trivial considerations.

2. The exercises of prayer-meetings consist principally of singing, prayer, and exhortation, in which all the members, male and female, are expected to take a part. The doctrine of the Methodist Church in relation to female speaking and praying is, that while it is manifestly improper for "a woman to speak in the church," in relation to church business; and that, while on all matters of a temporal character, or others where dictation and governing are required, the women should "learn to keep silence in the churches," yet in matters of a purely religious character, in the social meetings of the church, it is not only their privilege but their duty to improve the talents which God has given them, by singing, prayer, and exhortation. Indeed, in all revivals of religion it has been found that the women are among the most efficient laborers, and the most

honored instruments in the conversion of souls; and we hope the day is far distant when in the Methodist Church it will be considered unfashionable or unusual for a pious female to pray or exhort in a Methodist social meeting. If such a day ever does arrive "Ichabod" may be inscribed upon the title-page of her history.

SECTION V.

OF LOVE-FEASTS.

1. Love-feasts were instituted by Mr. Wesley in an early day in the history of Methodism. He derived the idea from the Moravians, or United Brethren, one of whose love-feasts he had the privilege of attending; and since their institution by Mr. Wesley they have always been considered as an essential part of Methodist usages, and have for many years been connected with each quarterly meeting as an interesting part of the same. They are held quarterly, or oftener, as occasion may require.

2. The exercises of a love-feast are singing, prayer, partaking of bread and water as a token of Christian fellowship and love, and the relation of Christian experience. These meetings are hailed with delight by every Methodist, and no marvel, for if there is one place on earth more like heaven than another, it is an old-fashioned Methodist love-feast, where the members, worshipping God "under their own vine and fig-tree," with all intruders and spies shut out, have "none to molest or make afraid," and where each member, in simplicity and honesty, may declare what the Lord has done for his soul. The speeches, on such occasions, are necessarily short, and are directly to the point of present Christian experience and enjoyment. Frequently as many as eighty or a hundred persons, in few words, express their gratitude to God in the course of a single hour, besides occasional singing.

3. These meetings, as to time, are limited expressly by the Discipline to an hour and a half. A similar rule exists in relation to admitting strangers not more than twice or thrice to love-feasts, as exists in relation to class-meetings, and for the same or similar reasons. The preacher in charge, by virtue of his office, is required to hold love-feasts, but by common consent the presiding elder, when present, invariably presides during such occasions.

SECTION VI.

OF CAMP-MEETINGS.

1. These appendages to American Methodism originated, as stated in the historical part of this work, in the year 1799,* among the Methodists and Presbyterians in Kentucky. By the latter church they have long since been abandoned, as unsuited to their views of order and propriety; while by the Methodists they have been retained as a highly useful and interesting means of doing good.

2. Camp-meetings are usually held annually, in the summer or autumn, in a grove or forest in some central or convenient place, where water, pasturage, &c. may be obtained. The ministers and members from different parts of a presiding elder's district, and frequently of two adjoining districts, and from a distance of ten, twenty, thirty, and even fifty miles, assemble together in one place to enjoy this "feast of tabernacles." They bring with them their canvass tents, provisions, &c. &c. The snow-white tents are arranged in a circular form around the camp ground. At one end is the "stand," or pulpit, fitted up so as to accommodate twenty or thirty ministers with seats. In front of the stand is an enclosure called the "altar," fitted up with seats for any that may be seeking the

* Some authors state 1797. We have taken Bang's date.

pardon of sin. Beyond the altar, and in front of the stand, are arranged, in proper order, seats for the congregation, who, when seated, are surrounded on all sides by the circle of tents. The rear of the tents is devoted to culinary purposes, while in the interior of the circle, during religious services, nothing is expected to take place unbecoming the sanctity of a place of worship. The exercises consist of preaching four or five times each day, interspersed with prayer, singing, exhortation, &c. The meeting usually lasts five or six days, and on the morning of the last day of the meeting a love-feast is held, and frequently the Lord's Supper is administered; and before dispersing it is customary for all the congregation present to march round within the circle of tents, in solemn procession, singing appropriate farewell hymns. After marching round once or twice, the ministers arrange themselves in front of the stand, and receive the parting adieu of each person who passes before them. This "parting scene" is usually very solemn and affecting, and those who can refrain from weeping under these circumstances are favored with stronger nerves than usually fall to the lot of humanity. Many, who having participated in the previous exercises of the camp-meeting without much apparent conviction, have during this closing scene been pricked to the heart, and been forced to beg the prayers of God's people before leaving the ground. After the benediction has been pronounced by the presiding elder or senior preacher, all retire to their homes better qualified than before to labor for the conversion of souls. Thousands, no doubt, are every year converted to God through the instrumentality of these means of grace.

SECTION VII.

OF WATCH-NIGHT MEETINGS.

1. These meetings were instituted by Mr. Wesley. Before their conversion to Methodism the colliers of Cornwall, England.

were accustomed to spend every Saturday night, to a late hour, at the ale-house, or tavern, drinking, swearing, and carousing. After having been converted, through the labors of Whitefield and Wesley, the latter was providentially led to substitute the chapel for the ale-house, and prayer and praise for oaths and blasphemy. These meetings were held generally once a month, at the time of the full moon, and subsequently were introduced into all the Societies in England. In America, watch-nights have been confined to two evenings in the year—Christmas and New Year's eve—and are usually seasons of great spiritual profit.

2. The exercises at such meetings vary according to circumstances. On New Year's eve it is customary to have one or two sermons, interspersed with other appropriate exercises. As the hour of twelve passes away all are kneeling in solemn silent prayer before God, and as the old year becomes lost in eternity, and time gives birth to a new one, each Christian heart is being laid upon the altar in the act of self-consecration. After silent prayer, a New Year's hymn of praise is sung, salutations are exchanged, and the worshippers return to their homes, profited and blest by the interview.

SECTION VIII.

OF PROTRACTED AND OTHER MEETINGS.

1. At an early day in the history of American Methodism, two-days' meetings were quite common, and were seasons of great power and spiritual refreshing. As time elapsed, these meetings were continued to three, four, and five days. Still later, days gave place to weeks and even to months of continued effort for the salvation of souls, so that now it is by no means a strange thing among the Methodists for a protracted meeting to be continued during the greater part of fall or

winter; during these meetings hundreds are frequently converted to God; and although it is to be regretted that the church, as well as the unconverted in many places, scarcely expect a revival of religion except in connection with such meetings, yet it by no means follows that such extra efforts should be dispensed with, but rather continued from year to year, and from place to place, "if by any means we may save some."

2. The meetings of the general and annual conferences are, more or less, rendered a blessing to the places where they are held, as in connection with them there is much precious seed sown, which must sooner or later produce abundant fruit. Still it is a question, whether less preaching and more of the social means would not be more profitable at such seasons. Our own opinion is, that at every session of an annual conference not only should the sacrament of the Lord's Supper be administered, but a ministerial love-feast, in accordance with the rule of Discipline, should be held, in which, of course, the laity should be invited to participate. These, in connection with prayer-meetings, or a conference general class-meeting, would, in our humble opinion, do more good than a continued round of preaching, even by the greatest and best of men.

3. The meetings of district ministerial associations are becoming quite frequent, and are productive of great good, not only to the ministers themselves, but to the people where the sittings are held. So far as the author has been able to obtain authentic information in regard to the origin of these associations, Potsdam district, Black River Conference, has the honor of being the first district in the connection to form a regularly organized district ministerial association. This occurred in the fall of 1836. Rev. John Loveys, being presiding elder, was the first president, and Rev. Jesse T. Peck—now Dr. Peck—was the first secretary, the author and others of his brethren, being members of the said association. Since that period, district ministerial associations have been organized in different districts and conferences, and we may hope, from the experience we

have had of their utility, directly and indirectly, that they will be continued and multiplied throughout the connection. At these meetings sermons are preached, essays read, examinations held, discussions introduced, resolutions passed, and experience related. On the whole, they are a source of intellectual and spiritual profit, and we can but hope that they will become a common thing among us, be universally adopted, and be properly and prudently conducted.

CHAPTER VI.

OF THE SUPPORT OF THE MINISTRY AND FINANCIAL INTERESTS OF METHODISM.

SECTION I.

OF THE ANNUAL ALLOWANCE TO MINISTERS.

1. THE annual allowance of the bishops in the Methodist Episcopal Church, is as follows: If unmarried, one hundred dollars and his travelling expenses; if married, two hundred dollars and his travelling expenses; if he have children, for each child under seven years of age, sixteen dollars; and for each child over seven, and under fourteen, twenty-four dollars annually. Besides the above allowance, the bishops are allowed an amount annually for house-rent, fuel, and table expenses. The latter amount is estimated as follows: each annual conference within whose bounds a bishop may reside, appoints a committee, annually, of three or more, whose duty it is to estimate the amount necessary to furnish a house, fuel, and provision, for the bishop. This amount will of course differ according to the size of the bishop's family, and the place where he may reside, as house-rent, fuel, &c., may be much greater in some places than in others. The last amount, when estimated, is drawn from the funds of the book concern in New York and Cincinnati, while each annual conference is required to bear its proportionate part of the former amount, including salary and travelling expenses.

2. The annual allowance of the presiding elders is the same as that of the bishops, and is raised as follows: There is an annual meeting in each presiding elder's district, of one steward

from each station and circuit, who is appointed by a previous quarterly conference. These district stewards estimate the amount necessary to furnish a house, fuel, and table expenses, and apportion his entire claim, including his salary and travelling expenses, among the different circuits and stations in his district, according to their ability. When such an apportionment has been made, if there should be a deficiency in the receipts of any preacher in his district, he must share his proportionate loss of such deficiency ; and if all receive their full claim, the presiding elder receives his, thus sharing with each preacher in proportion to what the latter receives.

3. The annual allowance of all the travelling ministers and preachers is the same as that of the bishops and presiding elders, and is raised in the following manner : The quarterly conference appoints a committee to estimate the amount necessary to furnish a house, fuel, and table expenses of the preacher or preachers who may be sent to them. The sum estimated by the committee, if approved by the quarterly conference, is either raised by subscription, slip-rent, or voluntary contribution. The penny-a-week system, which obtains so largely among the Methodists in England, has not succeeded to any great extent in the United States.

4. Local preachers have an allowance in certain cases. Where they preach only on the Sabbath, and spend their week-days in pursuing their secular business, they do not expect any remuneration, unless they are very poor ; but where they spend any considerable portion of their week-time in the service of the church, and are employed by the presiding elder to fill the vacancy of a travelling preacher, they are entitled to the same allowance as a travelling preacher.

5. In making the estimates for travelling and table expenses, the various committees—except it may be in the case of bishops—are scarcely ever governed by the rule—How much will it take to supply the preacher and his family with provisions, and his horse with provender ? but—How much can we raise ?

In the former case two hundred—perhaps three, or more—would be thought necessary; in the latter, sometimes but half the necessary sum is estimated. We have known the estimate for the table expenses of a preacher with a wife and three or four children, to be as low as thirty dollars, with nothing for travelling expenses! Such an estimate is a mere evasion of the disciplinary requirement, and ought to be discountenanced by every preacher, steward, and leader in the church. The true policy appears to be, to estimate what is actually necessary for the above purposes, and if the circuit or station cannot, or will not raise it, as all know, the members are not holden as in case of debt. In making such estimates, committees should always inquire how much of each article their preacher will probably need. We will suppose he has a wife and four children, and is under the necessity of keeping a servant-girl. Such a family will consume, in the course of the year, at least

40	bushels of	Wheat,	at $1 00	$40 00
30	" "	Potatoes, at	25	7 50
200	lbs.	Butter, at	12½	25 00
100	"	Cheese, at	6¼	6 25
200	"	Meat, at	10	20 00
		Groceries, &c. &c.,		30 00
		Fuel,		20 00
		Hay, and provender for horse		50 00
		Incidentals,		1 25
				$200 00

Add to the above his salary, out of which he must find himself and his family in clothing, schooling, books, periodicals, postage, medicine, medical attendance, help, wear of carriage, horse, harness, crockery, furniture, &c.,	280 00
To this should be added the claim of the presiding elder, say $40,	40 00
Aggregate of the whole,	$520 00

By adopting some such method of estimating a preacher's claim, committees would arrive at a more correct conclusion than they generally do, and instead of our preachers being obliged—as is sometimes the case—literally to beg a living, they would have enough, and nothing more; but as long as the present wretched policy of making estimates is pursued, the church must expect to lose, from year to year, some of her best ministers, for the good and sufficient reason, that they do not, and cannot, as parents and husbands, consent to see their families in want, as long as it is written, "He that provideth not for his own house, hath denied the faith, and is worse than an infidel."

6. The annual allowance of the supernumerary, superannuated, or worn-out preachers is the same as that of the effective travelling preachers and bishops. The superannuated preachers, however, receive nothing for table expenses, house-rent, and fuel. Their allowance, paltry as it is, is scarcely ever paid them in full; what is paid, is raised partly from the fifth collection, and partly from the proceeds of the book concern, and chartered fund.

7. The widows and orphans of deceased preachers are also allowed one hundred dollars for the widow, and the same amount for each child, as before mentioned, but nothing for table, travelling expenses, house-rent, or fuel.

8. The fifth collection—so called because it usually comes after the four quarterly collections—is required by discipline to be taken up on each circuit or station in the connection, once in each year. This collection, in the year 1850, in all the conferences, amounted to $15,750, or an average of $543 to each conference.

The proceeds of the Book Concern, for the same year, amounted to $17,400, or, $600 to each conference.

The proceeds of the chartered fund, for the same year, amounted to $1,885, or $65 to each conference.

The income from all other sources, such as ten-cent collections, legacies, interest on conference funds, &c. &c., amounted to about $6,200. The whole making an aggregate of $41,135. This sum at first sight appears large, but if it is divided by the number of superannuated preachers, and widows, and orphans, in the connection, it will be found that but a portion of their disciplinary allowance is given to these worthy claimants on the funds of the church.

The number of superannuated preachers returned on the minutes of conference for 1850 is 352.

The number of widows returned on the same minutes, as nearly as we can ascertain, is 275.

The number of orphan children depending on the same funds, more or less, cannot be less than 300.

In addition to the above claimants, the bishops must receive their portion of the funds, which amounted in 1850—with the allowance to a bishop's widow—to $1,813, or $62.53 to each conference. If we add together the above number of claimants, and divide the gross receipts, we shall find that the average dividend to each claimant is $44, and a fraction. But as each one receives in proportion to the number in the family, and the age of the child, or children, the actual receipts differ greatly from the average to each. Hence, in the minutes, we find that the lowest amount given to any one orphan is one dollar and twenty-eight cents ! or about eight per cent. on their claim of sixteen dollars ! In the same conference, widows with probably one or two children, received the sum of $10.70, as an annual allowance, and the greatest amount to any one superannuated preacher, in the same conference, was $26.53, and this "worn-out" man probably had a wife, and six or seven children. On the other hand, the Genesee Conference had the honor of paying up the claims of the superannuated preachers, the widows and orphans, in 1850, each married man having received $200, with the full allowance for children. Both of these cases, however, are extreme ones, and the probability is.

that not more than fifty per cent., on an average, is realized from these funds, to support the various claimants.

It should be remembered, also, that if an *effective* travelling preacher receives less on his circuit than would amount to the dividend of the worn-out men—let it be more or less—he is entitled to have the deficiency of per centage made up, so that his gross receipts for the year shall equal theirs. This should be remembered, for two reasons. (1.) Many think that if an effective preacher fails to receive his allowance on his circuit, the deficiency will all be made up from the conference funds; this is a mistake. (2.) If a circuit or station allow their preacher to remain unpaid, for the above reason, they are taking bread from the mouths of the aged and infirm preachers, and from the widow and the orphan.

We have thus stated as fully as possible the polity of the church, and the requirements of the Discipline, in relation to the allowance of ministers.

SECTION II.

OF CHURCHES, AND CHURCH PROPERTY.

1. Churches, chapels, meeting-houses, and parsonages, built for the use or occupancy of the members and preachers of the Methodist Episcopal Church, are invariably deeded to the trustees of the local church or Society erecting or purchasing the same. Some have embraced the idea that all such property is deeded either to the bishops, or preachers; or to the general or annual conferences. This, however, is a mistake, in regard to which any one may satisfy himself, who will examine the subject.

2. The trustees—as stated in a previous chapter—are required to hold the property for the purpose for which it was erected, purchased, or donated, which purpose is, that the

members of the Methodist Episcopal Church may use the same as a place of worship, according to the rules and discipline of the church; and in further trust, that they shall always permit the ministers and preachers of such church, who may be duly appointed by the annual conference, to preach and expound God's holy word therein.

3. For the manner of appointing trustees, the reader is referred to Book III. Chapter III. Section IX. Paragraph 4.

4. Parsonages, burying-grounds, &c., are held by a similar tenure as churches, and the only control the conferences or ministers have over them is, to use them and the churches according to the design of the donors or purchasers. The preachers, bishops, or conferences have no right to dispose of them nor use them for any other purpose whatsoever than the one named in the deed of conveyance.

5. As churches and parsonages increase in the church, there is an increasing desire on the part of both preachers and people, to have the parsonages furnished with at least heavy furniture. Indeed, one of the greatest clogs to the itinerancy is the necessity of removing furniture from place to place. What with the wear and tear of furniture, and the enormous expense annually incurred in such removal, besides the time occupied in packing and unpacking, it begins to be seriously agitated as a question, whether the preachers had not better sell all their own furniture, and throw themselves at once on the generosity of the people for such articles of furniture as they need for housekeeping. If such arrangements could be made, the saving in expense for a few years, would, in a pecuniary point of view, more than meet the necessary outlay. But to have the plan operate well, it must be generally, even universally adopted.

APPENDIX TO BOOK III.

DECISIONS, AND RESOLUTIONS ON THE ADMINISTRATION OF THE DISCIPLINE OF THE METHODIST EPISCOPAL CHURCH.

THE Author begs leave to append the following decisions and resolutions for the special benefit of junior preachers and others, who may not be acquainted with the same. The authorities may be found at the end of the appendix.

1. When does the conference-year commence and terminate? ANS. When the appointments are announced in conference.

2. When a member of conference has been brought before a committee, during the interim of an annual conference, and has been by said committee acquitted, can the annual conference take up the case and decide the final issue, except in case of appeal? It can, the action of the committee being only to determine whether the accused shall be suspended, or allowed to discharge his ministerial functions during the interim.

3. Can a local preacher be tried by a quarterly conference before having been brought before a committee of local preachers? He can, but when it is practicable, he should be brought before a committee of his peers in the first instance. The quarterly conference, however, is the only body that can properly try, and finally acquit or suspend a local preacher. "It has original jurisdiction."

4. When a bill of charges is presented against a local preacher for imprudence, and the necessary disciplinary labor has not been performed, may the quarterly conference reject said bill of charges? "If any illegality is found, the conference may reject any part of the bill."

5. Are the characters of local elders and deacons subject to annual examination in the quarterly conference? They are.

6. If a local preacher or minister is proved guilty of some offence, who determines the degree or kind of punishment? The quarterly conference. The same rule applies to a travelling preacher on trial.

7. Can quarterly conferences, under any circumstances, try a member of an annual conference? They cannot. They may, however, state their grievances, as a quarterly conference, to the presiding elder.

8. Can exhorters, stewards, and leaders be tried by a quarterly conference? They cannot. Exhorters and stewards are responsible for only official misconduct to, and may be deprived of their office by, the quarterly conference, but can only be tried and expelled by the Society, or select number. Leaders, as such, are responsible only to the preacher in charge.

9. When it is asked in quarterly conference, "Are there any complaints?" what is intended? Complaints against local preachers for immorality or imprudence, or against them, and exhorters, stewards, and trustees—in certain instances—for official misconduct.

10. In case of a decision by a quarterly conference adverse to the membership of a local or travelling preacher on trial, and no appeal is presented to the next session of the annual conference, is such decision final? It is, in ordinary cases, especially in cases of law questions.

11. In granting or renewing licenses in a quarterly conference, if there should be a tie vote, will the tie vote grant, or renew the license? It will not. There must be a *majority* of votes of all the members present.

12. May a quarterly conference refuse to renew the license of a local preacher, without showing cause? It may, but cannot deprive him of it in less than a year, except for cause, formally proved.

13. Can a quarterly conference adjourn to a distant day?

They may adjourn from day to day, to finish pending business, only.

14. Is a travelling preacher on trial amenable to the quarterly, or annual conference for his administration of discipline? To the annual conference, only, in such case.

15. Who presides at the examination of a local elder, deacon, or preacher, who is accused of crime, and is brought before a committee of local preachers? The preacher in charge.

16. If found guilty, who is to suspend him? The committee.

17. In the trial of a member before the "select number," should the preacher in charge remain with them while making up their verdict? He should, but ought not to express an opinion in reference to the guilt or innocence of the accused, until the decision is made, nor even at any time during the progress of the trial.

18. If the member is found guilty, who is to determine and award the punishment? The preacher.

19. If an accused person object to any one or more of the select number, should his objections be overruled? They should, unless they are reasonable; in that case, the person or persons objected to, should be changed for others.

20. If the preacher in charge is a party interested in the issue of the case, when a member is to be tried, should he act as chairman of the trial? He should not. The presiding elder should appoint a chairman for the occasion.

21. When a verdict of guilty is rendered against an accused person, must the preacher expel the offender, or may pardon be granted? In cases of scandalous crimes, expulsion should follow; but for crimes of a moderate degree, if there is humility, and a promise of amendment, the person may be borne with, but then only by general consent of the committee or Society.

22. If a member refuse to arbitrate a disputed matter, after being recommended to do so, may the preacher in charge pro-

ceed to expel him? Not before he is tried for the offence and proved guilty, before the Society or select number. *In all cases of expulsion whatsoever*, the person must first be properly and formally tried for the offence for which he is expelled, before expulsion can ensue.

23. When a preacher differs in judgment from the Society or select number in relation to the guilt or innocence of an accused person, and refers the case to the quarterly conference, is that reference an appeal? It is not; it is a new trial. The power to refer should scarcely ever be used by a preacher, because by many good judges the rule is considered unconstitutional, as it destroys the privilege of appeal in the case, to the quarterly conference.

24. Who shall decide whether a person absents himself from trial, in the sense of the discipline? The select number, or the Society.

25. Is a preacher in charge obliged to present all appeals from expelled members to the quarterly conference? He is, when notified to that effect.

26. May a preacher receive a person into the church, living within the bounds of another charge, when it is known that such person could not be received in the charge where he resides? He may not, except in extreme cases.

27. When a member wishes to remove his residence, and the preacher believes there are good reasons why a certificate should be withheld, what shall be done? If the member is willing to be tried, the preacher must proceed to the trial of the person; otherwise, he will be guilty of maladministration. In case of a refusal to be tried, a certificate may, nay, ought to be withheld.

28. When a member wishes to withdraw from the church, is the preacher under obligation to grant him a certificate of membership? If the member wishes to unite with another evangelical church, a certificate may, as a matter of courtesy,

be given, otherwise, there is no obligation, nor even propriety, in doing so.

29. How long may a person retain a certificate of membership, before it becomes null, and void? There is no prescribed time. But a person presenting a certificate becomes responsible to the Society receiving him upon such certificate, for his moral conduct while he held the same in his hands.

30. Can a preacher or Society refuse to receive a member who presents a proper certificate of membership? They cannot, but if guilty of immorality, may proceed to try him, as above stated. All such evidences of membership must be duly honored.

31. When an expelled person confesses and gives proper satisfaction, and applies for re-admission, may he be received in full membership, or must he be received on trial? He may be received in full connection.

32. Is a preacher at liberty to refuse to call an accused member to trial, when charges have been preferred by respectable members of the church? He is, if there are sufficient reasons existing why he should not do so.

33. Must a preacher call a member to trial who is credibly reported to be guilty of crime, even if no charges are formally preferred against him? It is the duty of the preacher to do so.

34. Should a preacher proceed to try a member on a bill of charges prepared, and preferred by a complainant out of the church? He should not; all formal bills of charges should be preferred by members; but if, in the absence of the latter, the preacher believes the accused guilty, he should make out charges against him himself.

35. How long a time should elapse between a citation to trial, and the time of the trial? This will depend on circumstances; but generally at least a week's notice should be given.

36. If a different crime is proven against an accused person, from the one specified in the bill of charges, what should be

done? If the accused plead that he is not prepared for trial on that point, the trial should be adjourned to a future day.

37. In preparing a bill of charges, how should a preacher proceed? He should give the charges, with all the specifications under those charges; and he should be as specific as possible, both in regard to time, and place, where the alleged offence was committed. In case of a charge of falsehood, or slander, the exact words used should be given; a correct copy should be furnished the accused, with the name of the accuser, if any, and a proper notice of the time and place of trial.

38. At the time of the trial, how should he proceed? He should cause correct minutes of the charges, specifications, testimony, and decision, to be kept in writing, together with all the proceedings in the case, so that in case of an appeal, the same may be presented in due form, to the quarterly conference.

39. When a member is charged with crime, and wishes to withdraw, for the purpose of evading a trial, is the preacher under the necessity of considering him withdrawn? He is not; the accused member should not be allowed to withdraw without permission from the Society.

40. If an expelled person is restored to membership by the action of an annual conference, on account of incorrect administration, can such person be tried over again for the same offence? He can; the action of the conference simply places him where justice may be done by a new trial.

41. Can an expelled member avail himself of the action of an annual conference in his case, unless he first uses his constitutional privilege of an appeal to the quarterly conference, as described in the discipline? He cannot; his first and chief redress is in his right of appeal to the quarterly conference.

42. Should an accuser be allowed to be a witness? In cases of personal dispute, in the issue of which the accuser has a *direct interest*, he should not; but in cases where he has no other interest than is common to all the members of the church, he should be permitted to give evidence.

43. Has a preacher a right to give a love-feast *ticket* to any person not a member or probationer of the church? He has no such right. Tickets with the word "*member*" printed on them, should be given only to members; tickets without the word member, should be given only to probationers: "*notes*" of admission should be given to those who are neither members nor probationers.

44. Has an annual conference a right to *require* its members to take up an annual collection for the purpose of sustaining the literary institutions under its care? It has such right.

45. Can an annual conference refuse a location to one of its members in good standing, when such location is demanded? It cannot, and is obliged to give him a certificate of such location.

46. Is the recommendation of a quarterly conference, in the case of local preachers, candidates for the travelling connection, &c., of any force after the ensuing annual conference? It is not.

47. Has the presiding elder of a district a right to give leave of absence to any of his preachers? He has not.

48. Has the president of an annual or quarterly conference a right to decline putting the question on a motion, when in his judgment such motion does not relate to the proper business of the conference? He has.

49. Are questions relating to the admissibility of testimony, questions of law? They are. (Consequently the president or chairman of a trial must decide on the admissibility of testimony.)

50. To what quarterly conference or Society does a superannuated preacher belong? If he resides within the bounds of his own conference, he belongs to such bodies where he resides; if in the bounds of another conference, he belongs to no Society, or quarterly conference, but has a right, as all preachers have, to meet in class.

AUTHORITIES.

Question.		Question.	
1	Bishop Waugh	26	Bishop Morris
2	" Hamline	27	Gen. Con. 1848
3	" Morris	28	Gen. Con. 1848
4	" Janes	29	Bishop Morris
5	" Morris	30	Various
6	" Hedding	31	Bishop Hedding
7	" Morris	32	" Hedding
8	" Morris	33	" Hedding
9	Various	34	Various
10	Bishop Hamline	35	"
11	" Waugh	36	Bishop Hedding
12	" Waugh	37	Various
13	" Hedding	38	"
14	" Hedding	39	All the Bishops
15	" Hedding	40	Bishop Janes
16	" Hedding	41	B. R. Con. 1851
17	" Hedding, Morris	42	Bishop Janes
18	" Hedding	43	Discipline
19	" Hedding	44	Gen. Con. 1840
20	" Morris	45	Gen. Con. 1840, & 1844
21	" Hedding	46	Gen. Con. 1840
22	" Hedding	47	Gen. Con. 1840
23	" Hedding	48	Gen. Con. 1840
24	" Hedding	49	Gen. Con. 1844
25	Various	50	Gen. Con. 1844

The above decisions and resolutions are given, not in the exact words of the authorities referred to, but so as to embrace the substance in the fewest words possible, and yet retain the meaning.

BOOK IV.

BENEVOLENT AND LITERARY INSTITUTIONS AND STATISTICS OF METHODISM.

CHAPTER I.

BENEVOLENT INSTITUTIONS.

SECTION I.

BOOK CONCERN.

1. THE Book Concern may properly be called a benevolent institution, as the design—in part, at least—is to furnish a fund for the relief of the superannuated, or worn-out preachers, the widows and orphans of those who have died in the regular work of the ministry, and the profits of that establishment are, in the main, sacredly devoted to that purpose. It is true that this is by no means the only design of its institution; the circulation of bibles, Sunday-school books, tracts, and religious works of various kinds, all prove that another prominent object is the furnishing of wholesome reading to the thousands of our Israel, who naturally look to their own church and ministry for a supply of their wants in this respect.

At an early period in the history of English Methodism, Mr. Wesley became an author, and indirectly a publisher on an extensive scale. The voluminous works which he found it necessary to print "for the use of the people called Methodists," demanded a press of his own, which was, and is, located in the city of London. Soon after the organization of the Methodist Episcopal Church, the importance of having Methodist books printed in America, was deeply felt. Hitherto, the minutes, Sunday service, hymn-books, &c., had been published at Mr. Wesley's press in London, and had to be imported at great risk and expense, besides loss of time. In the year 1787, the subject of printing and publishing books in America is first alluded to in the discipline. At the conference which assembled in the above year, it was resolved to print such books as the conference should recommend, and that the profits of sale should be applied "toward Cokesbury College, the preachers' fund, the deficiencies of the preachers, the distant missions, or the debts on our churches." The first attempt at publishing books was in Philadelphia, and in 1792, the Rev. John Dickins was appointed to manage the printing business. His annual allowance was, "two hundred dollars for a dwelling-house, and for a book-room; eighty dollars for a boy; fifty-three and one third dollars for fire-wood; and three hundred and thirty-three dollars to clothe and feed himself, his wife, and his children. In all, six hundred and sixty-six dollars, and one third. The first book-committee appointed to regulate the concern, were John Dickins, Henry Willis, and Thomas Haskins. In 1796, the publication of the Methodist Magazine was recommended by the conference, and in 1800, Ezekiel Cooper was appointed superintendent of the Book Concern, and it was made the duty of each presiding elder to see that his district was duly supplied with books; to order such books as were wanted; to distribute them among the different circuits, and to charge the same to the preachers. The latter were required to sell as many as possible, and account to the presiding elder for the same, and when they left a circuit, they were to collect all the books remaining on their hands in one place, and leave an inventory of the same with the presiding elder. No preacher was allowed to print or circulate any book or pamphlet without the consent of the conference, previously obtained.

In 1804, the Book Concern was removed to New York, and Ezekiel Cooper was re-appointed general book steward, and John Wilson, assistant editor and book steward. At this time it was resolved that the profits be applied to the support of distressed travelling preachers and their families.

In 1820, a book agent was appointed to reside in Cincinnati, and manage the Concern in the western country, under the direction of the editor in New York. The system of issuing books on commission still obtained, and it was only in 1828 that the General Conference resolved thereafter to issue no more books on commission. In 1826 the publication of the "Christian Advocate" was commenced in New York, and at the conference of 1828, an editor was appointed to superintend the same, and to edit the Child's Magazine. In 1832, a branch concern, or general depository, was established in New Orleans, and in 1836 the book concern at Cincinnati was made independent of the one in New York,* yet so "as to co-operate with the agents at New York" in the publication of books, &c. In the last named year, in addition to the Christian Advocate and Journal, and Western Christian Advocate, provision was made for issuing weekly papers from Charleston, S. C., Richmond, Va., and Nashville, Tenn.

In 1840, provision was made for the publication of the Methodist Quarterly Review, Youth's Magazine, the Christian Apologist, in German, Pittsburgh Christian Advocate, and the Ladies' Repository.

In 1844, the Northern Christian Advocate, in Auburn, was

* On the 18th Feb. 1836, the entire book establishment in New York, with its buildings, presses, books, papers, &c., was destroyed by fire. Through the liberality of friends, in and out of the church, however, the loss was partly made up, and better buildings were erected on the site of the old ones, so that the "glory of the latter house," far surpasses "that of the former."

adopted as a General Conference paper, and given in charge to Rev. N. Rounds, of the Oneida Conference, who was succeeded in 1848 by the present talented editor, Rev. William Hosmer, of the Genesee Conference.

2. The present state of the Book Concern is as follows :—In New York, there is one agent, and one assistant agent; an editor of the Quarterly Review, and books of the General Catalogue; an editor of the Christian Advocate and Journal; an editor of Sunday-school books and tracts, all of whom are under the supervision of a book committee of seven, appointed by the General Conference. A large number of clerks, salesmen, porters, printers, binders, &c. &c., are employed at this concern, which is located at 200 Mulberry-street.

At Cincinnati there are two agents, and three editors, with the necessary number of *employees*, and an editor for each of the General Conference papers. Depositories of books are found in Pittsburgh, and Boston, and Methodist book-stores are found in Auburn, Buffalo, Philadelphia, Baltimore, and other places. The number of distinct works published at New York and Cincinnati, from the ponderous imperial octavo of 5,528 pages, down to the lilliputian 48mo. of but a few pages, amounts to about two thousand in round numbers. These works may be classified as follows :—

On Biblical Literature,	21
On Doctrinal and Controversial Theology,	56
On Experimental and Practical Religion,	67
On Biography and History,	85
On Ecclesiastical Polity and History,	13
On Homiletics and Pastoral Duties,	9
On Methodist Usages, Church Polity, &c.,	23
On Missions, &c.,	16
Sermons and Addresses by different Ministers,	59
Poetical and Musical,	9
On Miscellaneous Subjects,	70
German Works,	9

Juvenile Works, ...	71
Fireside Library, ...	121
Tracts, &c., ...	400

SUNDAY-SCHOOL DEPARTMENT.

Youth's Library, VOLS.	400
Child's Library, "	300
Children's Tracts, ...	60
Gift Books, &c., ...	163
	1952

The publication of these books by thousands of copies annually, together with the printing of love-feast tickets, Sunday-school tickets, certificates of membership in the church, and Missionary Societies, Sunday School Union, &c. &c., and the printing of portraits, engravings, &c., will show to some extent the amount of capital required, and the labor to be performed, in that vast establishment in New York, and its sister establishment in the west.

The preparation of books, however, is but one part of the business performed at these establishments. About thirty thousand copies of the Christian Advocate and Journal are weekly printed in New York; about one hundred thousand copies of the Sunday School Advocate—a paper as large as the former—are published monthly at the same place; about fifty thousand copies of the Missionary Advocate are also published monthly, besides between two and three thousand copies of the Quarterly Review. At Cincinnati, besides the publication of books, the Western Christian Advocate, the Christian Apologist, and the Ladies' Monthly Repository, are published weekly and monthly by thousands.

3. The following table exhibits the present financial condition of the book concerns at New York and Cincinnati, as reported to the annual conferences at their sessions in 1851.

BOOK-ROOM AT NEW YORK.

Real Estate in New York city, consisting of buildings, &c.	$115,573
Cash in hand, and in bank, with State Stocks	66,605
Books on hand, bound and unbound, &c. &c.	191,681
Printing-office, including presses, type, stereotype plates, &c.	92,907
Foundry, &c. &c.	618
Bindery	8,868
Notes and accounts considered good	164,971
Deduct $14,819, due by the concern, leaves	$626,225
Nett profits of the year 1850	42,161
Paid conference dividends in 1850	19,700
Amount of sales in 1850	200,215

BOOK CONCERN AT CINCINNATI.

Real Estate in Cincinnati, &c.	$65,000
Books and stationery on hand	44,061
Printing-office, presses, type, &c.	29,912
Bindery	4,915
Furniture, &c. &c.	1,900
Notes and accounts considered good	79,782
Cash on hand, &c. &c.	3,567
Deduct $26,502, due by the concern, leaves	$202,637
Profits of the year 1850–1	15,095
Present value of both concerns	$828,862

Both concerns are incorporated by the Legislatures of the States wherein they are located.

SECTION II.

CHARTERED FUND.

1. THIS fund was instituted in the year 1796. The design of its institution was to relieve the distressed travelling preachers, the worn-out preachers, and the widows and orphans of preachers. It was raised by the voluntary contributions of the friends of Methodism, and from the first, has been located in Philadelphia, where the board of trustees are incorporated, and the fund chartered by the State of Pennsylvania. The trustees are chosen by the General Conference, and hold the funds in trust, for the purposes above specified. The interest only of the fund can be applied for such purposes, the principal remaining untouched. The amount thus funded is about $36,000, and yields an annual interest of about $2,500, which is equally divided among all the conferences in the connection, for the benefits of the claimants. The discipline requires the interest to be divided into thirty-nine equal parts, while there are but *twenty-nine* conferences—exclusive of mission conferences—in the connection. The reason for this apparent discrepancy, is found in the fact that the number of conferences in 1844, and before the separation of the Southern Church from the Methodist Episcopal Church, was thirty-nine, and as the South, since the separation, claims a portion of the said fund, it has been thought best to allow the discipline to remain as it is, till after the settlement of this question by competent authority.

SECTION III.

MISSIONARY SOCIETY OF THE METHODIST EPISCOPAL CHURCH.

1. THE Missionary Society of the Methodist Episcopal Church was organized in the city of New York, in the year 1819.

The Constitution of the Society has several times undergone alteration and revision, the last revision being by the General Conference of 1844.

2. The object of the Society is for the purpose of supporting missions and schools in our own, and in foreign countries.

3. The payment of two dollars annually constitutes a member, and the payment of twenty dollars at one time, a member for life. The payment of one hundred and fifty dollars constitutes a manager for life, and the payment of five hundred dollars a patron for life.

4. The officers of the Society consist of a president, vice-presidents, corresponding secretary, recording secretary, treasurer, assistant treasurer, and thirty-two managers.

5. The senior bishop of the church is president, and the other bishops are vice-presidents, according to seniority. These with the other officers—excepting the corresponding secretary—are all appointed by the Society at its annual meeting in April of each year. The corresponding Secretary is appointed by the General Conference, and is required to reside in New York, and conduct the correspondence of the Society, at home and abroad.

6. The receipts of the Society have gradually increased from the time of its organization. The receipts for 1849–50 were $107,835 73, and the disbursements for the same period were $100,989 63. The receipts for the year ending May 1st, 1851, were $133,317 41, and the disbursements for the same year amounted to $131,663 40. The appropriation for the present year—1851–2—by the missionary board for the support of the various Methodist Missions, is $167,000.

7. There are eight patrons of the Society, having paid each $500 or more at one time; thirteen life managers, having paid each $150 or more at one time, and about seven thousand life-members, who have paid each twenty dollars or more at one time.

8. The following table will exhibit at a single glance the

operations of the Society, which table we have compiled principally from the latest report of the Missionary Society of the Methodist Episcopal Church.

1. DOMESTIC MISSIONS:	Missions.	Missionaries.	Local Preachers.	Members.	Churches or Chapels.	Sunday Schools.
English Domestic Missions,	366	380	235	26,341		
German " "	103	116	56	6,325	115	99
Swedish, Danish and Norwegian Domestic Missions,	4	6		338	2	2
Welsh Domestic Missions	5	5		110		2
French " "	2	2		21		
Indian " "	13	23		1,470	7	8
Oregon " "	8	12	17	393	5	3
California " "	10	6	26	754	7	5
2. FOREIGN MISSIONS:						
Germany	3	7		113		
South America	1	1		40	1	1
China	5	5				
Africa	14	18	18	1,074	10	
Total	534	581	352	36,979	117	120

There are connected with the above missions, besides the members, 8,370 probationers, making an aggregate of members and probationers, of 45,349.

9. Besides the Parent Society at New York, there are auxiliary Societies in each conference in the church, besides numerous subordinate societies, such as Ladies', Youth's and Sunday-school Missionary Societies. All these operate through the Parent Society, except the Ladies' Home Missionary Society in New York city, which supports a mission in the vilest part of the city. Each circuit and station in the church is in fact a missionary society, as it is made the duty of each quarterly conference to appoint a mission committee of at least five persons, who shall, with the preacher in charge, superintend the interests of the missionary cause within their respective bounds, by organizing

missionary societies, taking up collections, having sermons or addresses delivered, and establishing missionary prayer-meetings.

10. Thus we see that Methodism is emphatically missionary in its character, not only in its foreign operations, but in its domestic, or home work. Indeed, in an important sense, every minister of the Methodist Episcopal Church—and indeed of all other branches of the Methodist family, where the itinerancy is preserved—is, in an important sense, a missionary, for instead of being called by a church or congregation, under a stipulated salary, to preach to them, they are annually sent forth without purse or scrip, into the highways and hedges, the fields and the forests, the city and the country, to invite men to Christ. We may further remark, that in proportion as a church is missionary in its character, does it give evidence of being a true church of Jesus Christ; evidence at once so clear, so convincing, that the chimera of apostolical succession sinks into utter insignificancy when compared with it. "Ye are the light of the world;" "the salt of the earth," said Christ to his disciples; and when he said to his ministers, "Go ye into all the world, and preach the Gospel to every creature," he stamped his church on earth as a missionary church.

For a farther view of Methodist missions in different parts of the world, the reader is referred to the statistical tables in this work, pages 348, *et seq.*

SECTION IV.

SUNDAY-SCHOOL UNION OF THE METHODIST EPISCOPAL CHURCH.

1. The honor of having originated Sunday-schools is generally—and we believe justly—ascribed to Robert Raikes, Esq., of Gloucester, Eng., who in the year 1781, at the place of his residence, engaged four persons for a stipulated sum each Sabbath, to teach such children as he might send to them.

2. The honor of having originated the system of gratuitous instruction in Sunday-schools, belongs, we think, with equal justice, to Mr. John Wesley, who, in 1785, urged his Societies to follow the laudable example of Mr. Raikes. The Societies took Mr. Wesley's advice, and shortly after, Sunday-schools, on the plan of gratuitous and religious instruction, were commenced in all parts of the Methodist connection in England.

3. As early as 1786, Sunday-schools were established in the Methodist Episcopal Church in the United States, through the agency of Bishop Asbury, who, being in constant communication with Mr. Wesley by correspondence, learned from the latter the fact of their establishment in England. But prior to this period (in 1784), the Methodist ministers and preachers were required by the discipline, wherever there were ten children, whose parents were members, to meet them at least an hour every week, for purposes of religious instruction; and in 1790, they were required to establish Sunday-schools in or near the places of worship, for the benefit of white and black children, and to appoint suitable persons to teach gratis all who would attend, and had a capacity to learn. As there is no authentic account of Sunday-schools in America prior to 1786, we may justly claim for Bishop Asbury and his co-laborers in the church, the honor of having established Sunday-schools on the gratuitous plan, in America.

4. In 1828, the Methodist Sunday-school, Bible, and Tract Union was organized, but the complexity of this organization rendered it expedient, in 1836, to discontinue the Bible department of the Union; and in 1840, the Tract department was also discontinued, and the Sunday School Union of the Methodist Episcopal Church was established on a new, and we trust a firm and permanent foundation.

5. Since the organization of the Sunday School Union in its present form, the cause of Sunday-schools in our church has received a fresh impulse, and has acquired a degree of importance secondary to no other cause in which the church is en-

gaged. Not only have its annual receipts increased, but its books have continued to multiply almost beyond conception. Its facilities for obtaining correct statistical reports have also been increased, and it is perhaps not too much to say, that no other Sunday-school Society in the land, is in a more flourishing and prosperous condition, at the present time, than the Methodist Sunday School Union, under the management of its very efficient corresponding secretary, the Rev. D. P. Kidder, D. D.

6. The receipts of the Union for the supply of destitute schools with books, fall very far short of what they ought to be. While the members generally evince a becoming degree of zeal in behalf of Sunday-schools in their own localities, they should not forget that there are thousands of poor children in the new and sparse settlements of our common country, who need to be aided in their thirst for religious knowledge, by the contributions of the more highly favored portion of our members and youth. Only about $5000 the past year was contributed for this purpose.

7. The actual condition of our Sunday-schools in the United States may be inferred from the following table, taken from the annual report of the Sunday School Union of the Methodist Episcopal Church for 1851. We give only the aggregate of the numbers in the various conferences.

No. of Sunday Schools.	No. of Teachers.	No. of Scholars.	No. of Vols. in Library.	Bible-Classes.	Scholars in Infant-class.	Annual Expense of Schools.	Sunday School Advocates taken.	Conversions past year.
8,021	84,840	429,589	1,117,083	5,486	32,826	$54,587	74,363	11,398
Increase past year.								
687	10,966	37,356	149 497	891	4,927	$6,508	8,648	2,384

SECTION V.

BIBLE SOCIETY.

1. The American Bible Society, although not a denominational nor Methodist institution, yet as it is largely supported by the Methodist Church, and the preachers are required to take up an annual collection in aid of its funds, it seems proper to give it a place among the benevolent institutions of the Methodist Episcopal Church. This Society was formed in New York, in the year 1816, and its declared object from the beginning has been to circulate copies of the Holy Scriptures without note or comment, which object it has faithfully carried out.

2. After the formation of the American Bible Society, up to the year 1828, the Methodist Church co-operated more or less with the same, but in the latter year a distinct Methodist Bible Society was formed in connection with the Sunday School and Tract Union of the Methodist Episcopal Church. This separate organization existed for about eight years, when in 1836 it was formally discontinued; and since that time the Methodist Episcopal Church has labored in this department of her work, in connection with the American Bible Society, and her various auxiliaries in different States, counties, and towns of the Union.

3. The gross receipts of the Society for 1850–51, amounted to the sum of $276,882, and the expenditures, to $276,899. Over half a million of copies of the Scriptures were issued during the same period, and since its organization no less than 7,572,967 copies of the Old and New Testaments have been circulated by the Society.

4. The precise amount contributed to the Society by the Methodist Church cannot be ascertained during the past year. Some of the largest conferences in the church, who have co-operated very efficiently in this good work, have failed to make

their report of the amount raised within their respective bounds for the Bible Society, and in many places the Methodist congregations co-operate in connection with other churches and congregations, in making collections; so that no distinction can be drawn between the contributions of the one, or the other. From the reports of the twenty-two conferences who have made returns, we learn that there was raised, in the year 1850, within their bounds, the sum of $19,330. If to this we add $5,000, as the probable amount raised in the six conferences not reporting, the total receipts from the Methodist Church in the North, will exceed $24,000. To this should properly be added the receipts from the Methodist Church South, which would swell the aggregate to between forty and fifty thousand dollars for the past year.

CHAPTER II.

LITERARY INSTITUTIONS OF METHODISM.

SECTION I.

UNIVERSITIES AND COLLEGES.

1. At an early period in the history of the Methodist Episcopal Church—as may be learned from the historical part of this work—strenuous efforts were put forth by Bishops Coke and Asbury, for the proper establishment of a Methodist college; and notwithstanding the promising aspect of things as connected with Cokesbury College for awhile, yet the hopes of these men of God, and the lovers of education in the church, were doomed to disappointment by the repeated destruction by fire of that institution. The failure in this early attempt in favor of education, produced discouragement in the church, and for a period of over thirty years, but little appears to have been done by the Methodist Church toward the establishment of colleges and seminaries of a higher grade.

2. The first Methodist minister in the United States who had enjoyed the benefits of a regular college education, was the late Rev. Wilbur Fisk, D.D., who graduated at Brown University in Rhode Island, in 1815. In 1818, Fisk joined the travelling connection, and after a few years' itinerant labor, was under the necessity of retiring from the field of active labor as a preacher. In 1825, having regained his health, he was called by the church to take charge of the Wilbraham Academy in Massa-

chusetts. From this period, the cause of education in the Methodist Episcopal Church was onward, and it is not too much to say, in honor of the memory of the dead, that to no man, living or dead, does the Methodist Church owe more for his efforts in the cause of education, than to Wilbur Fisk, while principal of the above named academy, and especially while President of the Wesleyan University, in Middletown, Conn.

The following is a list of the Universities and Colleges under the patronage of the Methodist Church in the Northern and Western States:

Wesleyan University,	Middletown, Conn.
Ohio Wesleyan University,	Delaware, Ohio.
Asbury University,	Green Castle, Ind.
Dickinson College,	Carlisle, Pa.
Genesee College,	Lima, N. Y.
Alleghany College,	Meadville, Pa.
M'Kendree College,	Lebanon, Ill.
Lawrence University,	Appleton, Wis.
Oregon Institute,	Salem, Oregon.

SECTION II.

BIBLICAL INSTITUTE.

THIS institution was opened in April, 1847, in Concord, N. H. The design contemplated in its formation, is the education of young men for the ministry in the Methodist Church. The object is not to *call* young men to the ministry, but to prepare more fully for the work in which they are about to engage, those young men who have previously been called by God and his church, to take upon themselves the sacred office. Hence, none are received as students, unless they bring a certificate from a quarterly or annual conference, of their being licentiates. Candidates for admission are also required to possess a previous knowledge of the common and higher branches of an English education, with the elements of the Greek language. The course of study is full, and particular attention is paid to the Scriptures in the original tongues. The endowment consists of bonds, notes, &c., to the amount of $33,000, the interest of which is applied annually for the support of the Institute. No tuition is required of any student, and although but in its infancy, a larger number of students are connected with it, than with any other similar institution in New England, excepting Andover. The number of professors is three, and of students, in July, 1851, fifty-four. John Dempster, D.D. of the Black River Conference, is the senior Professor, or President.

SECTION III.

SEMINARIES, ACADEMIES, &C.

About the year 1821, an academy, partly under Methodist patronage, was established in New Market, N. H.; and in 1825 the Wilbraham Academy, before mentioned, was organized, and the New Market Academy was merged in the same. Since that period, the number of Methodist seminaries, academies, and high schools, of a respectable literary character, have been organized from time to time, in different parts of the country. The following is a list of the same, with their places of location:

Amenia Seminary,	Amenia,	N. Y.
Falley "	Fulton,	"
Genesee Wesleyan Seminary,	Lima,	"
Governeur " "	Governeur,	"
Hempstead " "	Hempstead,	"
New York Conference "	Charlotteville,	"
Oneida " "	Cazenovia,	"
Jonesville Academy,	Jonesville,	"

Asbury Seminary,	Chagrine Falls, Ohio.
Greenfield "	Greenfield, "
Oakland Female Seminary,	Hillsboro', "
Worthington Female Seminary,	Worthington, "
Wesleyan Female College,	Cincinnati, "
Ohio Conference High School,	Springfield, "
Baldwin Institute,	Berea, "
Bakersfield Academy,	Bakersfield, Vt.
Newbury Seminary,	Newbury, "
Troy Conference Academy,	West Poultney, "
Wesleyan Seminary,	Springfield, "
Dickenson College Academy,	Williamsport, Pa.
Wyoming Seminary,	Kingston, "
Flushing Female Institute,	Flushing, L. I.
Fort Wayne Female College,	Fort Wayne, Ind.
Illinois Conf. Female Academy,	Jacksonville, Ill.
Maine Wesleyan Seminary,	Kent's Hill, Me.
Newark Wesleyan Institute,	Newark, N. J.
Pennington Male Seminary,	Pennington, "
Pennington Female Seminary,	" "
New Hampshire Conf. Seminary,	Northfield, N. H.
Virginia Academy,	Clarksburgh, Va.
Preparatory School,	Middletown, Ct.
Providence Conference Academy,	East Greenwich, R. I
Rock River Seminary,	Mount Morris, Ill.
Wesleyan Academy,	Wilbraham, Mass.
Wesleyan Fem. Collegiate Inst.,	Wilmington, Del.
Wesleyan Female Institute,	Staunton, Va.
Wesleyan Seminary,	Albion, Mich.
Charlotte Boarding Academy,	Charlotte, N. Y.
Portland Academy,	Portland, Oregon.
California Institute, (not fully established),	California.

CHAPTER III.

STATISTICS OF EPISCOPAL METHODISM.

SECTION I.

THE NUMBER OF CONFERENCES, &C.

1. THE Methodist Episcopal Church is embraced in one General Conference, which extends from the Canada line on the north and north-west, to the States of Maryland and Virginia on the south—embracing the whole of the former and the western part of the latter; and from the Atlantic Ocean on the east to the Pacific on the west. Prior to the separation of the Southern portion of the Church, the General Conference embraced the whole of the United States and Territories. At present the above are its geographical limits, exclusive of foreign missionary ground.

2. The number of Annual Conferences represented in the General Conference is twenty-nine, exclusive of the California and Liberia Conferences. The following are the names of all the Conferences in the Church:

New York,	Troy,	Western Virginia,
New York East,	Black River,	North Ohio,
Providence,	Oneida,	Michigan,
New England,	East Genesee,	Indiana,
Maine,	Genesee,	North Indiana,
East Maine,	Erie,	Rock River,
New Hampshire,	Pittsburgh,	Wisconsin,
Vermont,	Ohio,	Iowa,
Illinois,	Baltimore,	New Jersey,
Missouri,	Philadelphia,	Oregon & California,

Liberia Mission Conference.

3. The number of Quarterly Conferences in the Church, is 3,174, exclusive of foreign work. Each of these Quarterly Conferences is under the supervision and presidency of a presiding elder. About the same number of distinct charges, including circuits, stations, and missions, is embraced in the work.

SECTION II.

NUMBER OF BISHOPS, PRESIDING ELDERS, AND PREACHERS.

1. Bishops, five—

	Residence.	Time of Consecration.
Elijah Hedding,	Poughkeepsie, N. Y.	1824
Beverly Waugh,	Baltimore, Md.	1836
Thomas A. Morris,	Cincinnati, Ohio,	1836
Leonidas L. Hamline,	" "	1844
Edmund Storer Janes,	New York City,	1844

2. Presiding elders: of these there are 174 in the United States, besides two in Oregon and California, three in Liberia, and one in Germany.

3. Travelling Preachers, including elders, deacons, and preachers: of these there are, in the United States and Liberia, 4,129, besides several in Oregon and California.

4. Local Preachers: the number of this highly useful class of men in the Methodist Episcopal Church, exceeds that of the travelling ministers, it being in 1850 not less than 5,420—making a total of travelling and local preachers in the church, of 9,549.

SECTION III.

NUMBER OF MEMBERS AND PROBATIONERS.

Conference.	Members.	Probationers.
Baltimore, ...	46,620	6,433
Philadelphia, ...	36,668	8,406
Providence, ...	11,940	2,059

Conference.	Members.	Probationers.
New Jersey, ...	27,594	5,435
New England, . . .	11,859	1,782
New York, ...	22,609	4,002
New Hampshire, . . .	8,017	1,016
New York East, . . .	19,022	2,346
Troy, ...	22,640	2,996
Western Virginia, . .	12,202	1,597
Vermont, ...	7,079	770
Pittsburgh, ...	31,429	3,864
Black River, ...	15,838	2,566
Wisconsin, ...	6,205	1,796
East Maine, ...	8,342	1,678
Maine, ...	9,654	1,354
Erie, ...	18,852	2,553
Rock River, ...	14,035	3,024
North Ohio, ...	24,325	3,108
Oneida, ...	23,639	3,137
Iowa, ...	9,183	1,897
East Genesee, ...	15,769	1,941
North Indiana,. . . .	25,598	4,782
Missouri, ...	4,262	790
Michigan, ...	14,377	1,912
Ohio, ...	58,116	6,474
Genesee, ...	9,860	881
Illinois, ...	26,784	5,058
Indiana, ...	31,747	5,874
Liberia, ...		
Oregon, &c., ...	754	76

In addition to the above, there are 28,139 colored members and probationers, including 1,117 in Liberia—making the total number of members and probationers in the Methodist Episcopal Church, 703,571, which, being added to the 9,549 preachers as stated in the preceding section, will give the total number of members, probationers, and preachers, at 711,120.

SECTION IV.

STATISTICS OF THE METHODIST EPISCOPAL CHURCH SOUTH.

It seems proper that we should give, in this chapter, a condensed statement of the statistics of this branch of the Methodist Episcopal Church, inasmuch as it occupies as its field of operations so large a portion of the United States. It has one General Conference, and twenty Annual Conferences, all being in the Southern and South-western slaveholding States. It has four bishops: Joshua Soule, James O. Andrew, William Capers, and Robert Paine; the two former having been bishops of the Methodist Episcopal Church previous to the separation, and the two latter having been elected since that period. They have also a Book Concern at Charleston, S. C., with a Branch Concern at Louisville, Ky. They publish five weekly papers, namely, the Southern Christian Advocate, at Charleston; the Richmond Christian Advocate, at Richmond, Va.; the Nashville and Louisville Christian Advocate, at Louisville; the Holston Christian Advocate, at Knoxville, Tenn.; and the Texas Wesleyan Banner, at Houston, Texas. Besides these, they issue from the press at Richmond, the Southern Methodist Quarterly Review; from the press at Nashville, the Southern Ladies' Companion; and from the press at Charleston, the Sunday School Visitor.

The Church South has a very efficient Missionary Society, the head-quarters of which is at Louisville. The number of missionaries among the destitute white population, is 117; among the colored population, 104; among the Indians, 39; among the Germans, 8; two in China, and three in California. These missions embrace a total membership of 59,540 souls. The receipts of the past year, 1850, were about $86,000.*

* The receipts for the year 1850-51, amounted to $93,470. Missions, 271; missionaries, 244.

This Church has also a number of flourishing Colleges and Universities: Emory College, Ga.; Emory and Henry College, Va.; La Grange College, Ala.; Centenary College, Miss.; Randolph Macon College, Va.; and Transylvania University, Ky.

The number of ministers in the travelling connection at the South, is 1,700; in the local ranks, 3,955; the membership numbers 514,601. They have 1,262 Sunday Schools; 7,409 teachers; and 44,500 scholars. In regard to the latter institution, they are far behind their Northern brethren, while in some other respects their statistics show very favorably.

SECTION V.

SUMMARY OF EPISCOPAL METHODISM IN THE UNITED STATES, NORTH AND SOUTH.

1. General Conferences, &c.,	2
Annual Conferences,	49
Bishops,	9
Travelling Ministers,	5,899
Local "	9,491
Total Preachers,	15,390
Members and Probationers, with Preachers added,	1,220,317
2. SUNDAY SCHOOLS,	9,429
Teachers,	94,283
Scholars,	507,125
3. MISSIONS:	
Missionaries,	854
Mission Members,	70,697
Expended last year,	$217,637
4. EDUCATION:	
Colleges and Universities,	15
Seminaries, &c.,	40
(No report from the South.)	
Biblical Institute,	1

5. Religious Periodicals:

Weekly,	11
Monthly,	6
Quarterly,	2
Individual and unofficial,	6

SECTION VI.

TABLE OF MINISTERS AND MEMBERS OF EACH METHODIST DENOMINATION IN THE UNITED STATES.

	Trav. Preachers.	Local Preachers.	Members.
1. M. E. Church,	4,129	5,420	703,571
2. M. E. Church South,	1,700	3,995	514,601
3. Prot. Meth. Church,	740	1,141	64,313
4. Wes. Meth. Church,	400	300	30,000
5. African M. E. Church,	300		20,000
6. African Methodist Zion,	200		5,000
	7,369	10,856	1,337,485
Local Preachers,			10,856
Travelling Preachers,			7,369
Grand total,			1,355,710

From the above it will be seen, that the number of Methodist ministers, travelling and local, in the United States, is over 18,000; and that the number of members, including the ministers belonging to all the Methodist Churches in the Union, approximates toward a million and a half of souls.

SECTION VII.

ENGLISH AND CANADIAN METHODISM.

1. Wesleyan Methodist Church: England.

The following table will show the statistics of this branch of the Methodist Church:

	Circuits.	Trav. Preachers.	Members.
England,	386	1,086	331,250
Wales,	35	77	16,210
Scotland,	13	25	2,934
Ireland,	70	157	21,107
British Islands	10	29	7,883
Foreign Missions,	308	399	97,861
	824	1,773	477,245

The Wesleyan Methodist Missionary Society extends its operations to nearly every part of the world. The receipts of the Society for the year 1850, were $502,775, averaging more than a dollar for each member, including those on missions.

2. Primitive Methodist Church: England—Circuits, 303; Travelling Preachers, 551; Local Preachers, 9,077; Members, 108,781.

3. New Connection Methodists: England—130 Travelling Preachers; 22,062 Members.

4. Wesleyan Association: England—97 Travelling Preachers; 22,178 Members.

5. Wesleyan Methodist Church: Canada—Circuits, 127; Travelling Preachers, 204; Members, 26,213.

6. Methodist Episcopal Church: Canada—Bishops, 2; Circuits, 58; Travelling Preachers, 103; Local Preachers, 105; Members, 8,500.

SECTION VIII.

RECAPITULATION OF STATISTICS.

	Trav. Preachers.	Local Preachers.	Members.
In the United States,	7,369	10,856	1,337,485
In England, &c.,	2,551	9,077*	630,266
In Canada,	307	105	34,713
Total,	10,227	20,038	2,002,464
Add Preachers, ...			30,265
			2,032,729

In viewing the above result, and in comparing "METHODISM AS IT IS" with "METHODISM AS IT WAS" a century ago, we are led to exclaim, "What hath God wrought!" and while the success of Methodism, and especially of Episcopal Methodism, demands our heartfelt gratitude, we, as Methodists, should be incited to humility, and to increased activity in the glorious work of spreading "Scripture holiness" throughout these and all other lands. "Be not high-minded, but fear."

* There are no returns of Local Preachers from the Wesleyans in England or Canada.

THE END.

The Life of Gen. Zachary Taylor, 12th President of the United States, brought down to his inauguration Steel portrait, 12mo., muslin; a new edition, by H. Montgomery.

*** 18,000 of the above work have been sold by us.

"THE LIFE OF GEN. Z. TAYLOR."—*H. Montgomery*, Esq., editor of the Auburn Daily Advertiser, has found leisure, amid the multitude of his engagements, to get up the most respectable looking and carefully prepared biography of the old General we have yet seen. It makes a neat volume, and is printed on excellent paper and new type, and bound in the very best style. It cannot fail to find a tremendous sale, a result due alike to the book itself, and the enterprise of its busy publishers.—*Albany Evening Journal.*

"LIFE OF GENERAL ZACHARY TAYLOR, by *H. Montgomery*," is the latest and most complete of the numerous volumes purporting to be 'Lives' of the General. The author of this work — likewise editor of the Auburn Journal — is already known as a forcible and pleasing writer, handling his subject with a masterly hand; these characteristics are fully developed in the book before us. The stirring incidents of General Taylor's life, and the recent battles on Mexican soil are well portrayed — the very fair and impartial style of narration being a rare quality in depicting battle scenes. The book will repay an attentive perusal.—*N. Y. Tribune.*

THE LIFE OF MAJOR GENERAL ZACHARY TAYLOR. *By H. Montgomery.*—Another and still another "illustrated" Life of the great American, (would that he had as many lives as the publishers give him,) the American whom Carlyle would recognise as "a hero" worthy of his pen's most eloquent recognition; THE MAN OF DUTY in an age of Self. An American in everything; in valor, in strong muscular sense; in simplicity and directness and cordiality of feeling; an American in every thing, save in devotion to our new political God of Expediency.

The volume before us is put forth in Auburn, by the editor of the Auburn Daily Advertiser, whose vigorous, fluent style, and skill in compressing his materials, must make his elegant volume very generally acceptable. Many of the traits ascribed to General Taylor have been assimilated by some of his admirers to the leading military characteristics of Frederick the Great. But, unlike Frederick, Taylor is anything but a martinet in discipline; and, though his movements of small bodies of troops against vast odds, are characterized by the vigorous will and iron determination of Frederick, the arbitrary disposition of the Prussian despot is wholly alien to his tolerant and candid nature. Taylor's affectionate and almost parental relation to his soldiers, perhaps, alone first suggested the parallel, as we find it hinted in the following stanza of some verses upon one of his battles, quoted by Mr Montgomery:

"'OLD ZACH!' 'OLD ZACH!' the war cry rattles
Among those men of iron tread,
As rung 'OLD FRITZ' in Europe's battles
When thus his host Great Frederick led."

Literary World.

Golden Steps to Respectability, Usefulness and Happiness; being a series of Lectures to the youth of both sexes on Character, Principles, Associates, Amusements, Religion, and Marriage. By JOHN MATHER AUSTIN. Derby, Miller & Co., Auburn, 1850. 243 pp.

The author of this book is a writer of superior attraction, and has here selected a subject of deep interest. Could the youth of the country be induced to exchange the Buntline, Lippard, and Ingraham literature of the day, for such reading as this, the benefits to themselves and society would be incalculable.—*Lockport Courier.*

We honor the heart of the writer of this volume as well as his head. He has here addressed an earnest and manly appeal to the young, every page of which proves his sincerity and his desire for their welfare. The subjects treated of in the different lectures are those indicated on the title page. Integrity and virtue, usefulness, truth and honor, are the "Golden Steps" by which the young may ascend to respectability, usefulness, and happiness. We trust the seed thus sown will not be without its fruit, and that his readers will imbibe the spirit of the motto he has chosen—

"Onward! onward! toils despising,
Upward! upward! turn thine eyes,
Only be content when rising,
Fix thy goal amid the skies."

—*Albany State Register.*

The work of Mr. Austin, written in a pleasing style, and nervous and pointed in its argumentation, will hold a prominent position among the fortunate endeavors by which the rising generation are to be influenced. The volume before us is beautiful in its exterior, and this, combined with the aim of the author, in which he has admirably succeeded, will give it a wide range, and secure for it, we hope, an invaluable influence.—*Buffalo Christian Advocate.*

A plain, familiar, forcible exposition of the duties and responsibilities of Youth, which can hardly be read without exerting a salutary and lasting influence. Judging from the popularity of Mr. Austin's former works, we predict for it a wide circulation.—*New York Tribune.*

If the precepts eloquently and forcibly urged in these pages could be brought home and impressed upon the minds of the mass of youth in our land, they would confer lasting and incalculable benefits upon the rising generation. We cordially commend this work to the attention of the young and all who have charge of them.

The publishers have executed their work admirable, and have brought out an elegant and beautiful book. Their work will compare favorably with any of the New York houses.—*Troy Post.*

The following extract has reference to the "golden steps" of the President of the United States, Millard Fillmore:—(See page 69.)

The American Lady's System of Cookery, comprising every variety of information for ordinary and Holiday occasions. By Mrs. T. J. Crowen.

The "American System of Cookery" is a capital book of its class, and for which we bespeak the good word of all thrifty housekeepers. It introduces us into a wilderness of sweets, where no rude surfeit reigns! The almost innumerable variety of good things, clearly and orderly set forth, is most apetizing for the hungry reader, just before dinner.

Here is an American housewife, sensible and thrifty, who has laid down directions for making all sorts of dishes, baking all kinds of cakes and pies, manufacturing every variety of confectionery, preserving, pickling, &c., so plainly that a housekeeper of a week's standing can easily act upon her directions, and yet taken so comprehensive a scope, that the very best and most skilful will find something new. We take for granted, that as the latest, it is the best book of its class.

The writer of this volume has previously published a similar work, on a smaller scale—"Every Lady's Book"—of which more than two hundred thousand copies are said to have been sold. If this is not popularity, we know not what is.—*Literary World.*

The "American System of Cookery," is the title of a goodly sized duodecimo, published in New York. The authoress of this work has obtained considerable celebrity, by a work which she entitled "Every Lady's Book," and we believe she will add to her deserved credit by the present volume, which comes home to the stomach of every man. The receipts are abundant and practical.—*North American.*

Of all the reforms, none is more loudly called for than one in American Cookery—that being one in which everybody is interested. That the national health would be better, if the national kitchen were more philosophically and phyorologically managed, there seems to be no doubt anywhere. Even morals suffer, beyond question, through the influence of crude, ill-selected aliment. Who knows but the Mexican war may be traced to an ill-cooked, ill-assorted, contradictory, and irritating cabinet dinner?

A Lady of New York tells us how to make a great many nice, wholesome things, and we beg our readers not to imagine we speak rashly, or even theoretically, upon this all-important subject—we have tasted, and we testify without a misgiving. "The proof of the pudding," etc.—*Union Magazine.*

Thus *our* wife settles the question. The same author's "Every Lady's Book," she said, might be useful for some folks, but the real simon pure, Yankee, American Cook Book, was the thing exactly, just such a book as she should have made, if she had cooked it up herself. She says it is made on common sense principles; the rules are exactly such as sensible folks follow in this democratic land, who regard taste, health, and economy. Our wife says, that, with some Cook Books, one has to deduct half the spice, shortning and sugar. Our book, however, as our wife declares, is practicable, and is to be followed to the letter.—*Central Washingtonian News.*

This book is compiled by a person of practical knowledge of the subject, who, as stated in the preface, has been for the last eight years employed in collecting information on the subject of the work, and in reducing to practice the receipts obtained. —*Evening Post.*

By the spiciness of the preface, and by the very funny epistle with which the authoress of this book sends us a copy, we cannot doubt her to be a woman of talent; and as Mrs. Child has applied her genins to the making of such a book, we can believe even a Cooking Book may be better for genius in the writer.—*Home Journal.*

This appears to be the most complete and satisfactory collection of receipts in the culinary art, which the skill and enterprise of American ladies, devoted to the subject, have produced. It contains a large amount of matter in a volume of very good siz as a manual, and we have confidence, from the decided testimony of those who ha tested its merits, in recommending it to house-keepers.—*Protestant Churchman.*

THE LIFE OF LOUIS KOSSUTH,

GOVERNOR OF HUNGARY; INCLUDING NOTICES OF THE MEN AND SCENES OF THE HUNGARIAN REVOLUTION: TO WHICH IS ADDED AN APPENDIX, CONTAINING HIS PRINCIPAL SPEECHES, &C. WITH AN INTRODUCTION BY HORACE GREELEY. BY P. C. HEADLEY. Auburn: DERBY & MILLER.

"What an age! A great man steps upon our shores—the fact is telegraphed in an instant to every city in the Union. He speaks—immediately a thousand newspapers carry his words to every house in the land. While he is yet speaking, some rapid writer sketches the history of his life, and the press—prone to miracles—scatters in beautiful volumes, both Life and Speeches through all the country. Mr. Headley has written an excellent memoir of Kossuth. It details, in easy, perspicuous narrative, the principal events of his life, bringing down the history almost to the present hour."—*N. C. Advocate.*

"This volume, containing a full biography of the noble Hungarian from his birth to the present time, with copious notices of the revolutionary movement, is a seasonable and interesting publication. It will be read by great numbers, whose interest in Kossuth's career has been awakened by his presence in this country; and it cannot be read without profit. The principal events in his life are related with sufficient minuteness; numerous anecdotes are introduced, illustrative of his character; and brief comments made on the progress of his history. The course of the Hungarian Revolution is described with clearness and accuracy, correcting many prevalent errors on the subject, and presenting a comprehensive view of the principles involved in that patriotic struggle."—*New York Tribune.*

"In no part of this composition does the author betray an appearance of carelessness or imperfection, yet it is a wonder among the world of critics, 'how Headley can write so much, and write nothing that is incomplete.' His power to give his writings a clearness and vivacity of style, has already obtained for him a reputation that will ever secure for him a passport with the illustrious in the world of letters. And in this instance he has a theme that is happily adapted to his style of composition. The life and character of the 'political Luther of Europe,' furnishes ample material for his brilliant and discriminating genius, and he seems to have spared no pains to make his book worthy of both the theme and the author."—*G. M. Aegis.*

"It is written in an eager, animated style, adapted for the special purpose of the book. It is reliable and exceedingly interesting. A brief introduction by Mr. Greeley pitches the key-note of the volume, and will find a response, we doubt not, in the popular heart."—*New York Organ.*

"We consider the book worth its weight in gold."—*P. Ryson Gaz.*

History of the War with Mexico, from the commencement of hostilities with the United States, to the ratification of Peace; embracing detailed accounts of the brilliant achievements of Generals Taylor, Scott, Worth, Wool, Twiggs, Kearney, and others; by John S. Jenkins, 8vo., 20 illustrations, morocco gilt.

A History of the late war prepared for popular circulation. The writer takes a patriotic view of his subject. His narrative of the commencement of the war would, we presume, not displease Mr. Polk. He follows the campaign throughout with industry and spirit, drawing from public documents, diplomatic correspondence, and the newspaper letter writers by the way. More facts, we believe, are brought together than in any single publication of the kind. The narratives of adventure in California, Col. Doniphan's march, and other passages, are told with interest; the writer evidently seeking to make a useful book. The portraits and illustrations of scenes are numerous; the mechanical execution of the whole work being highly creditable to the Auburn publishers.—*Literary World.*

This is a volume of over 500 pages. The publishers have brought it out in excellent style. The paper, type, printing and binding, are admirable. The book has been written with due regard to accuracy, and in a popular style. It is the most elaborate, and probably the best History of the War yet published.—*Albany Evening Journal.*

We have been unable to notice, until now, this new work from the pen of the author of "The Generals of the last War with Great Britain, etc." In this volume we have at last a complete and interesting history of the late collision between the two Republics of the Continent. To a minute and detailed account of the position and policy of Mexico, the origin and causes of War, are added soul-stirring descriptions of the brilliant and successful engagements of our army with the enemy. This narrative is written after a careful examination of the diplomatic correspondence and the various publications, of a public or private character, that have appeared from time to time, calculated to throw light on the subject. To render the work still more interesting and desirable, it has been illustrated with portraits of the most distinguished officers of our own and the Mexican army, with views of the ever memorable battle-fields of Buena Vista and Cerro Gordo. The reputation of the author will insure for this history a very general circulation.—*Albany Atlas.*

The Odd Fellows' Amulet: or the principles of Odd Fellowship defined; the objections to the order answered; and its advantages maintained; with an address to the public, the ladies, and the order. By Rev. D. W. Bristol, Pastor of the M. E. Church, and P. G. of Osco Lodge, No. 304, at Auburn, N. Y.

The Rev. Mr. Bristol, the author of the above work, is a popular clergyman of the Methodist church. He appears to have written the work not merely for Odd Fellows, but to disabuse the public mind, if possible, of prejudices formed against the Order. A spirit and design of apparent sincerity appears to pervade the entire work, and the writer discusses his themes and meets the objections urged against Odd Fellows, with a great deal of candor and respect. No person, we think, can read it, whatever may have been his prejudices hitherto, without having those prejudices at least, considerably softened, if not wholly taken away. The style of the writer is captivating, while the arrangement and classification of his subjects adds interest to the volume. We have no hesitancy in recommending the Amulet as a book that may be read by the public —*Genesee Evangelist.*

We have wiled away several hours pleasantly and profitably in its perusal, and can recommend it as a work deserving of a large circulation. The principles of the Order are set forth by its author, the Rev. D. W. Bristol, a distinguished Methodist clergyman, in a masterly manner, objections instituted by many to the Order, are fairly tested, and answered in a mild and satisfactory way. It is a cheap and useful work, and we cheerfully recommend it to public favor.—*Mirror of the Times.*

Able and exceedingly interesting articles, that we would most cordially commend to the attention of every reader, while we are gratified at being able to bring them under the notice of members of the great Order. The work contains also Addresses by Rev. D. W. Bristol, and is embellished with several fine Steel Engravings. Fully and correctly defining the principles of O. F., it should fill a niche in the library of every Odd Fellow, where it will furnish a mine of valuable matter whence he can draw at all times for the facts illustrative of the great principles of the noble institution of Odd Fellowship.—*Golden Rule.*

It is an excellent work, and worthy of the patronage of the Order. The objections often urged against our institution, are most thoroughly examined, and ably answered. The book is got up in good style, and is offered at a low price.—*The Ark.*

We should think that every lover of the Order which this book upholds would adorn his library with it; and every person that is opposed to it should also have one so that they could see their objections answered. We would say to every lover of the poor and afflicted, buy one and peruse it for yourselves and see what the Odd Fellows do for them. Its motto is "Do unto others as ye would have others do unto you."—*The Bee.*

This is a clear, forcible, and well written exposition of the subjects above named; and a book that every Odd Fellow in the country should be in possession of. The work is well got up, and embellished with several fine engravings appropriate to the subject of which it treats. It is sold at the low price of *one dollar*, and can be mailed to any part of the United States.—*Banner of the Union.*

www.ingramcontent.com/pod-product-compliance
Lightning Source LLC
LaVergne TN
LVHW020122110826
845151LV00001B/248

* 9 7 8 1 4 2 5 5 4 1 0 5 7 *